RIGHT

OF

BOOM

R I G H T
//// OF ////
BOOM

THE AFTERMATH OF NUCLEAR TERRORISM

BENJAMIN E. SCHWARTZ

The Overlook Press
New York, NY

This edition first published in hardcover in the United States in 2015 by
The Overlook Press, Peter Mayer Publishers, Inc.

141 Wooster Street
New York, NY 10012
www.overlookpress.com
For bulk and special sales, please contact sales@overlookny.com,
or write us at the address above.

Cataloging-in-Publication Data is available from the Library of Congress

Book design and typeformatting by Bernard Schleifer
Manufactured in the United States of America
FIRST EDITION
1 3 5 7 9 10 8 6 4 2
ISBN 978-1-4683-0994-2

This book is dedicated to the late Harvey Sicherman.
A man who understood the power of words and how to wield
that power in service of American statecraft.

May his memory be a blessing.

CONTENTS

INTRODUCTION The Explosion   1

ONE The Persistent Danger:
Two Days "Right of Boom"   21

TWO The New Threats:
Three Days "Right of Boom"   53

THREE The Lessons of Nuclear Deterrence:
Three Days "Right of Boom"   81

FOUR The Lessons of Countering Terrorism:
Four Days "Right of Boom"   115

FIVE Global Impact:
Five Days "Right of Boom"   155

SIX The Red Line:
Fifteen Days "Right of Boom"   199

CONCLUSION The New Order:
Twenty-Three Days "Right of Boom"   221

NOTES   239

ACKNOWLEDGMENTS   264

INDEX   265

INTRODUCTION

THE EXPLOSION

O N AN OTHERWISE CALM AND UNEVENTFUL MORNING, A small nuclear weapon explodes in downtown Washington, DC. The device generates a yield of fifteen kilotons, roughly the same force unleashed by the bomb Little Boy over Hiroshima. The casualty count rises to over a hundred thousand, and the destruction is measured in hundreds of billions of dollars. The blast's electromagnetic pulse burns out electrical components across the metropolitan area. Radiation leaves the center of the city uninhabitable for the first time since it was declared America's capital in 1790, and the scientific community predicts that it will remain so for a decade. The stock market plunges as investors anticipate draconian customs regimes that will choke global trade. Fear of further attacks paralyzes America and much of the Western world.

Hours after the explosion, a little known terrorist group claims responsibility. It is the first time the president, who was not in Washington at the time of the blast, and his surviving cabinet members, including the director of national intelligence, have heard of the group. After searching intelligence databases, analysts report that the group is linked to three hostile governments, all of which have issued statements condemning the attack and denying involvement. It will take weeks for the remnants of the US intelligence community to assess that one of these three governments is probably lying, but even then the US government won't have irrefutable evidence of complicity. Unlike a ballistic missile or bomb delivered by enemy land-, air-, or seacraft, the origin of what analysts will call a "container-based improvised nuclear device" is difficult to determine and impossible to prove.

Nuclear forensics will ultimately provide strong evidence that the fissile material used in the device originated from the country under suspicion. Signals intelligence will record celebrations and praise of the attack by midlevel officials in that country's military and intelligence establishment. However, the intelligence reporting taken as a whole will suggest that negligence within that country's weapons industry and at its nuclear complexes is at least as plausible a scenario as a deliberate transfer by government officials to the terrorist group. Yet there is no conclusive reporting that points to either willful negligence or human error. Either way, there is no way to know if the transfer occurred through official policy, the machinations of a venal or ideologically motivated individual, or simple incompetence. There is almost nothing about the origins of the attack that the president of the United States knows for certain.

The world awaits a response from the White House. What happens next?

Many books have been written on the topic of nuclear weapons, and many others have been written on terrorism. A smaller but still sizable number of authors have focused on nuclear terrorism, particularly since al-Qaeda's attacks of September 11, 2001. Purveyors of popular culture, from American novelists to Hollywood directors, have also addressed the subject. Author Tom Clancy envisioned terrorists targeting the Super Bowl with nuclear weapons in *The Sum of All Fears* in 1991. Hollywood offered us the George Clooney vehicle *The Peacemaker* in 1997. The acclaimed post-9/11 TV drama *24* presented a bleak, dangerous world in which terrorists were always only a few ticks away from nuclear disaster. Americans have had so much entertainment on the issue that they may feel sufficiently educated.

Yet there are very few authors, academics, or entertainers who have really thought through the scenario described above or examined in detail the question of what happens in the days, weeks, and months after such an attack. Presumably, part of the reason for this is that the US government's response to nuclear terrorism is unknowable. Ask anyone who has spent time at the White House on the National Security Council staff and they will tell you that decisions of war and peace are in no small part the product of fickle factors like the personality of the president and the people who surround him. Thoughtful national security practitioners also know that happenstance and dumb luck have a prominent role in shaping discussions in the White House Situation Room. These conditions make realistic speculation difficult to formulate. The wide range of possible scenarios and the salience of unknowable factors make it difficult to anticipate hypothetical policy prescriptions.

Another reason that this question hasn't demanded an answer is that most people understandably consider it to be far less relevant than "How can nuclear terrorism be prevented?" Speculating on responses to a nuclear attack is a bit like contemplating the day after any number of disasters that involve an unprecedented scale of devastation. Does the national security community focus on the US government's potential response to an asteroid striking the planet or the aftermath of a war between China and the United States? It does not, because these types of scenarios fall into the realm of the surreal or at a minimum envision a situation in which there is such massive social disruption and such a severe diminution of US government capacity that it is difficult to even know where to begin. Admitting the limits of American power, particularly the "hard power" of the US military and intelligence community, is also not a popular pastime. A politician would need to be unusually brave to publicly focus on the day after an act of nuclear terrorism instead of the days before. Accepting nuclear terrorism is an unacceptable position, his opponents would surely retort.

There are also no precedents, history, or cases of nuclear terrorism to provide context or demand consideration. People —particularly pundits and politicians—who have not studied much history often use the term *unprecedented* to describe the unfamiliar, but the scenario laid out above is truly something new under the sun. Since a successful nuclear terrorism event has not happened before, and it is not happening now, there is less appetite for thinking deeply about it than there is for considering more traditional security issues. From the sinking of the *Lusitania* by a German U-boat, to the Japanese empire's attack on Pearl Harbor, to al-Qaeda's attacks that culminated in the events of 9/11, Americans are conditioned to contemplate surprise attacks and expect that the US government can respond swiftly and severely, to manifest the prediction made by Japanese admiral Isoroky Yamamoto that a surprise attack against America would "awaken a sleeping giant."

People may assume that the answer to nuclear terrorism is tragic but quite straightforward: retaliation with nuclear weapons. But it won't be that simple. First, in a nuclear terrorism scenario the adversary has every incentive to obscure the origins of the attack and to conduct its activities in countries and through entities that are unaffiliated with the belligerency. This approach is consistent with the well-established practice of using civilians and noncombatants as both targets and human shields. Consequently, it wouldn't be clear to the US government who or what to target for retaliation. Second, unlike US retaliation plans developed during the Cold War, an American nuclear response wouldn't necessarily set the conditions necessary to prevent follow-on attacks. The ultimate outcome of the US government's response must be to deny the adversary the ability to access nuclear materials. Given the global nature of the nuclear industry, striking back with atomic bombs wouldn't guarantee that outcome. Third, we don't live in a world where the moral, legal, and political environment is likely to legitimize a retaliation that results in the violent death of hundreds of thousands of people who had nothing to do with perpetrators who could number fewer than a hundred. In 1957 Henry Kissinger wrote a treatise titled *Foreign Policy and Nuclear Weapons* in which he noted, "As the power of modern weapons grows, the threat of all-out war loses its credibility and therefore its political effectiveness. . . . The American people must be made aware that with the end of our atomic monopoly all-out war has ceased to be an instrument of policy, except as a last resort, and that for most of the issues likely to be in dispute our only choice is between a strategy of limited war or inaction." When Kissinger wrote these words he was thinking about the Soviet Union and was concerned about the ability of the United States to prevent communist expansion through coercion and low-intensity conflict, but his words are just as applicable to the type of nuclear terrorism scenario imagined above. Unfortunately, few have thought about what a "limited war" against nuclear terrorism would look like.

The great Prussian military theorist Carl von Clausewitz is renowned for his observation that the fog of war is a permanent condition of armed conflict, but it is also true that the density of this fog shifts over time, growing and dissipating with changing conditions—especially changes in technology. The atomic bomb has been in existence for six decades and in this time that fog hasn't threatened to obscure the origins of a nuclear attack. In the first two and a half decades after its creation, only five countries—China, France, the Soviet Union, the United Kingdom, and the United States—possessed the bomb. The acquisition of the weapon by Israel, India, and Pakistan ushered in what Yale University professor Paul Bracken termed "the second nuclear age." During neither period were these weapons and their components completely secure. Accidents happened. In 1961, the US Air Force mistakenly dropped two hydrogen bombs over North Carolina with a multi-megaton combined payload—hundreds of times more powerful than the bombs dropped over Hiroshima and Nagasaki—and all but one of the bombs' safety systems failed.[1] Nevertheless, the second half of the twentieth century—the high modern industrial age—was an era of strong centralized governments during which a small number of nuclear suppliers were closely watched by government regulators. Massive governments oversaw weapons of mass destruction. In this environment, attribution of a nuclear detonation would have been straightforward and culpability would have been clear.

The United States was able to avoid nuclear war during this time, despite repeated standoffs with the Soviet Union and China, because a significant number of Americans thought very seriously about the day after a nuclear attack. Tremendous time, energy, and resources went into planning for nuclear war. The US government made it official policy—articulated publicly by presidents and cabinet secretaries—to respond to a Soviet invasion of West Germany with nuclear weapons. It backed up this policy by deploying a massive nuclear arsenal and establishing a comprehensive nuclear command-and-control system. Just as today, during the Cold War no one could truly know how the United States would react if Soviet tanks actually crossed the Fulda Gap. Even presidents and cabinet officials who articulated these threats couldn't know if their vows were promises or bluffs, but their words possessed enough credibility to keep the Soviet Army at bay.

In the case of nuclear terrorism, it is not the uncertainty of America's response options that is notable today—uncertainty has always existed and always will—but the degree of it that is alarming. Since the dawn of the nuclear age and the devastation inflicted on Hiroshima and Nagasaki, the most powerful force preventing the use of nuclear weapons has been the plausible threat of effective retaliation. The articulation of this threat—which the US defense establishment calls declaratory policy—is manifest through public warnings. But words are not enough. To be effective, declaratory policy requires that the target audience understand the threat and that the threat be credible.

Credibility rests on a foundation of capability, interest, reputation, and risk propensity. The United States has substantial defense capabilities, but because the use of capabilities accrues costs, credibility requires that US interests be seen to be of such importance that Americans will bear costs and accept risk to defend them. To deter the Soviets, the US government not only declared its intention to use nuclear weapons but also created first- and second-strike capabilities through a nuclear triad. It also deployed American servicemen and -women to serve as a human trip wire in Europe. Having suffered the calamities of two world wars in two generations and having employed two atomic bombs, the American public was perceived by the world as willing to support the use of those weapons in order to protect vital interests of national and international security.

Today the United States possesses no comparable credible threat to compel governments to prevent the transfer of nuclear weapons and related materials to terrorist groups. Effective compellence requires both a perception that attribution of identity (where the weapon came from) is likely and the establishment of a "return address" (a target that can be held at risk). The inherent opacity of nuclear terrorism frustrates these conditions. Foreign governments don't have much reason to believe they will be held accountable if terrorists exploit their country's territory, markets, or other resources to attack the United States. Adversarial governments such as the regime in North Korea would be in a much stronger position vis-à-vis the United States if an atomic bomb happened to go off in Washington DC. Countries that have good relations with the United States, such as China and Malaysia, have even less reason to be concerned than countries like Iran and North Korea because they are unlikely to be targets of a wounded and angry American public in the days after a nuclear terrorism event. Ultimately, the incentive for governments to do nothing can be high. European and Chinese companies make a sizable profit from trading in nuclear-related technology.[2] These governments have an incentive to cooperate with the United States just enough to claim due diligence and to avoid responsibility, but not enough to actually eliminate threats emanating from their territory that are directed at the United States.

Since the Peace of Westphalia in 1648, international politics has been premised on the principle of state sovereignty, which holds that states are responsible for maintaining the peace or at least preventing the export of violence from the territories over which they are the supreme authority. In truth, this condition has always been honored more in word than in deed. The international security system and the powers that defend it don't really hold the Lebanese government responsible for Hezbollah's actions, the Mexican government responsible for the gang violence in the American Southwest or the US government responsible for the flow of automatic weapons into Mexico. The United States did not retaliate against Germany for hosting many of the al-Qaeda operatives who conducted the 9/11 attacks. Yet this is a gap in the international security system that poses a problem of an entirely different order of magnitude when it comes to nuclear terrorism.

Arguably the most likely reason why planning for the day after an act of nuclear terrorism hasn't been the focus of US national security policy is that doing so is difficult. But this is only part of the reason. Another is that the US national security community continues to divide the problem in a manner that obscures the issue. The bureaucratic structure of the federal government is demonstrative in this respect. There are offices with names like Missile Defense that deal with the issue of nuclear weapons primarily by formulating policy to deter nuclear weapons states. There are other offices with names like Counterterrorism that focus on kinetic operations aimed at dismantling al-Qaeda and countering other terrorists who threaten the United States. And then there are Counterproliferation and Nonproliferation offices charged with managing policies to prevent nuclear proliferation. These three types of offices have broader functions, but the point here is that the issue of nuclear terrorism crosses all three yet isn't any single office's primary responsibility. There is no office singularly focused on the problem of state-enabled terrorism or state failure to prevent terrorist use of nuclear weapons that is capable of marshaling all instruments of national power to meet this threat.

This isn't the product so much of poor thinking as it is of learned and applied history. The trifurcation reflects the history of three distinct national security problems, each of which spawned specific policies based on unique premises. The problem that gave birth to Missile Defense was the need to manage the US nuclear arsenal in a manner that deters other states from employing nuclear weapons, reassures allies that they are protected under the US nuclear umbrella, and dissuades states from developing and/or expanding nuclear weapons capabilities. Those tasked with addressing this problem are focused intently on providing advice on nuclear declaratory policy and US nuclear weapons posture, which are expressed officially in the Nuclear Posture Review. As might be expected (and quite appropriately), they are steeped in the literature, philosophy, and traditions of nuclear brinkmanship and international security theory. Such people are committed to the proposition that nuclear war can be deterred and military balances managed in order to promote peace.

The US counterterrorism community is a separate and very different tribe. In one respect, these people are the product of al-Qaeda and the post-9/11 wars. But terrorism and the essential premises behind US policy for combating terrorism existed long before Osama bin Laden. "The deliberate targeting of civilians and noncombatants with violence to achieve political purposes"—a standard description of terrorism—is far from a novel form of violence. However, the fundamental challenge posed by an unattributable nuclear attack isn't terrorism as a tactic, but terrorism as a phenomenon. Terrorism emerges from a sociological, geographical, and political condition that's been around since the dawn of civilization: the existence of groups that can organize and effectuate violence without occupying fixed territory. Groups like al-Qaeda follow in the footsteps of desert nomads and mountain dwellers who for centuries have harassed settled polities by raiding and then retreating into terrain inhospitable to pacification.[3] This dynamic remains the central problem posed by terrorism, and it lends itself to a time-tested response: isolation and preemption. After much trial and error, this has become the de facto strategy of the US counterterrorism community.

The weapons of mass destruction (WMD) proliferation people, who represent the third arm of the US national security bureaucracy in question, have a very different mandate from both the missile defense and counterterrorism communities. In essence, they manage two types of approaches: (1) nonproliferation supported by multilateral regimes, treaties, and UN sanctions; and (2) counterproliferation effectuated by military and covert action. The former comprises an alphabet soup of agreements and activities, including the G-8 Global Partnership against the Spread of Weapons and Materials of Mass Destruction, the Global Initiative to Combat Nuclear Terrorism (GICNT), the Non-Proliferation Treaty (NPT), the Nuclear Suppliers Group (NSG), the Nunn-Lugar Cooperative Threat Reduction (CTR) program, the Proliferation Security Initiative (PSI), and UN Security Council Resolutions 1540 and 1874, among others. The latter includes kinetic action such as the US-led invasion of Iraq (an event that represented only one chapter in a longer counterproliferation campaign dating back at least to the Israeli raid on Iraq's Osirak nuclear reactor in .1981), the US-led interdiction in 2003 of the motor vessel *BBC China* transporting components to Libya's nuclear program, the 2007 Israeli air strike on Syria's clandestine nuclear reactor, and the covert actions that have reportedly been conducted against Iran's nuclear program.[4]

Each of these three tribes in the national security community has done a reasonably successful job of fulfilling its mandates. Nuclear weapons states have deterred each other from employing atomic bombs for nearly two-thirds of a century. America's military and intelligence professionals removed Osama bin Laden from the battlefield and nearly vanquished al-Qaeda's original senior leadership while managing the broader terrorist threat in a manner that preserved Americans' way of life with minimal disruptions. By all reasonable measures, the nonproliferators also have exceeded expectations. At the time the Non-Proliferation Treaty was signed in 1968, experts predicted that the world would confront twenty-five to thirty nuclear weapon states within twenty years. Over forty years later, only four states are not parties to the NPT, and they are the only additional states that possess nuclear weapons. Military action played a role in this success. At tremendous cost, the US-led wars against Saddam Hussein's Iraq in 1991 and 2003 put an end to that government's ambition to acquire nuclear weapons. Interdictions on the high seas pushed the Libyan and North Korean proliferation efforts back on their heels. Israel's raid into Syria appears to have ended Bashar al-Assad's nuclear program.

Unfortunately, these policies may no longer be able to sufficiently manage the threat posed by nuclear terrorism. Ten years ago, Graham Allison—the founding dean of Harvard University's John F. Kennedy School of Government, adviser to secretary of defense Caspar Weinberger under president Ronald Reagan, and himself assistant secretary of defense under president Bill Clinton—wrote *Nuclear Terrorism: The Ultimate Preventable Catastrophe*. The book achieved international acclaim, becoming the standard on the subject in many colleges and graduate schools as well as think tanks and military academies. In his book, Allison puts forward a doctrine of "Three No's": "no loose nukes, no new nascent nukes, and no new nuclear weapons state." While characterized as general conditions, each *no* was targeted at the activity of a specific country. "No loose nukes" was a reaction to the proliferation of nuclear materials emanating from the former Soviet Union, principally Russia, Belarus, Kazakhstan, and Ukraine. "No new nascent nukes" responded to the growth of the Iranian nuclear complex. And his warning about "no new nuclear weapons state" was directed squarely at the Democratic People's Republic of Korea (DPRK, or North Korea).

A decade later, Allison's "Three No's" have become three yeses. Today North Korea is a member of the nuclear weapons club; it has conducted three live nuclear weapons tests, in 2006, 2009, and 2012. The regime has enough fissile material for anywhere between six and eighteen atomic bombs, according to public estimates, as well as the knowledge acquired from over twenty years of work on nuclear weaponization. The DRPK began a plutonium route to the bomb in the late 1980s when it built a clandestine separation plant at Yongbyon despite signing the NPT in 1985. A uranium enrichment program was later exposed as well, first brought to light in October 2002 when American officials in Pyongyang accused North Korea of having a secret, relatively large such program and then confirmed it in November 2010 when the DPRK invited an American scientist to a production-scale gas centrifuge plant at the Yongbyon site.[5]

With respect to "loose nukes," the threat faced today is unprecedented. The good news is that the danger that Allison focused on—fissile material leaking out of the former Soviet republics—has been substantially curtailed, though not eliminated. When Allison served in government he was confronted by a slew of nuclear smuggling cases. Between 1992 and 2002, eleven cases of attempted sales of highly enriched uranium and two cases of attempted plutonium sales occurred. In contrast, between 2002 and 2012 there have been only four cases—all but one of which was linked to a single country, Georgia. This is a good news story, which is probably due in no small measure to the efforts of the United States to provide rapid security upgrades as part of the Nunn-Lugar Cooperative Threat Reduction program.[6]

Unfortunately, this good news has been accompanied by extremely dangerous developments in Pakistan. The country is in the midst of a massive expansion of its nuclear weapons complex at a time when radicalization is on the rise and its military is under frequent attack from insurgents. Moreover, the size of the nuclear complex is not only expanding but, according to Feroz Khan, a thirty-year veteran of the Pakistani program, the military is also planning to produce miniaturized tactical nuclear weapons, deploy them in a ready-to-launch state, and mate them with new delivery vehicles. From a proliferation perspective this is a frightening prospect, particularly considering that Pakistan has an unparalleled history of proliferation. This is all occurring in a country that hosted Osama bin Laden and the senior leadership of al-Qaeda for over a decade and where the military intelligence service continues to court, co-opt, and coordinate with a wide array of terrorists groups.[7]

With respect to the issue of "nascent nukes" the Islamic Republic of Iran has progressed well past the point of having uranium enrichment capability. Despite robust international sanctions, Iran has procured a wide range of nuclear-related goods from illicit foreign suppliers. Today it possesses two gas centrifuge plants and has the ability to build more if it chooses to do so. In addition, the Bushehr power reactor is now operational and in 2013 the government nearly completed the Arak heavy water reactor that experts assess is better suited to making plutonium for nuclear weapons than to producing medical isotopes, as the Iranians claim. These facilities are fed by Iran's large uranium conversion and fuel fabrication plants. In November 2013, Iran and the P-5 + 1 reached a six-month agreement that eliminated dangerous stocks of low-enriched uranium, granted increased access to International Atomic Energy Agency (IAEA) inspectors, froze expansion of the program, and lengthened the time it would take Iran to "break out" of IAEA safeguards and "dash" to a bomb. Yet Iran's massive nuclear infrastructure remains in place and experts publicly estimate that the breakout time has only expanded by a month or so. Using its declared facilities, Iran could produce enough weapons-grade uranium for a bomb in a few months' time.[8] If ayatollah Ali Hosseini Khamenei gave a green light today for the production of a uranium-based weapon, it is possible that the

IAEA would not detect it and the United States would not be able to act in time to prevent Iran from producing sufficient highly enriched uranium for a bomb. The bottom line is that Iran now possesses a sizable nuclear industry composed of multiple facilities spread across the country, some of which have been built deep underground in locations that are difficult for foreign airpower to attack. Iran is a large and wealthy country; Iranian scientists are capable; and the atomic bomb is 1940s technology.[9]

The reality of the three yeses represents a tipping point because the atomic bomb and its ingredients are now so dispersed that loss of government control is both a viable and plausible scenario. The latter condition actually increases the incentive for some governments to exacerbate the former. It is time to think as seriously about the day after nuclear terrorism as Cold War strategists thought about a "hot war" between the United States and Soviet Union. The fog of war won't be eliminated, but examining the issue can help dissipate it, promote effective preparation, and help identify actions that can be taken prior to a crisis - "left of boom" – in order to diminish the probability of attack. First and foremost, defining and developing credible response capabilities would not only leave the United States with just that but would also boost our ability to compel states to regulate nuclear trade, enhance nuclear security, and increase counterterrorism activities within their own countries.

This is uncharted territory, but history is the best guide. The methodology of this work is to integrate lessons from the past—the successful deterrence of nuclear weapons states, enduring approaches to combating terrorism, and effective counterproliferation regimes in the context of evolving cultural and international legal norms—in order to promote practical thinking about the days after a nuclear terrorism attack. The theory and practice of nuclear weapons deterrence, reassurance, and compellence contain lessons for managing the unique dangers of the nuclear age. Centuries of irregular warfare and special operations provide lessons on how to effectively respond to terrorism. The evolution of the legal and political foundations of the international security system is also relevant for consideration because morality, legality, and legitimacy directly affect the political feasibility of retaliatory actions. The issues of morality and justice have direct and tremendous security implications because the political will for a nation such as the United States to engage in violent retribution for WMD terrorism depends on the issue of legitimacy. The threat of total war, which could cost hundreds of thousands or millions of lives, simply isn't a credible response to nuclear terrorism committed by only a few dozen people.

Belligerency was clearly transparent when the movement of massive military formations across borders was necessary to inflict massive destruction. This is no longer the case. The world's reaction in 2013 to chemical weapons use against Syrians is a case in point. Despite clear evidence that Assad's government deployed chemical weapons and that sarin-filled rockets were fired from government-controlled territory into opposition areas, culpability still became a contentious issue with Russia and China, whose governments asserted that Syrian opposition forces could be to blame. One can only imagine the potential for disagreement in the event a government chooses to facilitate, rather than directly use, WMD. The transfer of a nuclear weapon by a state to a nonstate actor violates treaties and UN resolutions and comes closest to a direct act of aggression, but what about less direct assistance? For example, is the transfer of fissile material a form of aggression? What about the transfer of funds? Or simply providing a sanctuary? If terrorists utilize a banking or transportation system to support their operations, are companies culpable?

Consider the following hypothetical situation. The North Korean government helped build a nuclear weapons complex for Syria that was destroyed by an Israeli air strike in 2007. What if the Israelis hadn't struck, and atomic bombs were eventually produced, acquired by Hezbollah in the midst of the chaos of Syria's civil war and then employed by Hezbollah operatives. Would North Korea be held accountable and retaliated against? If so, does the North Korean regime know this? In other words, what is the legal standard for culpability in the case of nuclear terrorism?

The most dangerous thing that governments can do with respect to nuclear terrorism is to do nothing at all, to not build institutions capable of securing nuclear weapons–related materials. Holding governments responsible for policing their own territory was relatively straightforward when nuclear weapons could only be built and deployed by governments. It is far more complicated when it is plausible for nonstate actors to acquire these capabilities. In a Hobbesian world bereft of a Leviathan —either in the form of a multinational world government or a superpower—national governments are the first and best line of defense against nuclear terrorism. But unlike during the Cold War, today there isn't a credible security framework that suggests that national authorities and their citizens will be held accountable.

The emergence of conditions that make it plausible for terrorists to acquire and employ nuclear weapons without an evidentiary chain that implicates a government is a fundamental change in the international security system that warrants new plans and policies. In charting a way forward, it is worth consulting some pertinent history and considering together topics that often are studied in isolation: (1) nuclear proliferation and efforts to contain the spread of the bomb; (2) conflict escalation among nuclear powers; (3) counterterrorism; (4) the evolution of the international system of states; and (5) the effect of moral considerations on warfare. This book brings these subjects together in an attempt to highlight lessons from the past in order to generate ideas for the future.

CHAPTER ONE

THE PERSISTENT DANGER
TWO DAYS "RIGHT OF BOOM"

WHILE MANY IN THE MEDIA AND THE POLITICAL ESTABLISH-ment have long debated whether or not the threat of nuclear terrorism was real, this isn't a question on any-one's mind in the days after the nuclear explosion in downtown Washington, DC. World leaders are unanimous in their expressions of shock, and defensive of their conduct.

"We always knew this was a possibility," remarks the president, flanked by prime ministers and presidents from the closest allied nations, "but there were no signs of a new threat."

While most Americans are silenced by a collective horror, a small number search for someone familiar to blame: "If only the government had . . ." and "The administration hadn't . . ." These voices murmur with varying degrees of derision.

Yet even with the clarity of hindsight, intelligence officials, academics, and pundits can't point to any single event that marked the moment when nuclear terrorism became an urgent problem. A few thoughtful observers recall the warning of Paul Bracken, who stated that often during periods of rapid change "we are caught up in the spiral of events, lost in its energy, blind to the accumulation of slow changes remaking our world."[1] The proliferation of nuclear knowledge and materials occurred gradually for over half a century. A radioactive crater now testifies to the fact that a tipping point had been passed but gives no indication of how, when, or where. "How did this happen?" is the question on the lips of nearly everyone. But no one in a position of authority can identify a single cause.

The magnitude of the attack overwhelms all response resources. Public officials announce a twenty-four-hour curfew throughout Washington while emergency officials are dispatched to the blast site. They contend with the unique features of a nuclear detonation: the explosive blast, direct nuclear radiation, and thermal radiation. The blast's shock wave generated surface winds approaching one hundred miles per hour, blowing off building walls and breaking glass with enough force to cause injury throughout a three-mile radius. Few of the buildings in a half mile of the blast remain standing, and those that do are not structurally sound. The city's underground infrastructure—tunnels, the subway system, water mains, power, telecommunications and gas conduits—are now blocked and will remain so for weeks. One mile from ground zero, sturdy buildings are standing but have been rendered unstable, as have most family homes. People are desperate to get as far away as possible, but rubble and overturned vehicles clog streets and fires rage across the city.

Panic induced by the visible devastation is compounded by fear of unobservable dangers. There is no consensus on the geographic boundaries of radioactive dust and debris. Nuclear radiation and contaminants associated with building materials, such as asbestos and heavy metals, are detectable as far as ten to twenty miles from the blast site. Victims within this range are already experiencing nausea and vomiting. In the days ahead an agricultural embargo will be declared for the Chesapeake Bay, all of Delaware and parts of New Jersey, Maryland and Virginia, but that is far from the minds of the first responders.[2] While emergency responders deal with the immediate human consequences of the attack—treating the injured, stabilizing damaged infrastructure and rebuilding water, sewage, and electrical systems—the "experts" suddenly see a malign trend that had hitherto been obscured by other concerns: the slow but inexorable spread of the technologies of clandestine nuclear warfare.

COULD THIS REALLY HAPPEN?

Is the scenario above simply the product of an overactive imagination and a penchant for alarmism?

This is a reasonable question to ask. And it is worth answering before embarking on an exploration of potential responses to nuclear terrorism. Those who assert that there is a genuine threat of nuclear terrorism should acknowledge at the outset that there are legitimate reasons for skepticism. In fact, those who have paid closest attention to the issue over the years may be most conditioned to be incredulous. They have heard public officials repeatedly issue dire warnings of impending terrorist attacks, watched and seen that no attack materializes, and then have been presented with little or no evidence to support the initial alert.

It is also perfectly understandable that reasonable people question the competence and/or trustworthiness of US national security officials, particularly those responsible for nuclear issues. This is especially so in light of the second American-led invasion of Iraq—a war justified to the public largely on the basis of nonexistent nuclear weapons. Moreover, warnings of impending doom didn't originate with then vice president Dick Cheney. "I think we have to live with the expectation," remarked a Los Alamos atomic engineer in 1973, "that once every four or five years a nuclear explosion will take place and kill a lot of people." This statement is cited in John McPhee's *The Curve of Binding Energy*, which detailed concerns about the proliferation of nuclear weapons to nonstate actors over forty years ago.[3] In the context of this history, accusations of Chicken Little–like behavior aren't flippant reactions.

While exaggeration may mislead the credulous and offend the perceptive, neither the absence of a precedent for nuclear terrorism nor the intelligence failure regarding Saddam Hussein's WMD program change the growing threat. Many of these conditions aren't new; they have existed since the dawn of the nuclear age, and the world has been very fortunate that the danger has been effectively managed for so long. Other conditions are truly unprecedented. The world crossed from Graham Allison's "Three No's" into three Yeses with a whimper rather than a bang, but we have nevertheless entered an environment of extraordinary risk. Allison's contention that "[t]he detonation of a terrorist nuclear device in an American city is inevitable if the U.S. continues on its present course" is certainly debatable.[4]

Yet an objective assessment of the current nuclear security situation and its future trajectory leads to an unavoidable conclusion: We are more vulnerable to nuclear terrorism than at any time since the dawn of the nuclear age.

THE ENDURING THREAT

The greatest danger remains the great discovery—the knowledge that can't be unlearned. Physical matter is made up of atoms. An atom is composed of a nucleus, which is an assembly of bounded protons and neutrons that is orbited by electrons. The number of protons in an atom's nucleus defines the element, the basic category of physical matter. The total number of protons and neutrons, taken together, is called the atomic weight. Variations in an element's atomic weight reflect variation in the number of neutrons bonded with its protons. These variations are known as isotopes. Uranium-235 is an isotope that contains 143 neutrons (which we know by subtracting the 92 protons from the total atomic weight of 235). Bombarding a nucleus that has a large number of protons with additional neutrons can split the atom, a process known as fission. Uranium-235 is especially well suited for this type of reaction given the high number of protons. In keeping with Albert Einstein's famous equation $E=mc^2$, when fission occurs energy is released because the "binding energy" that holds the neutrons and protons together needs an outlet. The world has known this since 1938, when Lise Meitner and Otto Hahn figured it out while working at the Kaiser Wilhelm Institute in Berlin.

The tremendous energy unleashed by an atomic bomb occurs because a chain reaction takes place when neutrons emerging from one fission reaction trigger other fission reactions—a process that requires enough fissile material for "supercriticality." The concept of a chain reaction was investigated by Frederic Joliot-Curie in France and Enrico Fermi and Leó Szilárd in the United States in 1939. This work prompted Albert Einstein to sign his famous letter to president Franklin Delano Roosevelt in August of that year:

> In the course of the last four months it has been made probable—through the work of Joliot in France as well as Fermi and Szilard in America—that it may become possible to set up a nuclear chain reaction in a large mass of uranium, by which vast amounts of power and large quantities of new radium-like elements would be generated. Now it appears almost certain that this could be achieved in the immediate future. This new phenomenon would also lead to the construction of bombs, and it is conceivable—though much less certain—that extremely powerful bombs of a new type may thus be constructed. A single bomb of this type, carried by boat and exploded in a port, might very well destroy the whole port together with some of the surrounding territory.[5]

A year after Einstein's letter this theory was the subject of a fission weapons study produced by Suzuki Tatsusaburo and Sagane Ryokichi for the Japanese Army as well as the subject of a report drafted on the other side of the world by Rudolf Peierls and Otto Frisch for the United Kingdom's Military Application of Uranium Detonation committee. In 1941 Soviet scientists, Yuly Khariton and Yakov Zel'dovich calculated that twenty-two pounds of U-235 was sufficient to achieve a chain reaction, a measurement henceforth called the critical mass. From then it took only one year for theory to become reality. In 1942, Enrico Fermi initiated the first self-sustaining nuclear chain reaction in a Chicago laboratory. The journey from this physics experiment to weaponization was not long. In 1943, both the US and Soviet governments initiated separate atomic bomb programs. On July 16, 1945, the Fat Man design was tested in New Mexico in what became known as the Trinity Event and less than a month after that the US military dropped atomic bombs on Hiroshima and Nagasaki.

From the beginning no single person and no single government ever controlled the secret of the atomic bomb. The United States was the first government to own the weapon, but the device was designed by a multinational scientific community that built upon discoveries made primarily in Europe. It is notable that of the twenty-four intellectual "all-stars" at the Los Alamos National Laboratory from 1943 to 1945—that is, the directors, division chiefs, and their deputies—25 percent were from the United Kingdom and Canada; 21 percent were from the United States; 21 percent were from Germany and Austria; 17 percent were from Hungary; and 17 percent were from other European countries.[6] Japan, which was in many ways the most European of the non-European countries, also had a modest nuclear weapons program known as the N Project located at the Aviation Technology Research Institute of Tokyo as well as a parallel effort called F Project (for fission) at the Imperial University of Kyoto. The Soviets also weren't far behind by 1945. In Leningrad, Yuly Khariton and his associates replicated the atomic research conducted by their peers in Berlin, Paris, New York, and Chicago.

One month before the Trinity Event, a committee composed of prominent nuclear physicists involved in the Manhattan Project submitted a report; the *Franck Report*, named after committee chairman James Franck, was addressed to president Harry S. Truman, and its subject was the "political and social problems" associated with the atomic bomb. Among the conclusions of the authors was the assertion that it would be impossible for the United States to keep the knowledge behind the atomic bomb a secret. Written before the politicization of atomic secrets and the intrigues of the Cold War, it is a statement worth quoting at length:

> [A]lthough we undoubtedly are at present ahead of the rest of the world in this field, the fundamental facts of nuclear power are a subject of common knowledge. British scientists know as much as we do about the basic wartime progress of nucleonics—with the exception of specific processes used in our engineering developments—and the background of French nuclear physicists plus their occasional contact with our Projects, will enable them to catch up rapidly, at least as far as basic scientific facts are concerned. German scientists, in whose discoveries the whole development of this field has originated, apparently did not develop it during the war to the same extent to which this has been done in America; but to the last day of the European war, we have been living in constant apprehension as to their possible achievements. The knowledge that German scientists were working on this

weapon and that their government certainly had no scruples against using it when available, was the main motivation of the initiative which American scientists have taken in developing nuclear power on such a large scale for military use in this country. In Russia, too, the basic facts and implications of nuclear power were well understood in 1940, and the experiences of Russian scientists in nuclear research is entirely sufficient to enable them to retrace our steps within a few years, even if we would make all attempts to conceal them. Furthermore, we should not expect too much success from attempts to keep basic information secret in peacetime, when scientists acquainted with the work on this and associated Projects will be scattered to many colleges and research institutions and many of them will continue to work on problems closely related to those on which our developments are based. In other words, even if we can retain our leadership in basic knowledge of nucleonics for a certain time by maintaining the secrecy of all results achieved on this and associated Projects, it would be foolish to hope that this can protect us for more than a few years.[7]

One of the signatures of the report and principal minds behind its articulation was Szilárd, who had spent a great deal of time focused on this subject and was arguably the best qualified to make such a judgment. Szilárd and the other authors anticipated that a nuclear arms race was coming. Few, however, knew how quickly this would happen.

KNOWLEDGE PASSES FROM GOVERNMENT TO GOVERNMENT

Gleaning the security implications of the Manhattan Project's motley crew does not take the diplomatic acumen of a Benjamin Franklin, who once aptly remarked that "three can keep a secret if two are dead." The men of the Manhattan Project traveled freely after the war, and some talked. A select few deliberately transferred information to foreign governments. Among the Los Alamos affiliates who provided vital information to the Soviet Union, including full-dimensioned drawings of Fat Man, were Klaus Fuchs, Theodore Hall, David Greenglass, and Lona Cohen. After the war, Fuchs returned to his native Germany and explained the inner workings of Fat Man to Qian Sanqiang, who promptly became China's chief nuclear weapons scientist. The idea of a French bomb was born on July 11, 1948, when French veterans of the Manhattan Project working at Chalk River violated their oath of secrecy and informed Charles de Gaulle of the Allied nuclear weapons program. The Chinese atomic bomb was likely a product in part of Joan Hinton, a senior scientist at Los Alamos, an attendee at the 1945 Trinity Event, and an ardent communist. She moved to China in 1948, where it is very likely that she shared her insights on the implosion technology of Fat Man.[8]

Speaking to the UN General Assembly in December 1953, president Dwight D. Eisenhower proclaimed that "the dreaded secret, and the fearful engines of atomic might, are not ours alone. . . . If at one time the United States possessed what might have been called a monopoly of atomic power, that monopoly ceased to exist several years ago."[9] He didn't know how right he was. It wasn't until decades later that the full extent of atomic espionage became known.

The Greek historian Thucydides attributed the birth of empires to "fear, honor, and profit." The same attributes of human nature explain the spread of the atomic bomb two thousand years later. The Soviets' atomic capability was imperative in confronting the Americans during the Cold War. On August 29, 1949, a Soviet bomb based on the Fat Man implosion design detonated. The spies that provided this critical information not only propelled the Soviet nuclear program but also started the cascade of events that ended with a British bomb. In July 1946, the US Congress responded to the revelation that the most significant Soviet penetration of the Manhattan Project was carried out by British citizens and British-sponsored émigrés by passing a bill known as the McMahon Act that curtailed US-UK nuclear cooperation. Fearing US abandonment, the British launched a unilateral program; a British bomb detonated on October 3, 1952. The French defeat at Dien Bien Phu in 1954 and American opposition to French involvement in the 1956 Suez Crisis motivated the French cabinet on December 26, 1957, to authorize the development of an atomic bomb. A French bomb exploded less than three years later. President Eisenhower's threat to employ nuclear weapons if an armistice agreement wasn't reached in the Korean War spurred Mao Zedong to pursue atomic capability for China. To help their communist comrades, the Soviets codified an agreement with China on October 15, 1957, called the New Defense Technical Accord, which committed them to providing technical nuclear training, a supply of ballistic missiles, hands-on construction, and a prototype of an atomic bomb. A Chinese bomb detonated on October 16, 1964. Four years later, these five countries—the victorious powers of the World War II and the only permanent members of the UN Security Council—legitimized their atomic power as "recognized nuclear weapons states" under the Non-Proliferation Treaty.

But history didn't end there. Fear drove the Israelis to the French. In May 1957, the French cabinet approved an agreement to build a nuclear reactor in the Negev Desert; this development expanded upon Israel's 1955 purchase of a small nuclear research reactor from the United States under the Atoms for Peace program. During the following two years, France and Israel worked closely together to design an atomic bomb based on technology acquired by French scientists who had worked on the Manhattan Project.[10] Subsequently, Israel purchased heavy water from the United Kingdom via a Norwegian supplier, yellowcake ore from Argentina, South Africa, and Belgium, and enriched uranium from an Ohio-based corporation (one can be sure that this is only a partial list of Israel's international suppliers).[11] An Israeli bomb existed by 1967, though an overt test was never conducted, according to public sources.[12]

India went nuclear next. Jawaharlal Nehru's government received a nuclear reactor as a gift from Canada in 1955. In 1958, Nehru authorized construction of a plutonium reprocessing facility, and two years later India's reactor went critical. The reorientation of nuclear research toward weapons was certainly motivated in part by China's nuclear weapons status and India's military humiliation in the 1962 Sino-Indian War, but honor also was a strong component of Indian motivation. As Karsten Frey notes in *India's Nuclear Bomb and National Security*, "There was never a discussion among us over whether we shouldn't make the bomb. How to do it was more important. For us it was a matter of prestige that would justify our ancient past. The question of deterrence came much later. Also, as Indian scientists we were keen to show our Western counterparts, who thought little of us in those days, that we too could do it."[13] On June 7, 1972, Indian prime minister Indira Gandhi authorized the development and assembly of a nuclear weapon. Two years later the "Smiling Buddha" was tested, which Gandhi's government characterized as a "peaceful nuclear explosive." It was a gadget rather than an operational weapon, but in the geopolitical context this was a distinction without a difference.

Pakistan's reaction to India mirrored India's response to China. Pakistan was humiliated by repeated military defeats at the hands of the Indian military and vulnerable to India's nuclear capability. Zulfigar Ali Bhutto couldn't have expressed the motivation for Pakistan's decision more clearly than he did in 1965 when he told the *Manchester Guardian*, "If India makes an atom bomb, then even if we have to feed on grass and leaves—or even if we have to starve—we shall also produce an atom bomb as we would be left with no other alternative. The answer to an atom bomb can only be an atom bomb."[14] A Pakistani bomb exploded in 1998, nineteen days after India formally declared its nuclear weapons status and tested a fusion bomb.

South Africa's atomic bomb program built directly upon

the knowledge and expertise first employed by the scientists of the Manhattan Project. The Afrikaner government's motivation for a bomb was also far from unique: fear of its neighbors. In the 1970s, the communist buildup of tens of thousands of Soviet and Cuban proxy forces in neighboring Angola, and the UN's military embargo, spurred fears in the South African government of invasion by Soviet-backed forces. In 1974 the government gave the green light for weapons production. The decision of the Republic of South Africa to go nuclear according to a US national intelligence estimate was due to the country's "growing feeling of isolation and helplessness, perceptions of major military threat, and desires for regional prestige."[15] No test was confirmed, but by all accounts South Africa possessed atomic bombs based on the Little Boy design by the end of the 1970s. Israeli technical advice might have contributed to this effort, but by this time the most important atomic weapons information was widespread.[16]

The purpose of this brief history is not to provide a comprehensive documentation of the development and spread of atomic weapons; plenty of authors have written tomes on the subject. The rendering above also simplifies government decision-making processes that were complicated and multifaceted. It does, however, demonstrate that the secrets of atomic weaponization were proliferated among governments almost immediately after their discovery. It also highlights a trajectory and proves the first point that President Eisenhower made in December 1953 when he announced his Atoms for Peace program in a speech before the UN General Assembly: "Atomic realities of today comprehend two facts of great significance. . . . First, the knowledge now possessed by several nations will eventually be shared by others—possibly all others. Second, even a vast superiority of weapons and a consequent capability for devastating retaliation, is no preventive of itself. . . ."[17] Eisenhower's second point is equally true, but that's a topic best left until after a review of how critical nuclear weapons information traveled out of government channels and into the public domain.

THE KNOWLEDGE GOES PUBLIC

By far the most significant disclosure of nuclear weapons secrets that ever occurred happened on August 6 and August 9, 1945: the dates when Little Boy struck Hiroshima and Fat Man was dropped on Nagasaki. These events demonstrated to the entire world that atomic science could be weaponized with tremendous strategic and political effect. From that moment on it was only a matter of time before the science behind the bombs became public knowledge. On October 3, President Truman made his first address to the US Congress on what had only months before been a top-secret subject, declaring, "Scientific opinion appears to be practically unanimous that the essential theoretical knowledge upon which the discovery is based is already widely known. There is also substantial agreement that foreign research can come abreast of our present theoretical knowledge in time."[18]

Truman's speech was a political statement as much as it was a rendering of scientific fact. His words were accurate in their imprecision, but the devil was in the details. What exactly is "essential theoretical knowledge"? Well, it depends. For scientists and engineers of the Manhattan Project who had an eye toward postwar academic careers, entrepreneurs looking to develop a nuclear power industry, and those who believed that nuclear weapons should be controlled by an international body such as the United Nations, the answer was broad. Alternatively, for those in the US government and military who sought to extend the wartime military regime's classification policies and prolong America's atomic dominance, the answer was far more restrictive.

In the weeks after Truman's speech two camps formed to do battle over the future of atomic science in America. On one side a legislative initiative was crafted in the form of the May-Johnson Bill to extend wartime military secrecy protocols into peacetime. Arrayed against this effort, scientists and engineers affiliated with the Los Alamos and Oak Ridge National Laboratories and the University of Chicago coalesced together in favor of increased transparency. Politically engaged scientists at University of Chicago's Metallurgical Laboratory took the initial lead in what ultimately became known as the atomic scientists movement, which vigorously advocated for civilian control of atomic policy.[19] One of the movement's pamphlets made its way to the editors of the *New Republic*, who quoted from it in the October 8, 1945, issue: "There is no secret to be kept." The "principles required for the explosive release of atomic energy," the editors continued, "have been the common property of scientists throughout the world for the last five years."[20] Going forward, former employees of the Manhattan Project would remain deeply involved in the public fight over the future of atomic science under the advocacy group the Federation of Atomic Scientists (later renamed the Federation of American Scientists).

This debate culminated in the form of a two-hundred-page document published on August 11, 1945, with the long-winded title *A General Account of the Development of Methods of Using Atomic Energy for Military Purposes under the Auspices of the United States Government, 1940–1945*. Known as the *Smyth Report* after its principal author, Princeton physicist and Manhattan Project consultant Henry DeWolf Smyth, the document served as the official history of the Manhattan Project and aimed to explain to the American public what its authors believed an informed citizenry in a democratic society was entitled to know. It also set the standard for what was permitted to be publicly disclosed about nuclear weapons.

The function of the report was fairly straightforward: its authors sought to ensure that released information was restricted to information that was already known or could easily become known and would not directly contribute to the construction of a nuclear weapon. Smyth developed guidelines on disclosure with Richard C. Tolman, the scientific adviser to general Leslie Groves. Groves directed the Manhattan Project and its offspring the Armed Forces Special Weapons Project, which was created in 1947 to control the military aspects of nuclear weapons. They specified that information could be released only in the following cases:

I   (a) That it is important to a reasonable understanding of what has been done on the project as a whole or
      (b) That it is of true scientific interest and likely to be truly helpful to scientific workers in this country and

II   (a) That it is already known generally by competent scientists or

(b) That it can be deduced or guessed by competent scientists from what is already known, combined with the knowledge that the project was in the overall successful or

(c) That it has no real bearing on the production of atomic bombs

or . . .

(d) That it could be discovered by a small group (fifteen, of whom not over five would be senior men) of competent scientists working in a well-equipped college laboratory in a year's time or less.[21]

A premise that guided the authors as they worked to satisfy these conditions was that the secrets of the atomic bomb were not textual in nature but based on artisanal know-how and industrial production. In other words, it wasn't a physics equation that was important to protect but the metallurgical, electronic, and production capabilities. Accordingly, the majority of the *Smyth Report*'s discussion of the bomb focused on physics, while engineering, chemistry, and electrical designs were omitted or referenced through statements such as "security considerations prevent a discussion of many of the most important phases of this work."

While the *Smyth Report* formed the primary basis of declassification and the official guideline for nuclear weapons information release, its publication didn't end the controversy on the parameters of what could or couldn't be released publicly.

In testimony before Congress in October 1945, Szilárd asserted that "knowing that such a bomb can be made is half of the secret. I believe that the other half of the remaining secret was given away when the War Department released the Smyth report, because the report clearly indicates the road along which any other nations will have to travel."[22] An editorial in the *Bulletin of the Atomic Scientists* in early 1946 noted that "so much has already been told that if we gave other nations all our remaining 'secrets' we would probably shorten their work by only about six months."[23] *Newsweek* devoted an extensive article to the subject that posed the question, "Did the Smyth Report tell too much?" In his testimony before Congress, Chairman of the Atomic Energy Administration David Lilienthal condemned the US Army's release of the *Smyth Report* as "the biggest breach of security since the beginning of the project."[24] Secretary of commerce Henry Wallace echoed this judgment in his own testimony, noting that "with the publication of the Smyth report and other published information, there are no substantial scientific secrets that would serve as obstacles to the production of atomic bombs by other nations."[25]

Smyth and his fellow scientists denied these accusations, asserting that atomic bombs "are not matters that can be stolen and transmitted in the form of information." Smyth told reporters from *Life* magazine that "there is no 'secret' of the atomic bomb in the sense of a mysterious formula that can be written on a slip of paper and carried in the sole of a shoe or the handle of a hunting knife."[26] Correct or not, this was the position of the US government as reaffirmed in a joint declaration made by President Truman with his British and Canadian counterparts in November 1945. The declaration stated that "the basic scientific information essential to the development of atomic energy for peaceful purposes has already been made available to the world. . . . The military exploitation of atomic energy depends, in large part, upon the same methods and processes as would be required for industrial uses."[27]

It is not clear if the authors of the *Smyth Report* didn't realize the significance of the information it divulged or favored release because they believed that attempting to keep the critical information secret was futile. Perhaps General Groves was thinking like a bomb designer rather than a potential proliferator. Groves highlighted that the report didn't remove the veil of secrecy over crucial technical details, while his critics stressed the risk of disclosing the general outlines of the atomic program. What is certain is that Groves and his allies were wrong on two critical points. First, they vastly misjudged how far the Soviets were from getting the bomb. Two months before the Soviets detonated their first nuclear device, Groves publicly declared that it would take Russia fifteen years to do so. A second failure—and one attested to through the admission of foreign atomic weapons designers—is that the authors didn't realize that the *Smyth Report* would provide a useful guide to foreign nuclear weapons programs. Years later, Russian scientists confirmed that the report was "the most important open source feeding into the Soviet nuclear project."[28] Even a half century after the *Smyth Report's* publication, Khidhir Hamza, an Iraqi weapons scientist who defected in 1994, reported that he utilized the report to support Saddam Hussein's nuclear program: "I was sure that if U.S. officials knew how valuable its Manhattan Project reports would be to us years later, they would have kicked themselves."[29]

The 1950s and '60s witnessed the release of additional nuclear weapons–related information to the public at a pace suggesting secrecy was judged to be even less important after the Soviet Union got the bomb. In 1961, the history of the "Manhattan Project" was declassified and released under the title *Project Y: The Los Alamos Project*. Written in 1946 and 1947 when its contents were highly classified, the text provides technical descriptions of the problems that came up during the building of the first atomic bombs. On its inside front cover is a legal notice that claims, "Neither the United States, nor the [Atomic Energy] Commission, nor any person acting on behalf of the Commission assumes any liabilities with respect to the use of, or for damages resulting from the use of, any information, apparatus, method, or process disclosed in this report." Three years after Project Y went to press, *The Los Alamos Primer*, which contains the mathematical fundamentals of fission bombs, was also declassified. Both documents became available to the public for less than four dollars a copy. The release of detailed information on the sizes, shapes, design, and construction of nuclear explosives—and on such topics as plutonium metallurgy and the chemistry of initiators—followed over the years.[30] On some subjects, such as the extraction of plutonium from irradiated reactor fuels, the Atomic Energy Commission declassified virtually all known information.[31]

The proliferation of atomic weapons information from governments to individuals wasn't at the forefront of US national security officials' thinking during this period, and with good reason. As noted above, the prevailing concept of critical nuclear weapons information held that the truly sensitive information was that which concerned practical production methods. As noted by Winston Churchill in 1945, "To be effective . . . disclosure would have to take the form of a considerable number of Soviet specialists, engineers and scientists visiting the United States arsenals, for that is what the manufacturing centers of the atomic bomb really are."[32] Moreover, this was the era of multimegaton nuclear detonations and "Mutually Assured Destruction (MAD)." Defense planners were examining nuclear fallout scenarios in which hundreds of millions of people died. The threat of a handful of people acquiring sufficient nuclear material for a bomb or a tactical nuclear weapon with a kiloton yield in the single digits paled in comparison to the apocalyptic possibilities of the 1962 Cuban Missile Crisis.

Yet the issue wasn't entirely ignored. Between 1964 and 1966, Lawrence Livermore National Laboratory gave three postdoctoral students the task of designing an atomic bomb. The Nth Country Experiment, as it was called, aimed "to see if a few capable physicists, unfamiliar with nuclear weapons and with access only to the unclassified technology, could produce a credible weapon design."[33] One of the students, Dave Dobson, described his rudimentary knowledge at the time: "I just had the idea that you had to quickly put a bunch of fissile material together somehow," he recalled in an interview years later. Yet Dobson and his fellow students quickly rejected designing a gun-style bomb like Little Boy, which would have used a sawed-off howitzer to crash two pieces of fissile material together, judging it to be too easy and unworthy of their time. Instead the students proceeded to design an implosion-type weapon like Fat Man. Less than three years later they had produced a design that experts eventually confirmed to be capable of producing a Hiroshima-type blast. "We produced a short document that described precisely, in engineering terms, what we proposed to build and what materials were involved," another student, Bob Selden, explained. "The whole works, in great detail, so that this thing could have been made by Joe's Machine Shop downtown."[34] The experiment demonstrated that the only significant barrier to nuclear terrorism conducted with an atomic implosion weapon lies in the practical challenges of acquiring materials, organizing assembly, managing people and employing the weapon. In other words, the students proved the veracity of the assertion made by Presidents Truman and Eisenhower as well as their scientific advisers that "the essential theoretical knowledge upon which the discovery [of atomic weapons] is already well known" and the common property of scientists throughout the world.[35]

The Nth Country Experiment is sufficient evidence to demonstrate that critical atomic weapons information lies in the public domain, but it is worth mentioning a subsequent case to highlight the inevitability of additional public disclosure. In 1978, the *Progressive*, a left-wing American monthly periodical commissioned freelance journalist Howard Morland to author an article on the secrecy involved in America's nuclear weapons program. The purpose of Morland's article was to "argue that nuclear bomb secrets are a hoax, and that public understanding of nuclear arsenals is a necessary step in the quest for nuclear disarmament."[36] With a scientific background consisting of little more than five undergraduate courses in physics and chemistry, Morland conducted a series of interviews that ultimately led him to identify the features of a hydrogen bomb.

In contrast to a fission bomb, the design of a hydrogen bomb, or fusion bomb, is highly complex and counterintuitive; at the time it was not public knowledge like the Manhattan Project designs. *Progressive* managing editor Sam Day, who had formally worked as an editor for the *Bulletin of the Atomic Scientists*, sent a draft of Morland's article out to reviewers. The draft made its way to the Massachusetts Institute of Technology, where a concerned professor forwarded it to the Department of Energy after the *Progressive* refused his plea to forgo publication. The government filed a lawsuit and achieved a temporary injunction against the *Progressive*, but ultimately was forced to file a motion to vacate the decision on the grounds that technically the information was already in the public domain. The basis for this claim was two reports from the Lawrence Livermore National Laboratory: UCRL-4725, *Weapons Development during June 1956*, and UCRL-5280, *Weapons Development during June 1958*, which contained detailed information on thermonuclear weapon design. They were apparently found in the Los Alamos library by a researcher working for the American Civil Liberties Union.[37]

Terrorists don't need a hydrogen bomb to inflict catastrophic damage and are very unlikely to acquire one, but the *Progressive* case demonstrates the feebleness of government efforts to control atomic information. The trend is clear: the gradual erosion of nuclear secrets cannot be stopped.

THE MATERIALS

Even before the first atomic bomb went supercritical, it was apparent to those in the know that the disposition and security of nuclear weapons materials was an issue of supreme importance. The most sensitive bomb component—and the one hardest to come by—has always been fissile material. The good news is that fissile material doesn't exist in nature; uranium ore requires extensive processing and enrichment before it becomes both fissionable and capable of sustaining a nuclear chain reaction. Plutonium is almost entirely a human creation; while miniscule qualities of plutonium exist in nature, a sufficient quality for nuclear weaponization can only be produced in a nuclear reactor.[38] The bad news is that it is not especially difficult to build a relatively small clandestine gas centrifuge plant capable of producing sufficient enriched uranium for a small number of nuclear weapons. Consequently, the tightest choke point on the path from intent to build an atomic bomb to a nuclear weapons capability is the acquisition of fissile material. In the words of the early advocates of nuclear controls, "the problem has definable boundaries."

The nuclear weapons community has always known that securing fissile materials is the most practical way of bounding the problem of nuclear proliferation. In June 1944 the UK and US governments created the Combined Development Trust to survey, produce, and procure sufficient uranium and thorium (a material that can breed fissile uranium-233) to meet the needs of the Manhattan Project, as well as to keep them out of the hands of the Germans and Soviets.[39] In February 1945

General Groves, who oversaw this effort, recommended direct action toward this end when he advised general George Marshall to order an air attack on the Auer uranium processing plant near Oranienburg, Germany.[40] On December 3, 1945, Groves reported to the secretary of war that the Combined Development Trust, controlled by Groves himself, had cornered 97 percent of the world's production of uranium and 65 percent of the production of thorium. Yet this proved to be a short-lived conceit. In the following years, geologists discovered that uranium and thorium are too widely dispersed around the globe to make a US-UK monopoly feasible.[41]

The Danish physicist Niels Bohr was the first and most prominent advocate of an alternative approach to fissile material security: international stewardship. Given that the development of atomic energy for peaceful purposes and the development of atomic energy for bombs are largely interchangeable and interdependent, Bohr concluded that attempting to forestall the spread of atomic capabilities was both immoral and impractical. As the Manhattan Project neared completion, Bohr urged President Roosevelt to forgo attempts to prevent the spread of atomic science and its industrial applications and instead establish plans to promote international control of sensitive materials. Over the course of the Cold War, the United States would vacillate between the alternative strategies proposed by Groves and Bohr.[42]

President Truman acknowledged the threat of material proliferation in his very first address to Congress on the atomic bomb when he declared a need to "establish control of the basic raw materials essential to this [atomic] power."[43] Soon thereafter, he issued a joint statement with the prime ministers of the United Kingdom and Canada calling for the establishment of a UN agency to provide recommendations for "eliminating the use of atomic energy for destructive purposes and promoting its widest use for industrial and humanitarian purposes."[44] Established the following year, the UN Atomic Energy Commission (UNAEC) would be the first of many forums in which American officials came to promote international cooperation to control fissile material.

After the Soviets agreed to support the UN commission, Truman tasked a committee headed by secretary of state Dean Acheson to develop policies that the United States would encourage the commission to adopt. To provide needed technical advice, Acheson appointed a board of consultants headed by David Lilienthal, the Chairman of the Tennessee Valley Authority. On March 16, 1946, the committee presented a study to the State Department titled *The Report on the International Control of Atomic Energy*, which soon became known as the *Acheson-Lilienthal Report*. The authors of the report argued that controlling fissile material was the most practical method of managing the threat of atomic weapons:

> This problem of building security against catastrophic use of atomic energy is not one without boundaries. This is important. For if the fact were that tomorrow or a year hence we might reasonably expect atomic energy to be developed from clay or iron or some other common material then it is apparent that the problem of protection against the misuse of energy thus derived would be vastly more difficult. But such is

not the case. The only scientific evidence worthy of regard makes it clear that in terms of security uranium is indispensable in the production of fissionable material on a scale large enough to make explosives or power. Absolute control of uranium would therefore mean adequate safeguard regarding raw materials.[45]

The report goes on to argue that inspections and policing operations are not likely to be effective. Instead it advocates for the creation of an agency to be called the Atomic Development Authority (ADA), which would own all fissile material, have access to the world's uranium and thorium deposits, and release small amounts to individual nations for the development of peaceful uses of atomic energy. The ADA would construct and operate all atomic reactors and separation plants that produce denatured plutonium, which the authority would lease for peaceful purposes. In exchange for this concession of sovereignty by nonnuclear weapons states, the report proposed that the United States offer to abandon its monopoly on atomic weapons, reveal nuclear weapons information to the Soviet Union, and agree not to develop additional atomic bombs.

Alas, this would be the first of many failed proposals. On June 14, 1946, US representative Bernard Baruch presented a slightly modified version of this plan to the UNAEC. Under the Baruch Plan the ADA would carry out the functions recommended by the *Acheson-Lilienthal Report* and also have the authority to seize facilities it administered, fine violators who interfered with inspections, and act to prohibit the illegal possession of an atomic bomb. In addition, Baruch stipulated that the ADA would answer to the UN Security Council, but no members would have veto power concerning the issue of UN sanctions against nations that engaged in prohibited activities. In light of the composition of the Security Council (China [then US-backed Nationalist China], France, the Soviet Union, the United Kingdom, and the United States) and its favoring the United States, as well as Baruch's further stipulation that only once the plan was fully implemented would the United States begin the process of destroying its nuclear arsenal, it was no surprise that the Soviets weren't thrilled with the idea.[46] Soviet ambassador Andrei Gromyko declared, "The USSR government has no intention of permitting a situation whereby the national economy of the Soviet Union or particular branches of that economy would be placed under foreign control."[47]

With Baruch's ADA doomed for the time being, efforts to control fissile material were essentially put on hold until the US government put forward a modified proposal in 1953 as part of President Eisenhower's Atoms for Peace initiative. Recognizing the absence of any force capable of compelling governments to give up core aspects of their sovereignty, Eisenhower aimed to create an international norm through voluntary participation. Speaking before the United Nations, he invited governments to make joint contributions from their stockpiles of fissionable materials to an international atomic energy agency set up under the aegis of the United Nations and mandated only to collect, store, and distribute fissile materials. The proposed agency would function as a "uranium bank" and wouldn't possess any coercive power. Eisenhower announced a sizable US contribution—twenty thousand kilograms of nuclear materials, an amount equal to that allocated for similar use within the United States—and stated that the US government had already entered into agreements with thirty-seven nations for nuclear cooperation. The idea behind this proposal was to use US technological and financial assistance to entice aspiring fissile material–producing nations, and potential Soviet clients, to establish nuclear security controls as well as links with the United States that would facilitate accountability. For example, export policy required recipients of US origin fissile material or reactors to transfer used fuel elements to American facilities for reprocessing, develop adequate production inspection and accounting, and eventually accept agency safeguards.[48] The official International Atomic Energy Agency (IAEA) was founded in 1957. The instrumental role that US exports under Eisenhower's Atoms for Peace played in the development of the Indian, Israeli, Pakistani, and South African atomic bomb programs ultimately proved that this approach had limited success at best.

The Atoms for Peace initiative and the Soviet Union's parallel effort to export nuclear research reactors and nuclear fuel catalyzed the process of fissile material proliferation. During the Cold War, the United States initiated nuclear cooperation agreements with over seventy-five countries.[49] Known recoverable resources of uranium exist in approximately twenty countries with sufficient qualities for mining in only fifteen: Australia, Brazil, Canada, China, the Czech Republic, India, Kazakhstan, Malawi, Namibia, Niger, the Russian Federation, South Africa, Ukraine, the United States, and Uzbekistan.[50] The proliferation of uranium enrichment facilities tracked the proliferation of atomic weapons with Argentina, Australia,

Brazil, Germany, Japan, and the Netherlands choosing to forgo
the bomb while maintaining a fissile material production capability.[51] Over the course of decades, the United States supplied
about 17.5 tons of highly enriched uranium to fuel foreign
reactors and exported approximately a ton of plutonium to
thirty-nine countries.[52] In time, over four hundred plutonium-
producing nuclear power reactors would be built across more
than thirty countries.[53]

Between the launch of Atoms for Peace and the establishment of the Non-Proliferation Treaty (NPT) in 1970, the history of international efforts to control fissile material
production is essentially a tale of draft declaration after draft
resolution submitted and vetoed by the Soviet Union on the
grounds that fissile material control was pointless without nuclear weapons disarmament. However, the NPT was a break-
through in committing its signatories to open up their fissile
material–related facilities to IAEA safeguards largely based on
nuclear material accountancy, complemented by containment
and surveillance techniques such as tamper-proof seals and
IAEA-installed cameras. While the primacy of state sovereignty
and the asymmetry in power between national governments
and a transnational organization limited the IAEA's ability to
effectuate this mandate, the NPT safeguards were and arguably
still remain the most effective mechanism for international fissile material control.

CHAPTER TWO

THE NEW THREATS
THREE DAYS "RIGHT OF BOOM"

THE SECRETARY OF STATE IS SKEPTICAL OF HER OWN TALK-
ING points. And she is privy to considerably more intelligence than she was authorized to share with foreign
capitals. The highly classified assessment of the US intelligence community on the perpetrators of the attack isn't a long
read. From what she can tell, it seems to be based largely on
SIGINT hits—signals interceptions—that reveal fragmented
thoughts of people who may or may not know what they are
talking about. And conjecture. Lots of conjecture. But she is
the voice of her country. And so, she speaks unequivocally in
her phone calls with foreign ministers. It was a weak case. She
knows it. But it is the best that a diplomat could do under the
circumstances.

An aide walks into the office and hands over a note. The
Foreign Minister of Russia is on the phone.

"Thank you for getting back to me. Is your government
willing to support my president's request?" This is the tenth
time today that she has spoken these words.

"I'm sorry, Madam Secretary, but we have reached a different conclusion from that of your analysts about the identity
of the perpetrators."

The secretary sighs. This is a significant blow to her diplomatic efforts, but she expected to be told as much.

"Based on our sources of information, we believe that the terrorist group that claimed responsibility for the attack is linked to one or a number of political dissidents and opposition groups. There isn't any reason to believe that any government had anything to do with the attack."

Ten minutes ago, the Chinese foreign minister had uttered nearly the exact same words to her. She wonders if the two men coordinated their talking points.

"Russia cannot support your request to publicly or privately pressure any of the governments you claim to be complicit. Nor can we lend our support to threats of military retaliation. American military threats will exacerbate the current crisis and if carried out will provoke a catastrophe. As you know, Madam Secretary, a number of weak states in volatile regions have nuclear weapons and special nuclear materials. It's plausible for a loss or theft to have been made in any of them. There is nothing to be gained by antagonizing these governments when there is no conclusive evidence that they are responsible for the recent tragedy in Washington. My people and my president are as horrified by the attack as you are and offer any humanitarian assistance that you request and that is in our power to provide . . ."

There is no point in continuing the phone call. She doesn't have time for words of sympathy. The United States will take some form of military and diplomatic action, likely directed at a "usual suspect," and the president needs an international coalition. But how, the secretary of state wonders, does one build a coalition against a clandestine network that has either penetrated or been granted access to a foreign country's most deadly materials?

THE PATH TOWARD PLAUSIBLE DENIABILITY

Over seventy years has passed since the dawn of the nuclear age without a nuclear shot fired in anger. In that time, the world's nuclear powers have built enough atomic bombs to destroy the planet many times over. It is no exaggeration to describe this arms race as humankind approaching the edge of a nuclear abyss, staring down at Armageddon and slowly stepping back. Today the historical record makes clear that a minor miscalculation during the 1962 Cuban Missile Crisis would have sparked a war with casualties in the hundreds of millions.[1] Not only was atomic warfare avoided during those fourteen days in October 1962 and during the subsequent decades of the Cold War, but today an apocalyptic scenario involving the exchange of multikiloton warheads is extremely unlikely. This accomplishment is a testament to the wisdom of world leaders and the effectiveness of the modern state, though surely some credit is due to divine providence, fate, or extraordinary good luck.

Yet just as this nuclear threat was receding another gradually emerged. Today, the risk of a single atomic bomb detonating in a city like Dubai, New York, Singapore, or Washington, DC, is higher than at any point in history. Why? Because the diffusion of nuclear weapons designs, materials, and know-how mean that it is or soon will be plausible for malign actors to

conduct a clandestine nuclear attack with limited or no attribution. In 2004, Graham Allison warned that the chance of this
type of attack taking place would be somewhere between "inevitable" and "highly likely" unless three conditions, which he
referred to as the "Three No's," were met: (1) "no loose nukes,"
meaning vulnerable nuclear weapons and/or fissile material;
(2) "no new nascent nukes," which means no new national capabilities to enrich uranium or reprocess plutonium; and (3)
"no new nuclear weapons states." Unfortunately, ten years have
passed and in that time each of the three conditions has been
violated.

NORTH KOREA ENTERS THE NUCLEAR WEAPONS CLUB

The most unambiguous violation of Allison's "Three No's"
was the entry of the Democratic People's Republic of Korea
(DPRK) into the club of nuclear weapons nations. On October
9, 2006, the hermit kingdom nudged one foot in the door when
the regime conducted its first test of a yield-producing nuclear
device. This event was a partial failure at best. An anonymous
North Korean official at the Beijing embassy admitted that the
yield, estimated to be below a kiloton, was smaller than expected. Three years later, however, whatever problems the design had were demonstrably resolved. On May 25, 2009, the
regime tested a second device, widely interpreted as a success.
The Russian government estimated that it produced a yield of
between ten and twenty kilotons.[2] Then, on February 12, 2013,
North Korean state media announced that its government conducted a third test with a "miniaturized and lighter nuclear

device." South Korea's defense ministry publically estimated that the detonation resulted in a six- to nine-kiloton blast. While of less destructive power, the diminished size of the explosion was greeted with increased alarm because it lent credence to North Korea's claim that it was testing miniaturized weapons that could be deployed on a ballistic missile or sold and easily transported to a foreign buyer.[3] "We have failed," admits Evans Revere, who has devoted much of his career at the State Department to trying to prevent this outcome. "For two decades our policy has been to keep the North Koreans from developing nuclear weapons. It's now clear there is no way they will give them up, no matter what sanctions we impose, no matter what we offer."[4]

The DPRK's weapons tests are a testament to the disturbing reality that with time and motivation even the world's most reclusive and isolated government is capable of achieving a nuclear weapons capability. North Korea's quest for nuclear weapons likely began as early as the 1950s. Recently declassified materials from the Soviet and Hungarian archives point to a range of specific motivations consistent with the contemporary international political environment. During the late 1950s and early '60s, the DPRK took note both of president Dwight D. Eisenhower's Atoms for Peace outreach as well as the Soviet Union's nuclear assistance to communist nations, particularly Czechoslovakia and East Germany. Like these nations, the DPRK was anxious to demonstrate its technological and industrial development through nuclear power. China's nuclear weapons test in 1964 and the speculation that Japan, South Korea or Taiwan would follow Mao Zedong's lead probably also contributed to the DPRK's calculations. As in the case of India's path toward the bomb, national honor was also apparently a factor. In January 1977, Soviet observers noted that Pyongyang insisted on the construction of a nuclear power plant "for reasons of prestige."[5]

The first step on North Korea's long road toward the bomb was taken in March 1956 when the Soviet Union signed a treaty providing technical nuclear assistance. This agreement became the basis for the Yongbyon nuclear research reactor that was completed in 1965. No substantial additional nuclear cooperation took place until after the DPRK signed the NPT on December 12, 1985, however, almost immediately the DPRK undertook a clandestine effort to construct a plutonium separation plant in violation of its NPT obligations. Estimates suggest that the reactor produced and separated enough plutonium for one or two weapons.[6] In 1992, the DPRK submitted its safeguards declaration to the International Atomic Energy Agency, but upon review the IAEA challenged the declaration and asserted that North Korea had produced more plutonium than it reported. Siegfried S. Hecker, a former director of Los Alamos National Laboratory and a frequent visitor to North Korea, estimated after a 2006 trip there that the DPRK had likely produced an inventory of between forty and fifty kilograms of plutonium before its 2006 nuclear test.[7]

The DPRK also secretly developed a relatively large uranium enrichment program to serve as an alternative source of fissile material that wasn't under IAEA scrutiny. Abduel Qadeer Khan of Pakistan contributed to this effort after reaching a deal with the DPRK in the late 1990s to trade advanced centrifuge technology for North Korean missile technology.[8] North Korea and Pakistan had dealings on missiles and conventional munitions starting as far back as the 1970s, which made it relatively easy for Khan to arrange for North Korean scientists to visit Pakistani nuclear facilities and use chartered flights to transport centrifuges and other nuclear weapons–related components.[8] In 2002 the US government officially accused North Korea of having a secret uranium enrichment program, but its full extent wasn't revealed until eight years later when Hecker was given a tour of the facility. In an interview with the *New York Times*, Hecker said that he had been "stunned" by the sophistication of the new plant, where he saw "hundreds and hundreds" of centrifuges that had just been installed in a recently gutted building that had housed an aging fuel fabrication center and were operated from what he called "an ultra-modern control room." The North Koreans claimed two thousand centrifuges were already installed and running, he said.[10] The Institute for Science and International Security (ISIS), a leading research center focused on nuclear proliferation, estimates that North Korea has enough fissile material to build anywhere between six and eighteen nuclear weapons and will be able to produce between thirty-seven and forty-eight bombs by 2016.[11]

While most Americans don't think twice about what's going on inside the hermit kingdom, the North Korean government still considers itself at war with the United States. Its people are living in desperate conditions; its military maintains a wartime footing and periodically takes violent and provocative actions, such as attacking a South Korean Navy ship and causing the death of forty-six seamen in 2010. North Korea's government engages in illicit trade with the world's most antagonistic regimes. And having conducted three nuclear weapons tests in less than seven years, the North Korean government has clearly violated one of Graham Allison's "Three No's," that of "no new nuclear weapons states."

IRAN DEVELOPS "NASCENT NUKES"

Allison's second edict, "no new nascent nukes," refers to a policy of allowing no new national capabilities to enrich uranium or reprocess plutonium. He was thinking primarily of the situation in the Islamic Republic of Iran. The current framework of the NPT allows nonnuclear states to develop enrichment facilities in order to produce fuel for civilian nuclear reactor, but these same facilities can be used to create the essential ingredients for nuclear weapons. For years American diplomats have offered to guarantee a supply of reactor fuel to Iran at a price substantially below any national production cost and provide for the disposal of the spent fuel. The Iranians turned down this offer and instead proceeded to develop a massive, dispersed, and well-defended fissile material production program that provides both uranium and plutonium pathways to a bomb.

Ironically, the United States provided the first ingredients for Iran's nuclear program through Eisenhower's Atoms for Peace initiative. On March 5, 1957, the Iranian and US governments reached an agreement that would allow American companies to invest in Iran's civilian nuclear industries in exchange for the US Atomic Energy Commission approving a lease to Iran of up to 13.2 pounds of low-enriched uranium (LEU) for research purposes. Over the next decade, the United States provided substantial quantities of fissile material and related nuclear equipment. Consistent with bilateral agreements with other Atoms for Peace partners, the objective of the United States in supporting this arrangement was to steer Tehran away from indigenous fuel–cycle research and toward American managed assistance. Iran eventually signed the NPT in 1968 and completed its Safeguards Agreement with the IAEA soon thereafter. Given Iran's solid nonproliferation and security record at that time, by the mid-1970s multiple Western firms including companies headquartered in France, Germany, and the United States entered into contractual agreements with Iran to construct nuclear plants and supply nuclear materials. India's nuclear test in 1974 and growing instability in Iran leading up to the Islamic Revolution of 1979 provoked concerns about potential weaponization and resulted in the cancelation of some of these projects, but by this time Iran had already laid the foundations for a nuclear program.

The Islamic Revolution obviously changed Iran's relationship with its Western nuclear suppliers. The hostage crisis in 1979, the Iran-Iraq War, Israel's invasion and occupation of southern Lebanon, the birth of Hezbollah, the first and second American led wars in Iraq, and the attacks of September 11, 2001, produced destabilizing security dynamics, to put it mildly. Then, in August 2002, Iranian exiles affiliated with the Mujahadeen-e Khaq, an Iranian opposition group, held a press conference exposing the secret construction of the Pilot Fuel

Enrichment Plant (PFEP) and the Fuel Enrichment Plant (FEP) at Natanz and a heavy water production plant at Arak. Two months later, the US government formally accused Iran of attempting to make nuclear weapons. While Iran has continued to allow IAEA inspectors access to a number of nuclear facilities, the regime's behavior demonstrates a "policy of concealment" in the words of the IAEA. Only after US president Barack Obama, French president Nicholas Sarkozy, and UK prime minister Gordon Brown presented the IAEA with evidence of another secret underground enrichment facility near Qom in September 2009 did Iran announce the existence of the Fordow Fuel Enrichment Plant (FFEP), which it had begun constructing in 2006. On top of this extensive effort to clandestinely develop the capability to produce large quantities of special nuclear material, the IAEA also learned from diagrams it acquired that Iranian scientists had run computer simulations calculating nuclear explosive yields, some of which would produce more than triple the explosive force of the bomb that destroyed Hiroshima.[12]

Considering that the Iranian nuclear program is over a half century in the making, it should be no surprise that it is quite large and well established. When Iran pledged to freeze its nuclear program in November 2013, the country had installed over 18,458 centrifuges and produced approximately 10,357 kilograms of 3.5 percent LEU, of which 3,150 kilograms had been enriched to 20 percent LEU. The FEP contained over 15,421 IR-1m centrifuges and nearly 1,008 fully or partially installed IR-2m centrifuges. The facility is designed to ultimately hold 21,000 IR-1m centrifuges and approximately 3,000 of those of the advanced IR-2m design according to design information submitted by Iran to the IAEA. To date, the FEP has produced the bulk of Iran's 3.5 percent enriched uranium. The aboveground PFEP also holds IR-1m centrifuges along with advanced IR-2m, IR-4m, IR-5m, and IR-6m centrifuges that have processed 3.5 percent enriched uranium into 19.7 percent purity. Of greatest concern is the underground and hardened FFEP complex near Qom, which contains approximately 2,710 IR-1m centrifuges. Moreover, Ali Akbar Salehi, who heads Iran's Atomic Energy Organization and publicly claims that Iran has tested a new generation of IR-8 centrifuges that have sixteen times the capacity of the IR-1m.[13] In layperson's terms, this is a very large nuclear program, and Iran has more than enough uranium to produce an atomic bomb. The republic is also nearing completion of the Arak reactor, which before the November 2013 freeze had been scheduled to be loaded with fuel in early 2014, and which provides a plutonium pathway to the bomb. Before the November 2013 agreement between Iran and the P-5 +1, Iran was on track to have a capacity to produce a bomb's worth of highly enriched uranium (HEU) in twelve to fifteen days , according to ISIS.[14]

The deal struck in 2013 successfully pushed back this date, but Iran has already passed the point of establishing "nascent nukes," to use Allison's phrase. This fact has been obscured by a decade of Israeli warnings that an Iranian critical capability is imminent and that the Islamic republic is near a "red line" and "nuclear threshold." By one estimate, Iran has crossed at least nine Israeli red lines:

1995: no contract for civilian nuclear reactor

2004: no operational uranium conversion plant

2006: no enrichment up to 5 percent

2007: no mastery of enrichment

2009: no bomb's worth of 5 percent enriched uranium

2009: no covert facilities

2010: no uranium enrichment above 5 percent

2011: no activation of the FFEP

2011: no enrichment up to 20 percent medium-enriched uranium[15]

2012: no bomb's worth (250 kilograms) of 20 percent enriched uranium in hexafluoride form

Arguably one of Israel's more significant red lines was the activation of the FFEP, which Israeli intelligence estimates is 220 feet underground and according to former defense minister Ehud Barak places the nuclear program in the "zone of immunity."[16] This line was crossed in December 2011. In 2012, prime minister Benjamin Netanyahu physically drew a red line on a sketch of a bomb that he presented in a speech before the UN's General Assembly, which specified the acquisition of 250 kilograms of 20 percent enriched uranium, an amount that can be quickly enriched to a 90 percent fissile purity level. His administration later clarified that the red line was a bomb's worth of medium-enriched uranium (MEU) in hexafluoride form. To calm tensions, Iran subsequently decided to convert most of its new MEU into oxide fuel for the Tehran research reactor.

But these red lines have confused as much as clarified the issue. The most intuitive definition of nuclear weapons capability is the acquisition of sufficient special nuclear material for an atomic bomb, which is typically identified as about 25 kilograms of uranium enriched to above 90 percent U-235. Yet this definition has also been criticized on the grounds that additional time and capabilities are needed to create a viable weapon.[17] Other commentators have gone even further arguing that Iran would need at least two nuclear weapons to be a genuine threat and therefore the red line is crossed when the regime has the capability to produce a nuclear arsenal composed of multiple atomic bombs.

Pundits and policy wonks have a tendency to fixate on numbers in an attempt to clarify inherently arbitrary distinctions, but the significance of Iran's advances are most clearly gleaned through a framework articulated by both President Obama and Defense Minister Barak. What makes Iran a de facto nuclear weapons state isn't its intention, which is indeterminate and debatable but obviously relevant. It is also not the quantity of 3.5 percent and 20 percent enriched uranium that it possesses, although this is certainly a necessary component for a bomb. People focus on these issues for good reason, but Iran has effectively maneuvered to make them of secondary relevance. During the final presidential debate in the 2012 campaign, President Obama characterized the critical threshold as when "we would not be able to intervene in time to stop [Iran's] nuclear program." Barak has been more specific in stating that it is when an attack could not derail the nuclear project.[18] This conceptual framework integrates not only Iran's potential timeline to a bomb—which is generally defined as the speed at which Iran's declared centrifuge capacity could allow the government to use its safeguarded stockpile to "dash" to a nuclear bomb—but also the myriad of military and political factors that would inhibit the outside world from intervening.

Among the most salient factors are time and distance: the time between the ayatollah giving a green light and US and/or Israeli detection of this decision, and then a decision to respond with military action; the time necessary to launch a strike; and the time required (over years) to continue air strikes to keep the facilities inactive. It is a question of the distances between Iran and the United States, between Iran and Israel, and between the earth's surface and the hardened underground rooms filled with spinning centrifuges.[19]

These would be the dominant considerations if the president were ever presented with the following scenario.

"Mr. President, we've intercepted communications indicating Iran has decided to make an atomic bomb. We don't know when this decision was made, but we do assess that they have the capability to produce a weapons sufficient quantity of fissile material in less than a month. Given Iran's size, we also can't be confident that we know where all their nuclear facilities are located. It is possible that Iran may already have enough material to retaliate with a nuclear weapon if we strike now. What are our orders?"

Does Iran have a nuclear weapon? Not yet. Does it have "nascent nukes"? Most certainly.

THE "LOOSE NUKE" PROBLEM:
FROM RUSSIA TO PAKISTAN

The breakup of the Soviet Union presented an entirely unprecedented challenge: the redeployment of thousands of nuclear weapons and the dismantlement of hundreds of nuclear installations. It was this challenge that focused a great deal of attention on the danger of "loose nukes," another of Allison's "Three No's." In 1991, it also spurred Sam Nunn and Richard Lugar to launch the Cooperative Threat Reduction program, which has since provided a half billion dollars each year to improve the safety and security of Russia's unconventional arms. These funds allowed the United States to remove nuclear weapons from Belarus, Kazakhstan and Ukraine and financed the demolition of thousands of Soviet weapons, including missiles, submarines, bombers, and warheads. The Nunn-Lugar CTR program also paid the salaries of tens of thousands of Soviet weapons scientists, engineers, and technicians who were impoverished by the economic crises of the early 1990s and helped discourage them from working for American adversaries and governments of proliferation concern.[20] The growth of CTR efforts corresponded with a significant decline in seizures of illicit highly enriched uranium, partially enriched uranium, and plutonium sales on the black market. Between 1992 and 2002 there were at least eleven cases of HEU seizures and two plutonium seizures reported to the IAEA. In contrast, only four seizures occurred during nearly a decade between 2002 and 2012, and they were all associated with a single country—Georgia. While correlation certainly doesn't prove causation, these statistics are a strong indication of CTR's effectiveness and suggest that the threat of loose Soviet nukes and fissile materials has been largely contained.[21]

Unfortunately, the threat of "loose nukes" has shifted rather than declined. Few have had greater access to information on this threat, and experience combating it, than Rolf Mowatt-Larssen. A twenty-three year veteran of the CIA's Clandestine Service, Mowatt-Larssen served multiple tours as a chief of station and rose to the agency's most powerful positions: chief of the European Division, chief of the Weapons of Mass Destruction Department, and chief of the Counterterrorism Center. After the September 11, 2001 attacks George Tenet, the director of the CIA, tapped Mowatt-Larssen to be at the point of the spear in America's response to the threat of nuclear terrorism. Mowatt-Larssen fulfilled this role first within the CIA and then from the basement of the Energy Department's headquarters as the director of its Office of Intelligence and Counterintelligence.[22] The centrality of Mowatt-Larssen's efforts is documented, among other places, in Tenet's memoir. After leaving government, Mowatt-Larssen articulated the problem in no uncertain terms: "The greatest threat of a loose nuke scenario stems from insiders in the nuclear establishment working with outsiders, people seeking a bomb or material to make a bomb. Nowhere in the world is this threat greater than in Pakistan."[23]

Pakistan is distinguished by an extraordinary combination of malevolent ingredients. It is the only country ever to have both the founding father of the nation's nuclear weapons program and a lead nuclear weapons scientist independently develop clandestine networks to proliferate atomic weapons for profit. The latter, and better known of the two, Abduel Qadeer Khan, stole uranium enrichment technology while working at a centrifuge manufacturing company in the Netherlands during the 1970s, went on to develop Pakistan's uranium enrichment pathway to the bomb, and then proceeded to go into business for himself. His clients included Iran, Libya, and North Korea. This became apparent to the world in dramatic fashion in January 2003 when US agents intercepted a German ship named the *BBC China* that was transporting a large stash of nuclear weapons components to Libya. Libyan officials later admitted to having reached an agreement with Khan Research Laboratories to provide $100 million in exchange for a "complete store-bought nuclear weapons program."[24] Khan also built upon Pakistan's long-standing relationship with North Korea in the field of missile technology to provide that country with dozens of centrifuges.[25] As early as 1987, Khan also sold to the Iranians and eventually provided them P-1 centrifuges, schematics of advanced P-2 designs, and hundreds of sensitive nuclear components.[26] Despite his public confession in 2004, Khan remains a hero to the vast majority of Pakistanis, a political reality that compelled president Pervez Musharraf to pardon Khan for his crimes.

Pakistan's other premier proliferator, Bashiruddin Mahmood, is less well known but was also a stalwart of the nuclear program during the 1970s; he occupies the singular position of being the most senior scientist to liaison directly with al-Qaeda. The chief designer and director of Pakistan's Khushab Plutonium Production Reactor, Mahmood retired from government service in 1999 and founded a nongovernmental organization called Umma Tameer-e-Nau (UTN; Reconstruction for the Islamic Community). The leadership of UTN was made up of retired Pakistani nuclear scientists, military officers, engineers, and technicians, including Chaudhry Abdul Majid, who had been a nuclear fuel expert at the Pakistan Institute of Nuclear Science and Technology. In the summer of 2001, Mahmood and Majid traveled to Afghanistan under the cover of the UTN in order to discuss nuclear weapons with mullah Mohammed Omar and Osama bin Laden. According to former director of the Central Intelligence Agency George Tenet,

> Mahmood was thought of as something of a madman by many of his former colleagues in the Pakistan nuclear establishment. In 1987 he published a book called "Doomsday and Life After Death: the Ultimate Faith of the Universe as Seen by the Holy Quran." It was a disturbing tribute to his skewed view of the role of science in jihad. The book's basic message— from the leader of a group that has offered WMD capabilities to AQ [al-Qaeda] —was that the world would end one day soon in the fire of nuclear holocaust that would usher in judgment day and thus fulfill the prophecies of the Quran . . .

Mahmood and Majid were detained after a tip from a foreign intelligence service prompted the CIA to inform the Pakistani government of their actions. The two scientists admitted to the meetings, noted that bin Laden was interested in nuclear weapons and that Majid had drawn a rough sketch of an improvised nuclear device for him, but denied that they assisted al-Qaeda. Despite failing several polygraph tests and a statement from Libya's head of intelligence claiming that the UTN had tried to sell Libya a nuclear bomb, the two scientists were soon released.[27] According to Tenet, the United States "knew that UTN enjoyed some measure of support from Pakistani military officers . . . notably the former director of Pakistani intelligence service, Gen. Hamid Gul."[28]

A second factor that makes the nuclear terrorism threat from Pakistan especially acute is its track record as a sanctuary and a patron of terrorist organizations. Even before Pakistan became a state after the partition of British India, its advocates decided that securing an Islamic polity required an investment in asymmetric proxies. India was destined to have conventional military superiority, so the Muslims of the subcontinent from the start invested in unconventional warfare. From the bloody battles of partition through the present day, the Pakistani military cultivated radicals, which for the first few decades were overwhelmingly Pathans/Pashtuns, but in recent time have come to include Punjabis as well. This isn't a temporary fad; it is an embedded component of Pakistan's national security system. The ability of Osama bin Laden to enjoy approximately a decade of hospitality just miles from Pakistan's premier military university likely had more to do with the sympathies of a handful of people then official policy, but his presence was entirely consistent with Pakistani support for radical jihadist groups such as Lashkar-e-Jhangvi, Lashkar-e-Taibai, the Haqqani Network, and the Afghan Taliban, among others.[29]

Third, and likely related, Pakistani public opinion polls consistently show widespread antipathy toward the United States and sympathy for jihadist organizations. As of June 2012, 75 percent considered the United States "an enemy."[30] Significant segments of the public not only hold anti-American views but also subscribe to radical militant ideology that is manifest in violence against Christians, Shi'ites (of which 375 were killed in 2012

alone), symbols of secularism, and even the Pakistani government. The assassination in 2011 of Pakistan's only Christian minister, Shahbaz Bhatti, was indicative of this trend, but even more
alarming than the murder was the subsequent outburst of public
support for the assassin. Thousands of demonstrators celebrated
the "execution," which they claimed was justified by Bhatti's efforts to reform Pakistan's blasphemy laws, which impose the
death penalty for insulting Islam. Before former prime minister
Benazir Bhutto was murdered in 2007, she expressed a belief
that al-Qaeda would march on Islamabad in a matter of years.[31]

These attitudes are worth bearing in mind in the context
of another statistic: the approximately nine thousand civilian
scientists, including two thousand who reportedly possess "critical knowledge" of weapons manufacturing and maintenance
who work in Pakistan's nuclear complexes.[32] There is arguably
no published figure more qualified to comment on Pakistan's
nuclear weapons program than Feroz Khan, who served for
thirty years in the Pakistani military and occupied senior positions at Pakistan's Strategic Plans Division, the country's nuclear decision-making and command-and-control apparatus.
Regarding the insider threat Khan has said, "Pakistan faces two
fundamental challenges in establishing its personnel reliability
requirements. First, religious extremism is increasing in Pakistani society as a whole. . . . Second, because Pakistan does not
have sophisticated technological controls over personnel, it has
to rely on the rationality and loyalty of individuals. . . ."[33] These
words don't inspire a great deal of confidence.

A fourth development of serious concern is that radical ideology and radical organizations inevitably have spawned radical

violence in Pakistan. According to Bruce Reidel, a CIA veteran and former lead Pakistan analyst for the Obama administration, government insiders have facilitated multiple terrorist attacks against the Pakistani state, including suicide bombings at air force bases that house nuclear weapons storage sites.[34] In 2011, Jeffrey Goldberg reported in the *Atlantic* that at least six facilities widely believed to be associated with Pakistan's nuclear program had already been targeted by militants. The Pakistani military's inability to protect its own assets was demonstrably apparent in early 2011 when it took forces over fifteen hours to regain control of a major Pakistani naval base near Karachi after militants overran it, destroyed two P-3C Orion surveillance planes and killed ten people.[35] These events, alongside a variety of other negative economic indicators, led Stephen Cohen, a leading expert on the country, to conclude, "The fundamentals of the state are either failing or questionable, and this applies to both the idea of Pakistan, the ideology of the state, the purpose of the state, and also to the coherence of the state itself. I wouldn't predict a comprehensive failure soon, but clearly that's the direction in which Pakistan is moving."[36]

Fifth and most alarming, Pakistan's nuclear arsenal and its nuclear doctrine are undergoing changes that exponentially expand the risk of terrorist acquisition of a nuclear weapon. With respect to sheer size, Pakistan was on track to displace France as the world's fourth largest nuclear weapons power.[37] This is a dangerous development in itself, but is accompanied by even more troubling indications of how those weapons will be managed. Feroz Khan has confirmed these facts, and his access to senior Pakistani officials, including former president Musharraf, lend great credibility to his account of the nuclear security situation in Pakistan. While a Pakistani patriot and strong supporter of the country's nuclear weapons program, Khan's account reveals a number of issues of grave concern from a proliferation perspective.

Khan cites two specific events as catalysts that pushed Pakistan to undertake unprecedented risks with respect to its nuclear arsenal. The first was instigated by India on January 25, 2000, when India's defense minister, George Fernandes, formally announced a new doctrine of "limited war under the nuclear umbrella"—a doctrine that would become known as Cold Start. The central idea of the Cold Start doctrine is that India could take conventional military action against Pakistan in a limited manner that would prevent escalation to nuclear war. This would allow India a viable response to Pakistani-sponsored terrorist attacks. Following Lashkar-e-Taibai's attack on the Indian Parliament in December 2001, India demonstrated that this doctrine was more than words by mobilizing 500,000 troops for the first time since the 1971 war. The subsequent ten-month standoff between the two countries convinced the Pakistan military that it needed to up its nuclear ante. In Khan's words, the standoff demonstrated that "Pakistan would lack the resources to begin major mobilizations whenever terrorists attacked India and instead would be forced to rely even more on nuclear deterrence."[38]

A second catalytic event was the US-led invasion of Afghanistan after 9/11, which placed US military assets in striking distance of Pakistan. As early as the 1960s, Americans had expressed alarm about nuclear security in Pakistan. None other than the famous Henry De Wolf Smyth of the *Smyth Report* once stated, "What I am concerned about internationally is power reactors in countries that have unstable governments. The Pakistani reactor, for example, builds up a stockpile of plutonium. Suppose there's a revolution. A totally new and crazy government comes in, and here's the plutonium just sitting there asking to be made into a bomb."[39] Islamabad has long been aware of these concerns, and when it conceded to Washington's demand for access to Pakistani airspace to support US military operations in Afghanistan its "decades-long fear of preventive strikes sent it to high alert."

India's Cold Start doctrine and the US-led invasion of Afghanistan spurred Pakistan to make changes in its nuclear posture that are entirely rational within a framework that assumes the Indian military to be an existential threat; but these changes are also extremely destabilizing when placed in the context of Pakistan's domestic instability. The first change is a massive expansion of Pakistan's plutonium production capacity. The Pakistan Atomic Energy Commission is constructing three additional heavy water reactors at the same site as its fifty-megawatt Khushab reactor. To reprocess the higher quantities of plutonium, Islamabad is also doubling the capacity of the reprocessing plant at the Pakistan Institute of Nuclear Science and Technology as well as completing a much larger commercial-scale reprocessing facility at Chashma that was abandoned by the French in 1978.[40] This is consistent with Pakistan's position with respect to the Fissile Material Cutoff Treaty, which Pakistani diplomats have worked for years to block; these diplomats declare that in order to maintain their country's minimal critical deterrent, Pakistan cannot be expected to accept any cap in fissile material production. Expansion of plutonium production is also reportedly being accompanied by greater HEU enrichment. According to Feroz Khan, the Khan Research Laboratories continue to produce at least one hundred kilograms of HEU annually and are expanding their capability by introducing and installing a new generation of P-3 and P-4 gas centrifuges that have a significantly higher separative work unit.

A second development, which is closely related to the first, is Pakistan's decision to build small tactical nuclear warheads. Plutonium-based nuclear weapons designs, which can require only four to six kilograms of plutonium, allow for substantial miniaturization.[41] This trend is consistent with the April 2011 test of the HatfXI/NASR missile system, which is a rocket launcher capable of being tipped with a nuclear warhead. According to Khan, "The implication of this system is that Pakistan has acquired the capability to build a miniaturized nuclear warhead . . . plutonium-based system that requires an implosion device with a diameter of less than twelve inches—quite a technological achievement."[42] From a proliferation prospective this is also quite a problem.

A third development of grave concern is the implication of the fielding of such a system. To be most effective, it would have to be "pre-deployed and combat ready."[43] Kahn suggests that given the current trajectory of the program, "at some point nuclear weapons would be mated with delivery systems in peacetime."[44] This is the same allegation that Goldberg made in his 2011 article in the *Atlantic* asserting that Pakistan is using civilian-style vehicles without noticeable defense to transport not merely the "demated" components of nuclear parts but "mated" nuclear weapons.[45] The Congressional Research Service has also cited lieutenant general Khalid Kidwai, the head of Pakistan's Strategic Plans Division in 2008, who made the same allegation.[46] This contention is conjecture rather than a sure fact, but the military dynamics of the conflict between Pakistan and India do encourage the predeployment of combat ready nuclear weapons and therefore make these assertions plausible.

Fourth, Khan confirms that Pakistan has prioritized preventing Indian or American disablement of Pakistan's nuclear arsenal above the danger of theft. As the United States prepared to launch an attack on the Afghan Taliban after September 11, 2001, President Musharraf reportedly ordered the dispersal of Pakistan's nuclear arsenal to "at least six secret new locations."[47] The dispersal of the arsenal apparently is also consistent with Khan's allegation that Pakistan is expanding its nuclear weapons delivery systems. Initially, Pakistan only had the capability to deliver atomic weapons by aircraft, but with assistance from North Korea and China, solid and liquid fueled ballistic missiles became an option. However, Pakistan interpreted India's bid for an Arrow antiballistic missile system and Patriot PAC-3 system to back up its S-300 system as a threat that could blunt Pakistan's offensive systems. Pakistan responded by developing the Babur cruise missile and, according to Khan, is also actively pursuing a sea-based deterrent that would "complete the third leg of the [nuclear] triad."[48] When considering the potential for a maritime nuclear capability, it is worth keeping in mind a statement that a retired Pakistani general made to Goldberg: "Different aspects of the military and security services have different levels of sympathy for the extremists. The navy is high in sympathy."[49]

THE NUCLEAR TIPPING POINT

It almost goes without saying that the president of the United States has access to more and better information than the public does when it comes to matters of national security. Therefore, even if we assume away all the facts relayed above, it is notable that men as different in temperament and philosophy as George W. Bush and Barack Obama both publicly declared that the single most important national security threat we face is nuclear weapons falling into the hands of terrorists. There is a good chance these presidents know something about the issue that we don't. But even in the absence of supersecret presidential eye–only intelligence, there is enough information in the public domain about the threat to reach the conclusion that a single atomic bomb going off in an American city is a real possibility.

A lot has been made of the fact that al-Qaeda seeks to acquire an atomic bomb and wouldn't hesitate to use one. Allegedly, Osama bin Laden decided sometime after the first bombing of the World Trade Center in 1993 that al-Qaeda should construct an "improvised nuclear device": a crude atomic bomb but one capable of generating a nuclear yield. The earliest evidence of this decision is the testimony of Jamal al-Fadl, an al-Qaeda defector, who reported that bin Laden attempted in 1993 to procure uranium from former Sudanese president Saleh Mobruk, who supposedly had fissile material of South African origin. In 1998, bin Laden declared that "acquiring WMD for the defense of Muslims is a religious duty," and his deputy Ayman al-Zawahari subsequently stated that al-Qaeda was working through the central Asian black market to acquire a nuclear weapon and/or fissile material. Former director of Central Intelligence Tenet also asserted that between 1999 and 2001, Abd al-Aziz al-Masri conducted nuclear-related explosive experiments in the Afghan desert.[50] The problem, however, is bigger than al-Qaeda, which has proven to be a far less capable adversary than was widely assumed in the immediate aftermath of 9/11.

We are at a nuclear tipping point because the three yeses effectively pave a road to a place where governments have plausible deniability with respect to nuclear terrorism. No single event can clearly mark when the world arrives at such a place. The breaching of Graham Allison's "Three No's"—in the form of the North Korean atomic bomb, the Iranian nuclear capability, and the threat of Pakistan's "loose nukes"—is a significant milestone, but these events in themselves aren't transformational. Rather, what is transformational is the cumulative effect of nuclear weapons supply and demand. Currently the stocks of nuclear weapons or weapons-usable nuclear material that are most vulnerable to theft exist in India, Pakistan, Russia, and countries with research reactors that use large quantities of highly enriched uranium such as Belarus, Japan, and South Africa. According to IAEA estimates there are over 250 metric tons of separated plutonium in the civilian nuclear energy sector alone.[51] This number will rise and the list of states with special nuclear material will grow. Middle Eastern states are already positioning themselves to develop nuclear capabilities in response to Iran's capability.[52] The next decade may witness the construction of nuclear weapons facilities and the deployment of foreign nuclear weapons in Japan and Turkey, as well as in such bastions of instability as Egypt, Qatar, Saudi Arabia, and the United Arab Emirates. Meanwhile, Chinese and European companies continue to supply sensitive nuclear components to the highest bidder, and North Korea is now able to offer tested nuclear warheads for sale along with the sensitive nuclear components it has been exporting for years.[53]

The former IAEA director Mohamed ElBaradei has repeatedly stated "the nonproliferation treaty is obsolete." This may be true, but the problem is worse than proliferation. State acquisition of nuclear weapons can at times be stabilizing, as it arguably was for the United States and Soviet Union during the first decade of the Cold War and probably has been for India and Pakistan. As publicly acknowledged by the US Department of Energy, "Classification may delay, but cannot prevent, acquisition of a first-generation nuclear weapon."[54] The problem is that the knowledge and the ingredients for atomic bombs are so widespread that governments can now plausibly claim that they are unable to control—and are therefore not responsible for—proliferation. At the same time, there isn't a national or international security structure in place that is designed to hold governments accountable for nuclear terrorism. This is a serious problem.

CHAPTER THREE

THE LESSONS OF NUCLEAR DETERRENCE
THREE DAYS "RIGHT OF BOOM"

I N A NONDESCRIPT VAN, FOUR MEN CROSS THE US-CANADIAN border. Their mission is complete, and within days they expect to return home. Their motive was not complicated, nor was it new: the conspirators hated their neighbors. They hated them for all the reasons that such enmity has always existed—because their neighbors refused to show them sufficient respect, because of their foreign religion and culture, because of their undeserved prosperity, and because of their moral weakness despite material strength. Because, as an Athenian general remarked twenty-five hundred years ago, and so still it remains, "the strong do what they can and the weak suffer what they must."

The conspirators felt very strong. They felt strong because they believed that their neighbors were nothing without the support of the US government, and they had struck a devastating blow against their neighbor's foreign patron. One of the conspirators worked in his government's nuclear weapons industry, and that had been enough. The location and storage provisions for nuclear weapons materials were all that the plan required. With this information, the conspirators knew whom to bribe; they purchased access and arranged a situation in which hired muscle was able to overwhelm the guards. This hadn't been difficult because special nuclear materials were widely dispersed and at a number of locations with limited security. Aware of the choke points in the logistics system, the operation was not especially risky.

The idea for the plot and much of the plan had come from an especially enigmatic figure: a young man who had served in the military and who exhibited a great deal of knowledge about the command, control, and transport of nuclear materials. Unlike the other conspirators, whose occupations were apparent, no one knew where the young man had come from or what he did for a living. Did he still work for the government? If so, was he operating on his own or at the direction of some higher authority? At one level, the role of the government in the plot was nonexistent. By all appearances, the conspirators constituted a private group and had acted of their own volition. But their plan would not have been possible in the absence of the government-regulated nuclear weapons complex and the opportunity for exploitation that it afforded.

As the three men journey home, the leaders of their country profess ignorance of the plot and claim innocence. From the start, the conspirators had accepted their individual vulnerability to reprisal, but believed that their country and its people would be largely immune from retaliation. They had understood what they were: an innovation; a new instrument of warfare; a military capability impervious to the existing mechanisms of nuclear deterrence.

DETERRING NUCLEAR WEAPONS STATES

When trying to solve a contemporary problem, it is often useful to plumb the past for similar problems and explore how those problems were effectively addressed. Since the issue at hand is nuclear terrorism, it therefore makes sense to consider how nuclear escalation has been prevented so far. After all, terrorists are only one type of delivery system for nuclear weapons, and the last seventy years provides a historical record of success in preventing the employment of nuclear weapons through other means. As the great theorist Thomas Schelling noted upon the sixtieth anniversary of the bombing of Hiroshima, "The most spectacular event of the past half century is one that did not occur. We have enjoyed 60 years without nuclear weapons exploded in anger."[1] That record owes a great deal to deterrence, which was the principal bulwark that prevented nuclear escalation. But this outcome was not easily achieved. "Deterrence," as Albert Wohlstetter wrote in 1959, "is not automatic." The purpose of this chapter is to describe how deterrence was accomplished and to apply these lessons to the problem of nuclear terrorism.

CLEAR (AND NOT SO CLEAR) RED LINES

In the late 1940s and early '50s, the apocalyptic power of the atomic bomb convinced some observers that nuclear weapons had made strategy obsolete because, as Bernard Brodie argued in "Strategy Hits a Dead End," their use was tantamount to committing suicide.[2] And yet, if the United

States had not convinced the world that it would launch nuclear weapons, it wouldn't have been able to achieve its core post–World War II objectives: keeping Germany militarily weak and keeping the Soviets out of Western Europe. Achieving these goals required the deployment of sufficient force to deter the Red Army from crossing the Elbe and in so doing prevent West Germany from developing nuclear forces to defend itself from Soviet coercion. The United States lacked both the ground forces required for such a mission and the political will to engage in another massive land war so soon after two world wars. It was only in the nuclear age that a country located across the Atlantic Ocean could deter the fully mobilized military of the largest land power on earth from completing the conquest of its historically militaristic neighbor. However, as Brodie noted at the time, threatening to commit national suicide is not the most credible of commitments. How did the United States pull it off?

STRENGTHENING INTERNATIONAL BORDERS

One of the policies that proved most effective in preventing nuclear escalation in the nuclear age was to reinforce one of the rules of the preatomic world: the sanctity of international borders. In this context it is clear that public pronouncement of US "red lines" was tremendously consequential. This was true in instances of policy failure as well as policy success.

The first major military confrontation of the Cold War—the Korean War—was due in significant part to an error in American articulation of US red lines. On January 12, 1950, secretary of state Dean G. Acheson gave a speech at the National Press Club in which he identified America's "defensive perimeter" in the Pacific as a line running through Japan, the Philippines, and the Ryukyus. His statement implicitly denied a guarantee of US military protection to the Republic of Korea and the Republic of China (Taiwan). Acheson's words signaled to all concerned that North Korea could invade the south without risking a major confrontation with the United States. This was not his intention, but declassified Russian documents show that prior to Acheson's speech, Joseph Stalin had warned the North Koreans as well as the Chinese against military action that risked provoking American intervention. Syngman Rhee, the first president of South Korea, also interpreted Acheson's statement to mean that the US government did not "intend to fight for the interests of South Korea." Similarly, North Korean leader Kim Il-sung assured Stalin that "the Americans would never participate in the war." The United States had not used military force to prevent Mao Zedong's victory in China, so why would America "participate in such a small war on the Korean Peninsula"? According to contemporary North Korean accounts, "We were absolutely sure in this." As historian John Lewis Gaddis put it, "The evidence now confirms that, after repeated attempts, Kim got a green light from Stalin early in 1950, while all Rhee received from Washington were yellow lights shading over into red."[3] In June, North Korea launched a military offensive across the Thirty-Eighth Parallel aimed at imposing communist rule over the entire peninsula. The Korean Peninsula became the most bitterly contested territory of the Cold War, the host of the only shooting war between American and Soviet pilots, and the topic of heated political debate within the United States over president Harry S. Truman's refusal to use all available means—including nuclear weapons—to achieve a military victory.

The United States learned from its failure to clearly communicate red lines and made extraordinary efforts during the first decade of the Cold War to bolster national boundaries vulnerable to communist aggression through an array of public defense commitments. The first and most enduring of these defense pacts—the North Atlantic Treaty—was actually made before the Korean War. Established on April 4, 1949, and originally composed of twelve members—Belgium, Canada, Denmark, France, Iceland, Italy, Luxembourg, Norway, Portugal, the Netherlands, the United Kingdom, and the United States—the North Atlantic Treaty Organization (NATO) expanded with the additions of Greece and Turkey (1952), West Germany (1955), and Spain (1982), eventually admitting Eastern European states after the collapse of the Soviet Union in 1991. The NATO collective defense system committed its treaty members to pooling together their military resources by declaring that "an armed attack against one or more of [it is parties] in Europe or North America shall be considered an attack against them all and consequently they agree that, if such an armed attack occurs, each of them, in exercise of the right of individual or collective self-defense recognized by Article 51 of the Charter of the United Nations, will assist the Party or Parties so attacked. . . ."[4] This commitment did more than help organize a collective self-defense; it also communicated a clear red line to the Soviet Union that a violation by Soviet forces of the frontiers of the Western world constituted a threshold for a military response.

During the 1950s, the administrations of presidents Harry S. Truman and Dwight D. Eisenhower proceeded to erect an array of formal alliances and military agreements beyond Europe and North America to bolster the borders of vulnerable states. The first such agreement in the Asia-Pacific region was the Australia, New Zealand, and United States Security Treaty (ANZUS), which was signed on September 1, 1951, and went into force in April 1952. The treaty bound together the three countries by communicating that an armed attack in the Pacific region on any of the parties would be perceived as a danger to all three nations' own security and trigger a response to meet the common danger. While the treaty didn't commit the United States to come to Australia or New Zealand's defense in the event either country was attacked, it did establish an arrangement that could be invoked if hostilities occurred and it therefore increased the credibility of US warnings against aggression. The principal objective of the ANZUS treaty was to allay Australians' and New Zealanders' fears regarding the US-Japanese security alliance, but it also set the foundations for a separate treaty aimed squarely at the communist threat. In 1954, the Southeast Asia Treaty Organization (SEATO)— following the NATO model—brought together Australia, Britain, France, New Zealand, Pakistan, the Philippines, Thailand, and the United States to combat the spread of communism. SEATO was a response to France's defeat at Dien Bien Phu in Vietnam and the fall of French Indochina. Substantially stronger than ANZUS, SEATO bound each member to provide aid in the event of external aggression against a member state, noting, "Each Party recognizes that aggression by means of armed attack in the Treaty Area against any of the Parties or against any State or territory which the Parties by unanimous agreement may hereafter designate, would endanger its own peace and safety, and agrees that it will in that event act to meet the common danger. . . ."[5] While not named in the treaty, Cambodia, Laos, and South Vietnam were listed in an attached protocol—a fact that years later allowed the United States to formally justify American military involvement in the Vietnam War.

A year after the SEATO agreement was signed, the United States and the United Kingdom acted to create a similar security framework for the Middle East. Their objective was to develop an alliance that would connect Turkey, the southernmost member of NATO, with Pakistan, the westernmost member of SEATO. Known as the Baghdad Pact because it was inaugurated with a signing ceremony of Turkish and Iraqi officials in Baghdad in 1955, Iran, Pakistan, and the United Kingdom soon joined the accord. The United States did not formally become a member but signed individual agreements with each of the nations in the pact and participated as an observer in committee meetings. After the 1958 coup d'état in Baghdad that ousted King Faisal II, and subsequent American military intervention in Lebanon, the new junta of major general Abdul Karim el Qasim withdrew Iraq from the pact and it was renamed the Central Treaty Organization (CENTO). While it proved largely ineffective as a means of organization military cooperation, it did serve as a communication mechanism. The

Baghdad Pact and CENTO demonstrated multinational support for the integrity of key international borders in the Middle East until its dissolution in the aftermath of the 1979 Islamic Revolution in Iran.

During the 1950s the United States also strengthened international borders by creating a series of bilateral defense treaties in Asia. On December 2, 1954, the United States signed the Sino-American Mutual Defense Treaty with Taiwan that included the provision that if one country came under attack, the other would aid and provide military support. That same year, the Mutual Defense Treaty between South Korea and the United States bound the two nations to act together to meet common military threats. Similarly, the United States revised its initial postwar treaty with Japan in 1960 under the new Treaty of Mutual Cooperation and Security that obligated both parties to maintain and develop their capacity to resist armed attack in common and provide assistance in case of armed attack on Japanese-administered territories.

DECLARATORY POLICIES

In additional to formal treaties, pacts, and security commitments, the United States also used declaratory policy to bolster the borders of the noncommunist world. With the Republican critique of the Korean War in the back of his mind, and in particular the unwillingness of President Truman to authorize the employment of nuclear weapons against North Korean and Chinese military forces, secretary of state John Foster Dulles announced a policy of massive retaliation before

the Council on Foreign Relations in January 1954. Dulles
stated that the United States would henceforth be "placing
more reliance on deterrent power and less dependence on local
defensive power," a shift that "must be reinforced by the further deterrent of massive retaliatory power." Unable to counter
communist aggression at the peripheries of the Soviet Union
or in the heart of Europe through conventional military power,
the United States would depend primarily upon "a great capacity to retaliate, instantly, by means and at places of our own
choosing." Dulles's words were a direct response to communist
advances in Indochina and the ability of the Soviet Union and
Red China to expand their spheres of influence by taking advantage of superior manpower. He added, "If an enemy could
pick his time and place and method of warfare—and if our policy was to remain the traditional one of meeting aggression by
direct and local opposition—then we needed to be ready to
fight in the Artic and in the Tropics; in Asia, the Near East, and
in Europe; by sea, by land, and by air; with old weapons and
with new weapons." The policy announced by Dulles, which
became known as "massive retaliation," aimed to shift the competition with the communist world from a contest between
conventional forces to one that allowed the United States to
utilize its atomic arsenal for political ends. This concept was
developed as a response and in contrast to the isolationist doctrine of "fortress America" that former president Herbert
Hoover had advocated. Dulles aimed to find an intermediate
option between the two extremes of reconstituting large-scale
conventional forces and withdrawing from Asia and the European theater.[6]

The period of the late 1950s through the early 1960s was a time of exceptional uncertainty in international affairs, with high risk of political miscalculation. Both the United States and the Soviet Union were probing each other for weaknesses while competing to establish international norms, shape diplomatic institutions, and legitimize military arrangements to their own advantage. The results of World War II set the grounds of the superpower contest. In his memoirs, President Eisenhower explained that at the time he had no intention of allowing Europe to be overrun as it had been twice already in the twentieth century. Eisenhower was also keenly aware, however, that the Soviets maintained something in the neighborhood of 175 active divisions in Europe at all times, while the United States had twenty divisions total, only five of which were in Europe. Only the interposition of nuclear weapons could stop a major communist aggression there.[7] In 1956, Dulles characterized America's strategy during that decade as brinkmanship resting on "the ability to get to the verge without getting into the war. If you cannot master it, you inevitably get into war. If you try to run away from it, if you are scared to go the brink, you are lost."[8]

The Eisenhower administration also used declaratory policy to communicate its red lines in Asia. In the years 1954–55 and again in 1958, the Communist Chinese attempted to take small offshore islands by force. President Eisenhower warned the US Congress that the government needed to speak with one voice to counter this threat; he requested a congressional resolution demonstrating the nation's "readiness to fight, if necessary, to preserve the vital stake of the free world in a free Formosa." Congress approved a resolution to that effect within a week. Asked later if he intended to use tactical nuclear weapons in such a conflict, Eisenhower remarked, "In any combat where these things can be used on strictly military targets and for strictly military purposes, I see no reason why they shouldn't be used just exactly as you would use a bullet or anything else."[9] He admitted in private, however, that it would be crazy to use the atomic bomb in Asia again, revealing that his public position was more exhortation than genuine policy, though at the time he did add heft to such rhetoric by ordering a conspicuous shipment of nuclear capable artillery to Taiwan.

The national security establishment in the Democratic Party never embraced "massive retaliation," and president John F. Kennedy's election in 1960 prompted a revision of US declaratory policy. The shift away from massive retaliation had been building for years. In 1957, Henry Kissinger wrote a treatise on the subject titled *Nuclear Weapons and Foreign Policy*. An outgrowth of a Council on Foreign Relations study group, the book criticized the doctrine of massive retaliation for lacking flexibility and leaving the United States unable to respond to the gradual expansion of communist power. Kissinger noted that the doctrine left the president with the impossible choice of using nuclear weapons in response to low-intensity Soviet provocations on the periphery of the superpower contest or doing nothing to confront communist aggression. In 1959 Dean Acheson, in a piece titled "Wishing Won't Hold Berlin," echoed this critique. In his view, "to respond to a blockade of Berlin with nuclear strategic attacks would be fatally unwise. To threaten this attack would be even more unwise . . . the only visible alternative is to use western conventional power."[10] The notion that the United States would be willing to suffer the tremendous losses associated with a nuclear war also lacked credibility among its European allies. Kennedy borrowed the idea in his campaign and denounced the policy of massive retaliation as confronting the president with a choice of "Suicide or Surrender; Humiliation or Holocaust."[11]

When President Kennedy entered the White House, secretary of defense Robert McNamara became the administration's champion of jettisoning massive retaliation in favor of a policy of "flexible response." This phrase was taken directly from general Maxwell Taylor's book *The Uncertain Trumpet*, in which he asserted that the United States should build its conventional forces to have the option of large-scale nonnuclear war. Speaking at the University of Washington in 1961, Kennedy asserted, "We possess weapons of tremendous power—but they are least effective in combating the weapons most often used by freedom's foes: subversion, infiltration, guerrilla warfare, civil disorder."[12] To combat these threats, on May 25, 1961, Kennedy implored Congress to fund a new military assistance program that would build "local defense against local attack." The underlying idea tied directly to Kennedy's fascination with Special Operations forces, especially the Green Berets, who are trained to assist foreign militaries in developing an ability to conduct foreign internal defense. Kennedy directed the Defense Department to increase "reinforcement of our own capacity to deter or resist non-nuclear aggression . . . a change of position to give us still further increases in flexibility." Toward this end, Kennedy conspicuously announced the reorganization of the US Army's divisional structure, an increase in its nonnuclear firepower, new investments in tactical mobility, and his intention to double the combat power that could be deployed in less than two months through a ten-division army and a 190,000-person marine corps. Kennedy was searching for a middle ground between total war and abandoning "our solemn commitments stretching back over the years since 1945," especially "our word that an attack upon that city [Berlin] will be regarded as an attack upon us all."[13]

To its advocates flexible response sent the message that the United States had a range of options available to control military escalation with the Soviets. To its critics it projected a hubristic and dangerous impression that escalation could be managed and nuclear war controlled. The policy spurred an array of concepts, such as "direct defense," which meant the use of NATO's European forces to halt a conventional assault on Berlin, to "deliberate escalation" and "counterforce," which characterized a limited nuclear war in which the Western alliance would employ tactical nuclear weapons to destroy Soviet military targets while refraining from striking "countervalue" targets (cities). Albert Wohlstetter introduced the concept of first and second strike and argued that stability required the United States to possess an invulnerable retaliatory force. Kennedy told Congress, "We will deter an enemy from making a nuclear attack only if our retaliatory power is so strong and so invulnerable that he knows he would be destroyed by our response."[14] This led to "assured destruction" and "mutually assured destruction," the latter of which entered the lexicon in 1964 and was defined as "the ability to deter a deliberate nuclear attack upon the United States or its allies by maintaining at all times a clear and unmistakable ability to inflict an unacceptable degree of damage upon any aggressor, or combination of aggressors—even after absorbing a surprise first attack."[15]

US defense policy continued to evolve throughout the duration of the Cold War, but the nation's publicly communicated deterrent framework remained largely consistent from the 1960s onward. The defense buildup of the 1960s and the Vietnam War marked the apex of US commitment to support "local defense against local attack." As American forces departed from Vietnam, these soldiers left behind America's aspiration to "pay any price, bear any burden, support any friend, oppose any foe" and demonstrated the United States' adoption of more modest goals. In 1969, president Richard Nixon highlighted this new realism when he announced that the United States would "look to threatened countries and their neighbors to assume primary responsibility for their own defense, and we will provide support where our interests call for that support. . . . Our interests must shape our commitments, rather than the other way around."[16] This ebb in America's defense commitments was followed in time by the military expansion of the 1980s. The "dovish" president Jimmy Carter committed the United States to use military force in order to keep the Soviets from attaining hegemony in the Persian Gulf, and president Ronald Reagan oversaw a range of aggressive policies focused on pushing back communism. Yet under every administration the United States sought to prevent nuclear escalation through a declaratory policy based on a combination of flexible response and assured destruction.

CREDIBLE STRATEGIC CAPABILITY

Red lines are necessary, but on their own they are an insufficient condition for effective deterrence. Means are needed to give meaning to any government's messages. As Brodie noted, "The first and most vital step in any American security program for the age of atomic bombs is to take measures to guarantee to ourselves in case of attack the possibility of retaliation in kind."[17] In other words, to effectively deter nuclear proliferation, the United States needed to make sure that its declaratory policy wasn't an empty threat. Credibility results from four basic factors: capability, interest, reputation, and risk propensity. In the immediate post–World War II era, the reputation and risk propensity of the United States was substantial. American military forces had crossed the Atlantic twice in half a century to fight and prevail in world wars. President Truman had ordered the use of Fat Man and Little Boy against Japan. With his military record and public pronouncement equating atomic bombs to conventional ordnance, President Eisenhower made clear that he would do everything in his power to avoid sending more Americans into combat when other military means were available. This was an era when there was also a unique political consensus regarding America's security interests. Having recently shed so much blood and having achieved such grand victories, the American people were willing to bear costs and accept risks in order to maintain their security commitments in Europe and Asia.

The most important means of bolstering the credibility of America's red lines was to develop an unassailable nuclear weapons retaliatory capability and an effective operational structure for nuclear war. A retaliatory capability and a capability to "win" a nuclear war are obviously distinct, yet they were often conflated during the Cold War because the United States publicly committed to defend its allies in Europe, which in practice would require the use of nuclear weapons, while privately recognizing that atomic weapons would only serve a retaliatory function because no side would win a full-blown nuclear war. This conflation affected not only American rhetoric but also the Defense Department's planning and the procurement of atomic weapons systems.

In the early years of the Cold War, the question of "how much is enough" in terms of nuclear weapons capability was answered by applying the targeting methodology of strategic bombing. The Defense Department worked to determine what it would take to destroy the industrial potential—the vital elements of warmaking capability—of the Soviet Union. In 1949, the Joint Chiefs of Staff approved a plan called Trojan that listed industrial facilities in seventy Soviet cities as military targets and asserted that their elimination would require a total of 133 atomic weapons. Yet even if this would have stopped the Red Army—an assertion that was rejected by many at the time who recalled that the estimated 2.7 million deaths that would be caused by the strikes were roughly comparable to the losses that the Soviets accepted and fought through in the first six months of World War II—the plan became operationally irrelevant once the Soviets acquired a robust atomic weapons capability. However, the function of a military is to plan, train, and equip to win wars; consequently, the procurement strategy of the Defense Department would be guided by both the goals of ensuring a retaliatory capability and winning a nuclear war.

In the aftermath of World War II, the US atomic arsenal was limited in both size and deployability. There were all of two atomic bombs in the stockpile at the end of 1945, nine in July 1946, thirteen in July 1947, and fifty in 1948. Nearly all of these weapons were ten-thousand-pound implosion bombs of the Mark 3 Fat Man design, which were relatively inefficient in their use of fissionable material and required thirty-nine men to assemble over two days' time. The Mark 3 also only had one delivery system—the B-29 Super Fortress—of which there were only thirty in the entire Strategic Air Command (SAC) with the necessary configuration to deliver nuclear bombs. There are some straightforward reasons for this state of affairs. First, the nuclear weapons industrial complex was still in its infancy. Second, America retained a nuclear monopoly and consequently there was less urgency to grow the program than there would be once the Russians got the bomb. Third, President Truman and members of his administration still held out hope that a nuclear arms race could be avoided through multinational institutions dedicated to peaceful nuclear cooperation.[18]

It was general Curtis LeMay who began to transform America's atomic program into a flexible and wide-ranging military capability. A strong personality and effective operational commander, LeMay became the commanding general of the SAC in October 1948. His first year of command coincided with the completion of the Harmon Committee report *Evaluation of the Effects of Atomic Bombing*, in which the authors concluded, "From the standpoint of our national security, the advantages of its [the atomic bomb's] early use would be transcending. Every reasonable effort should be devoted to providing the means to be prepared for prompt and effective delivery of the maximum numbers of atomic bombs at an appropriate target system."[19] LeMay acted immediately to meet this requirement and directed the establishment of an operational force that could deliver 80 percent of the nuclear stockpile simultaneously.

While LeMay linked the SAC's expansion to the growth of the nuclear stockpile, the stockpile's growth tracked the growth of the Defense Department's target list. Cognizant of that fact that Japan's surrender in World War II was never guaranteed and that the United States had only one remaining atomic bomb after the bombing of Hiroshima and Nagasaki, President Truman presided over a rapid expansion of America's fissile material production. The availability of this material allowed the Defense Department to develop and approve the first operationally oriented atomic target list in the summer of 1947. The Joint Outline Emergency War Plan—called Broiler—identified four cities to be struck with thirty-four atomic bombs. In the context of international efforts to outlaw the bomb, Truman ordered the development of alternative conventional plans. But in 1948 his administration endorsed National Security Council report NSC-30, *United States Policy on Atomic Warfare*, which stated that the United States must be ready to "utilize promptly and effectively all appropriate means available, including atomic weapons, in the interest of national security and must therefore plan accordingly." Soon thereafter, the Berlin Blockade of 1948 prompted Secretary of Defense James Forrestal to order the reinstitution of nuclear war plans under his own authority.[20]

The Berlin Blockade and the Soviet Union's first atomic bomb test in 1949 compelled the US Department of Defense to development the nuclear war plans that would structure America's nuclear posture for decades to come. The strategic bombing framework articulated in Broiler remained largely consistent with subsequent plans. In 1950, the Joint Chiefs of Staff designated three target sets in the Soviet Union: sites affiliated with atomic bomb delivery; "retardation targets" (sites that would degrade military capabilities); and liquid fuel, electrical power, and atomic energy industries. With some modifications these categories defined nuclear war plans until the development of the first Single Integrated Operational Plan at the end of the Eisenhower administration. According to analysis by David Rosenberg, who conducted an exhaustive review of declassified sources, the list of targets ultimately grew as large as 2,600 separate installations for attack, out of a target database of 4,100. This in turn translated into a list of approximately 1,050 designated ground zeros (DGZs) for nuclear weapons, including 151 urban-industrial targets. Under such plans, the United States would launch its entire strategic force carrying 3,500 nuclear weapons against the Soviet Union, Communist China, and satellite nations. At the very least, an "alert force" composed of 880 bombers and missiles would attack some 650 DGZs (including 170 defense-suppression targets) with over 1,400 weapons having a total yield of 2,100 megatons.[21]

The increased target list was made possible not only by an expanded fissile material stockpile but also by new weapons technologies. By 1954 the 10,000-pound implosion fission bombs of 1945–49 were being replaced with 1,000-pound Mark 12s that could be delivered by most air force bombers and navy attack planes, as well as surface-to-surface guided missiles, long-range artillery shells, depth charges for antisubmarine warfare, atomic demolition land mines, and, eventually, warheads for surface-to-air and air-to-air missiles.[22] Under the Eisenhower administration the United States developed its nuclear triad, and all three military services conducted research into intermediate range ballistic missiles. Moving at a speed of about ten thousand miles per hour, ballistic missiles reach their targets across continents in thirty minutes or less. Admiral Arleigh Burke oversaw the development of the Polaris submarines, capable of delivering Edward Teller's six hundred plus pound hydrogen bombs. Located closer to enemy targets, submarines decreased the time from launch to detonation to as little as ten minutes. The framework of mutually assured destruction was institutionalized through the creation of the Distant Early Warning Line to detect approaching bombers and the Ballistic Missile Early Warning System to warn of incoming missiles. In 1958, procedures were put in place to keep one-third of the US bomber force on fifteen-minute ground alert at all times, and exercises were conducted involving as many as fourteen bombers.[23] The system of reciprocal vulnerability to almost instant devastation created during this period would remain in place throughout the Cold War.

Between 1945 and 1990, the US nuclear weapons arsenal

grew from two primitive atomic devices to more than seventy thousand sophisticated bombs and warheads configured in sixty-five different designs, with a range of yields tailored for 116 delivery systems. The weapons ranged from atomic land mines and shoulder-fired rockets to intercontinental ballistic missiles tipped with multimegaton warheads to antiaircraft and antisubmarine devices. To fuel this arsenal, America's nuclear complexes churned out a total of 745.2 metric tons of highly enriched uranium and 103.5 metric tons of plutonium by the end of the Cold War. In 1960, when the explosive power of the US arsenal peaked, it was equivalent to 1,366,000 Hiroshima-sized bombs. Two years later, reaching the height of its atomic bomb test program, the United States detonated ninety-six warheads. By 1992, the United States had conducted 1,030 nuclear tests—215 in the atmosphere and 815 underground.[24]

The history depicted thus far demonstrates the great lengths that the United States went to in order to control nuclear escalation with the Soviet Union and China. It also highlights three strategies that were essential to this task: (1) the strengthening of international borders; (2) the communication of an effective nuclear declaratory policy; and (3) the development of military capabilities that could credibly carry out official policy. Since nuclear weapons were never used in anger during this period, it is understandable that many judge this effort to have been a tremendous success. While it is not possible to conclusively prove the cause of a nonevent, it can be said with certainty that America's deterrence policy did not demonstrably fail. This ought to be enough to inspire awe and appreciation, as well as sufficient grounds to treat these policies as a treasure chest of wisdom from which to draw lessons for future challenges.

FLEXIBLE MILITARY OPTIONS

We have thus far considered general policy at the strategic or even grand strategic level, but there are also important lessons that can be inferred about nuclear escalation and the limits of nuclear power—what nuclear weapons cannot accomplish in war—from specific case studies. Since 1945 there have been a number of international crises and military incidents involving countries with nuclear weapons that could have gone critical but didn't. These case studies are especially revealing in how they demonstrate the supreme importance of flexible and intermediate—typically, conventional military—options in providing governments under extreme pressure with the means of pursuing politicomilitary objectives without resorting to nuclear weapons. The common thread that connects the following examples is that in each incident there was a nonnuclear option through which the nuclear powers could protect their vital national interests. In addition, certain cases demonstrate that possessing nuclear weapons doesn't guarantee victory in asymmetric politicomilitary contests. Countries should not rely on their nuclear arsenals to prevail in unconventional conflicts.

The Berlin Blockade

Why didn't the United States take advantage of its nuclear monopoly and use atomic bombs in response to the Soviet Union's blockade of Berlin in the summer of 1948?

Following the defeat of the Nazis in 1945, the United States occupied a sector of the city of Berlin under arrangements concluded among the Allied Powers and in compliance with letters exchanged between Premier Stalin and President Truman. Berlin was entirely surrounded by Soviet-administered territory, with vital supplies and communication lines that went through Soviet territory in order to reach the American garrison in Berlin. The Soviets hoped to create a unified but demilitarized Germany under their own aegis that would be neutralized after Russia received what it considered to be adequate industrial reparations. In contrast, the US government believed that the prosperity of Western Europe depended on German industrial recovery and sought to develop the industrial portions of the country controlled by France, Great Britain, and the United States. This conflict came to a head in April 1948 when the Soviets formally denied the right of the United States to "free and unrestricted use of the established corridors." Weeks later Moscow severed all land and water communications between Western Berlin and Soviet-controlled East Berlin.[25]

The balance of conventional military power in Berlin strongly favored the Soviet Union. Nearly one and a half million Soviet military forces surrounded Berlin. This compared with American forces that numbered slightly less than 9,000, British contributions of nearly 7,600, and France's 6,100 men, all of which totaled only a fraction of the Soviets' strength. Given the correlation of forces, general Curtis LeMay, the commander of the US Air Force in Europe, favored ordering B-29s with fighter escorts to approach Soviet air bases in combination with moving ground troops toward Berlin. Lucius Clay, the American commander in Germany, vetoed this option given the risk of escalation.

General Clay and President Truman were able to avoid the choice of nuclear escalation or surrender because they had an intermediate option available. During the course of the Second World War, the United States developed the greatest air force the world had ever seen, and it maintained this unique advantage during the Berlin Blockade. A legal justification to utilize this advantage was also available. In November 1945, the victorious occupying powers agreed in writing that there would be a twenty-mile-wide air corridor that provided access to Berlin. These conditions allowed the United States to undertake a low-intensity military operation—the Berlin Airlift—that shifted the decision to escalate the standoff to a violent confrontation back onto the Soviet Union. Moreover, cargo aircraft couldn't easily be portrayed as militarily threatening in the same way that ground forces could; this further decreased the chance of Soviet escalation. The brilliance of Truman's decision was that it eschewed calls to solve the Berlin conflict and defeat the Soviets in favor of a course of action that aimed only to end the crisis and manage the East-West competition over Berlin. In other words, US objectives were limited and achievable. The combination of minimalist objectives and scalable military options can be inferred as the principal reason that the United States didn't resort to its atomic arsenal. Truman simply didn't need to employ an atomic bomb in order to protect the country's vital interests.

The Cuban Missile Crisis

The history of the 1962 Cuban Missile Crisis is well-trodden territory; it might well be the single most analyzed international security incident of the twentieth century. Yet it is nearly impossible to conduct a comprehensive study of nuclear escalation without reviewing what occurred over those fourteen days. The basic facts are as follows: In October 1962, an American U-2 spy plane took pictures that revealed the Soviet Navy clandestinely transferring nuclear-tipped missiles into Cuba. President Kennedy had previously gone on record committing his administration to preventing a military threat from Cuba. The deployment of nuclear weapons would have been a major blow to his and America's credibility. Kennedy's closest advisers initially provided him the binary option of accepting the nuclear weapons in Cuba or ordering a major military action. Given this choice, the majority of the president's Executive Committee advisers, including general Curtis LeMay, favored air strikes in the early days of the conflict. In retrospect, this would have been a disastrous decision of unprecedented proportions. Unbeknownst to Kennedy, Soviet commanders in Cuba already possessed the ability to retaliate without further instruction from Moscow and had made the nuclear missiles operationally capable. If these men came under fire from a US air strike, their response could well have triggered a conflict resulting in the death of hundreds of millions of people.

Like President Truman during the Soviet blockade of Berlin, President Kennedy rejected the choice between ordering a direct military assault and capitulating. On October 22, Kennedy delivered a national address in which he announced that the US Navy would impose a "quarantine" of offensive weapons headed for Cuba and that it would be the policy of his government to regard a nuclear missile attack from Cuba as an attack on the United States by the Soviet Union, requiring a full retaliatory response. Kennedy also later invoked the defense provision of the Rio Treaty (another example of an agreement that the US government supported in the early years of the Cold War to reinforce international borders in the face of communist expansion) to provide legal justification for what was essentially an illegal US blockade in international waters. That course of action—an intermediate, low-intensity military action—shifted the burden, escalating a violent level of conflict back onto the Soviets. It also demonstrated a recognition that the situation called for crisis management rather than a risky attempt at crisis resolution or "victory" against the Soviets.

A number of conditions contributed to the perilous character of this confrontation—not the least of which was the destructive power of the weapons in question. But one factor in particular that exacerbated the degree of risk was the inflexibility of the choices presented to President Kennedy. The plans that the US military initially provided, OPLAN 316 (a full invasion of Cuba carried out by US Army and Marine units) and OPLAN 312 (a more limited US Air Force and Navy operation to strike individual missile sites), were dangerously constraining. Moreover, if executed they would have narrowed the options available to the Soviet Union as well as the Soviet military forces on the ground in Cuba. In other words, they would have decreased the pathways out of the crisis rather than opened new routes to resolution. The initial lack of imagination regarding available options put the decision makers' backs against a wall.

If this type of situation happened today under the heighted scrutiny of the media, one wonders if the White House would have the time for creative, outside-the-box thinking. The increased transparency and public scrutiny of US government deliberations today suggests that having a range of flexible response plans on the shelf may be even more important now than it was even at the height of the Cold War.

The 1973 Israel-Arab War

On the afternoon of October 6, 1973—which fell on Yom Kippur, the holiest of Jewish holidays and a day of fasting—the Egyptian and Syrian militaries attacked the state of Israel. Within twenty-four hours Israel had lost much of the Golan Heights as well as its hold over the Suez Canal. Within forty-eight hours most of Israel's regular army units had suffered heavy losses and were no longer an organized fighting force. The Syrian Army was poised to cross the River Jordan bridges into Israel. Moshe Dayan, the defense minister, reportedly warned the Israeli cabinet that the country faced an existential threat and the Third Temple could soon be lost. According to various public sources, on October 8 prime minister Golda Meir's war cabinet agreed that the Israeli military would arm and make operational its Jericho nuclear tipped surface-to-surface missile launcher at Hirbat Zachariah, along with eight specially marked F-4s that were on twenty-four-hour alert at Tel Nof, the air force base near Rehovot. These weapons likely were tipped with atomic bombs with fifteen- to twenty-kiloton-yield payloads, roughly as powerful as the devices that destroyed Hiroshima and Nagasaki.[26] Facing defeat and possibly the dissolution of the young nation, why didn't Israel unleash its nuclear weapons?

A number of considerations certainly contributed to Israeli restraint, but the most significant factor was that the nation was not quite at the brink of catastrophe, as it may have seemed. One consideration in the minds of Israeli leaders was that nuclear escalation would mean violating their national commitment not to be the first to introduce nuclear weapons to the Middle East. This pledge was central to America's decision to abandon attempts to halt Israel's nuclear program and its tolerance of the nuclear capability following an oral agreement between Prime Minister Meir and President Nixon in September 1969.[27] Another factor—and one that is unique to Israel among the world's nuclear powers—is that Israel is a "one-bomb country." In a region where borders are defined by blood feuds, violence can break out over incidents that occurred thousands of years ago, and the phrase "an eye for an eye" was first coined, Israel's much larger neighbors would likely make every attempt to pay Israel back in kind if the Jewish state ever used its atomic weapons. And while its neighbors are large enough to survive an atomic strike, all it would take to destroy Israel would be a single weapon of mass destruction. Viewed from the perspective of history, a decision to employ a weapon that Israel couldn't endure itself, against an enemy it couldn't destroy, could be perceived as nearly as risky as the failure to prevent an invasion by the Egyptian and Syrian militaries. Even the destruction of the Third Temple and the loss of their state would likely cause less harm to the Israeli people than the detonation of a twenty-kiloton nuke over Jerusalem or Tel Aviv.

Despite this situation, the crucial factor in 1973 was that Israel simply did not face an imminent existential threat. Egypt's political and military objectives were limited; president Anwar Sadat sought to bloody the Israelis in order to compel them into a negotiation that would lead to the return of the Sinai Peninsula to Egyptian control. Moreover, on October 9, President Nixon ordered the commencement of Operation Nickel Grass, an American airlift of conventional military equipment to resupply the Israeli military. By the time Israel received these supplies, its army had already advanced deep into Syria and was effectively pushing back Egyptian forces in the Sinai. But the airlift sent a powerful message about Israel's military reserves as well as the commitment of the American superpower to its defense. The bottom line of this case is that Israel didn't go nuclear because it had other options: its conventional forces were sufficient to save the country.

POWERLESS NUCLEAR POWERS: COUNTERING INSURGENCY WITH ATOMIC BOMBS

While it is remarkable that nuclear powers under imminent threat have at times decided not to employ nuclear weapons, it is even more noteworthy that governments have been willing to accept defeat at the hands of weaker militaries rather than use atomic weapons. Every one of the world's five nuclear weapons states under the Non-Proliferation Treaty, except for China, has lost a war against a nonnuclear adversary. President

Truman could be called the father of this tradition; his decision to reject the counsel of general Douglas MacArthur to employ the atomic bomb in 1950 during the Korean War was a watershed event. On one level of analysis his decision was clearly understandable: he wanted to avoid escalation with China, and he wanted to avoid the loss of life and the perception of the United States as callous toward the lives of Asian peoples; and he didn't want to derail his nuclear nonproliferation agenda. However, at another level, his decision was unprecedented. Throughout the annals of military history, it is difficult to find examples of commanders withholding weapons from their military forces, especially when those forces are retreating. This was the situation in Korea after the North Koreans were reinforced by the Chinese Army. Indeed, considering the awesome destructive power of the atomic bomb, the restraint shown by Truman is truly without parallel.

Yet since the dawn of the nuclear age world leaders have repeatedly shown restraint. In the midst of the morass of the Vietnam War, national security adviser Henry Kissinger and his staff developed contingency military plans under the code name Duck Hook. "I refuse to believe that a little fourth-rate power like North Vietnam does not have a breaking point," Kissinger is reported to have remarked. "It shall be the assignment of this group to examine the option of a savage, decisive blow against North Vietnam. You start without any preconceptions at all." The president, Kissinger informed his staff, wanted a "military plan designed for maximum impact on the enemy's military capability," in order to "force a rapid conclusion" to the war. The documents on this activity analyzed by George Washington University's National Security Archive doesn't prove that Kissinger specifically requested plans involving nuclear weapons, but they do reveal the intent to consider this option; they also highlight the difficulty of utilizing nuclear weapons against an insurgency.[28] Years later, in a news interview on April 25, 1972, President Nixon admitted that he had proposed the employment of atomic bombs to shift the balance of power against the Vietcong, but he quickly rejected the "nuclear option" because, in his words, "the targets presented were not military targets."[29] The administrations of both Nixon and Lyndon Johnson before him unleashed a tremendous amount of violence in Vietnam, but out of moral considerations as well as out of the fear that atomic use would trigger nuclear action by the Soviets or Chinese, they didn't violate the "nuclear taboo."[30]

Other nuclear powers made the same decision in the midst of failed counterinsurgency wars. Between 1954 and 1962 the French fought a nasty insurgency in Algeria, to which they eventually succumbed. This traumatic ordeal occurred despite France's acquisition and successful test of atomic bombs in 1960. Similarly, the Soviet Union's 1979 expedition into Afghanistan ended in failure after years of bloodletting despite the potential power of the Red Army's nuclear weapons. While not comparable in scale or in the cost incurred in blood and treasure, the "Troubles" that the British military had in Northern Ireland between 1968 and 1998 demonstrate the irrelevance of nuclear weapons in the face of unconventional warfare. During the 1980s, Israel's failure to establish a friendly government in Lebanon or destroy Hezbollah while it occupied parts of southern Lebanon can also be included among examples of nuclear powers defeated by nonnuclear insurgencies. While less conclusive and depending on one's definition of success and failure, the US-led wars in Iraq and Afghanistan after the attacks of September 11, 2001 could be included on this list as well.

One indisputable lesson that can be drawn from this history is that nuclear weapons cannot be relied upon to counter unconventional violence—especially violence committed by substate groups. This precaution should inform not only prudent military planning but also deterrence posture. In light of these case studies, threats issued by nuclear powers to employ their atomic arsenal against nonstate effectuated violence—for example, terrorism and even nuclear terrorism—lacks credibility. As was the case for Nixon regarding the Vietcong, in the event of nuclear terrorism, it would be extremely difficult to find a military target to strike with nuclear weapons. If targets could be found, the dispersed nature of an insurgency and/or terrorist network would make it unlikely that striking those sites would actually result in the group's destruction. Moreover, it is extremely unlikely that the nuclear power would have the popular support and political legitimacy to permit the associated "collateral damage" that would affect tens of thousands of innocent people. Massive retaliation is simply not an effective deterrence against nuclear terrorism. To address this threat, consideration should be given to the enduring lesson of effective counterterrorism.

CHAPTER FOUR

THE LESSONS OF COUNTERING TERRORISM
FOUR DAYS "RIGHT OF BOOM"

T HE SECRETARY OF DEFENSE SPEAKS SLOWLY. "YOU ALL understand why we are here."

Flanked by the chairman of the Joint Chiefs of Staff and facing the US military's four-star combatant commanders, the secretary continues.

"The president expects a war plan on his desk by the end of the week."

The soldiers in the room know all too well that military campaign plans require clear objectives, specific targets, and operational parameters. They have been given none.

"Plan for a manhunt. You will be authorized to kill or capture the perpetrators. Prepare to go after the network."

There is a pause. The undersecretary of defense for intelligence fills it. "Mr. Secretary, the information we have suggests that the network extends into the corridors of foreign governments and potentially into components within foreign nuclear weapons programs. A conventional military response may draw us into a war with nuclear weapons states."

The secretary turns to the commander of Special Operations Command (SOCOM). "A show of conventional military force will be necessary, but I need you to prepare for an extensive campaign of low-intensity operations. The military component of our nation's response will need to be indirect and conducted in the shadows. Plan to use the tools developed to fight terrorism against the network of nuclear proliferators."

A Navy Seal responds, "Mr. Secretary, as you know we've conducted manhunts before, but nothing approaching the scale or scope of this mission. And frankly, sir, I'm hesitant to even call it a *mission* before the geographic parameters of the campaign have been defined. Individuals in multiple countries and multiple governments are suspects. Are we authorized to put boots on the ground anywhere in the world? Should we plan for armed hostilities with all of these governments? There is no combat doctrine for this type of military campaign. While we possess applicable capabilities, Special Operations forces are not trained and equipped to dismantle entire foreign nuclear weapons programs. It will take time to identify achievable objectives and prepare the force for executing operations."

The undersecretary of defense for policy interjects, "By the end of this week Congress will pass legislation granting the president expansive authorization to launch wide-ranging military operations. The language of the bill will be vague regarding both the enemy and our end state. For good or ill, our elected representatives will leave it to the executive branch to set the parameters of the nation's response to the attack. Congress will provide a mandate to eliminate the threat, but it will be up to us to translate this into realistic objectives. I've conveyed to the House and Senate leadership that the current emergency will be made more dangerous by precipitous military action, but there is a political reality that we all must contend with. Right now the American people are rallying around the flag, but this won't last for long in the absence of a show of strength. No one knows if a second attack is coming, but we all know that the United States needs to demonstrate our ability to respond."

The undersecretary shifts his gaze from the Special Operations forces commander toward the chairman of the Joint Chiefs of Staff. "What can we do to buy time for our special operators to set the conditions for dismantling the nuclear threat network?" he asks.

The secretary of defense speaks up before the chairman can respond. "What I'm about to say will not be expressed in any formal guidance or any planning order, but it is my direction to the Joint Staff and the Combatant Commanders. You will develop two distinct sets of operational plans. One set will be focused on a clear military objective—identifying, locating, degrading, and dismantling the network of individuals and entities that are responsible for the nuclear attack on our nation's capital. I understand that this will take time. The second will address a more abstract but no less important target—the political realities of domestic and international perception. The president needs immediate military options that demonstrate that the United States is going on the offensive. I want to see concepts of operations in a manner of days for repositioning forces, conducting raids, and launching strikes that may have limited military utility but high political impact. These operations will provide covering fire for SOCOM and give our Special Forces time to prepare for a protracted campaign."

The Special Operations community is a unique breed. Its members are trained and equipped for unconventional activities, but they still work for the United States Department of Defense—the largest bureaucracy on the planet, an organization not known for its agility and flexibility. The Special Operations forces commander knows his people will have to adapt from the bottom up; they will need to draw upon the enduring lessons of unconventional warfare and apply the best traditions of special operators against a new type of threat. And they will need to do so quickly.

TERRORISM AS BARBARIANISM

Terrorism was not a central concern of American national security officials or the world's military and diplomatic establishment during most of the twentieth century, but in previous eras it received a tremendous amount of attention. Of course, the focus returned after al-Qaeda's attacks on September 11, 2001. The phenomenon of terrorism, which is a distinct form of organized violence, has existed since time immemorial. Throughout history its significance to national and international security dynamics has ebbed and flowed, with variations in the balance of power between centralized territorially defined governments and loosely organized nonstate entities. Yet terrorism has consistently prompted states to develop and employ unconventional tactics, techniques, and strategies. Despite the unprecedented characteristics of nuclear terrorism, past and current approaches to managing conventional terrorism contain lessons and clues as to how the United States and other governments could respond to a limited or nonattributable nuclear attack.

Terrorism has come to mean different things for different people. While terminology tends to be a matter of agreement for the purpose of common understanding, not all definitions are equally coherent. Two Dutch researchers collected 109 different academic and official definitions of terrorism and found that 85 percent of them included the use of violence, 65 percent identified political objectives as a motivation for violence, slightly over 50 percent emphasized the infliction of fear, and 17.5 percent included the targeting of civilians.[1] One of the more typical definitions focuses on the objective of violence. For example, the United Kingdom's Terrorism Act of 2000 defines terrorism in part as "the use of threats made for the purpose of advancing a political, religious or ideological cause." Such definitions distinguish terrorism from violent criminal acts that are associated with personal and pecuniary matters. A central problem with this description, however, is that it encompasses nearly all military actions undertaken by governments, which are inherently political, as well as acts of violence committed by individuals whose motivations aren't self-centered.

Another common definition of terrorism is based on an action's tactical effect—the instilling of fear and intimidation in a targeted population. For example, another section of the UK Terrorism Act identifies terrorism as acts that are "designed to influence the government or to intimidate the public." According to this characterization, terrorism is distinct from traditional military actions that serve primarily to degrade or destroy an enemy's ability to organize violence. The implication is that terrorism is illegitimate because it causes damage and loss of life that is excessive and disproportionate to the concrete and direct military advantage anticipated. Yet the trouble with this definition is that striking at an enemy's morale is a tried and effective tactic of traditional warfare and consequently it fails to distinguish terrorism as a unique phenomenon. Another common basis for defining terrorism is reference to extremism. As such, the character of the perpetrators—members of warrior cults who exist outside of mainstream society—is dispositive. In other words, terrorists are, by definition, violent fanatics. The challenge with this conceptualization is that the charge of terrorism is based on who carries it out and whether or not the individual or group is generally accepted by society at the time of the event. The fluidity of this definition militates against its utility.

One of the more cogent definitions of terrorism is found in title 22, chapter 38 of the United States Code, which reads,: "The term 'terrorism' means premeditated, politically motivated violence perpetrated against noncombatant targets by subnational groups or clandestine agents." This definition is focused on intention and the fact that the targets of the violence are nonbelligerents. Customary international law and most traditions of "just war" distinguish between legitimate targets and innocents who are beyond the scope of honorable violence. The US Congress' definition makes violation of this practice the chief determinant of what constitutes terrorism. Furthermore, this definition circumscribes the phenomenon by excluding national entities as potential perpetrators (and presumably state and governmental bodies that are typically conflated with national entities). As such, traditional military operations carried out by governments, such as air strikes against military targets in which noncombatants are acknowledged to be present, do not fall within the scope of terrorism; examples include the fire bombings of Dresden and Tokyo during World War II. With respect to questions of morality and legitimacy, this definition is likely the most compelling and intellectually coherent.

Yet the definition of terrorism that best distinguishes the phenomenon from other security challenges, and the one that is most relevant to the issues of nuclear terrorism, is based on a separate distinction. The greatest challenge posed by groups like al-Qaeda is a characteristic that they share with what were referred to in premodern times as "barbarians." The Greek etymology of the name—which derives from an antonym for *polis*, "city-state"—shows that the term wasn't fashioned to convey a moral judgment, as it does today, but to reflect the condition of peoples who do not dwell in cities. Those most far removed from cities were naturally those who dwelt in territories, such as mountain wilderness and deserts, which are difficult to pacify and govern by a central authority. Barbarians tended to organize themselves around close-knit family, clan, and tribal units that dispersed authority through networked rather than hierarchical structures. As such, they struggled unsuccessfully to mass forces sufficient to challenge territorially administered polities, but they did pose asymmetrical threats that could prove devastating. Extremely mobile and resilient, barbarian hordes were offensively oriented and, at times, capable of swarming maneuvers that overwhelmed their foes in short order. Similarly, hill tribesmen and desert nomads could ambush isolated outposts and convoys without warning and vanish into uncharted territory.

Most important, however, and most analogous to the issue of nonattributable nuclear terrorism, such forces had no city walls to protect, and no fields or crops to defend. In other words they were, and remain today, very difficult to deter or eliminate.

THE FOUR COMMON STRATEGIES OF COUNTERTERRORISM

Every political and military contest that has pitted centralized states against roaming terrorist entities is unique in its own right, but a broad review of the history of this type of conflict reveals that governments have employed four common strategies. These include (1) establishing barriers to restrict movement, (2) promoting accountable governmental institutions, (3) developing and employing specialized paramilitary forces to operate through periods of consistent low-intensity conflict, and (4) conducting punitive and preventative expeditions premised on collective culpability. These strategies appear and reappear repeatedly throughout history and remain relevant to the unique challenges associated with nuclear terrorism.

Restricting Movement

One of the most visible and consequently one of the most discernible counterterrorism strategies has been the use of barriers. While warfare has changed tremendously in the last three thousand years, the high wall has endured the test of time. From the foundations of the Great Wall of China that were laid as early as the eighth century BCE to the Roman emperor

Hadrian's wall that was constructed across Britannia in 122 CE to the modern state of Israel's 430-mile West Bank barrier, walls remain a consistent response to violence conducted by networked mobile nonstate entities. Different in scale, but not in kind, checkpoints and roadblocks also have been used by territorial states to serve the same purpose. To pacify the Irish clans, the English constructed networks of rural settlements and urban estates overlooking strategic nodes throughout Irish lands. Administered by poor but devout Welsh, Scottish, and English Protestants, these estates controlled the movement of people and food for centuries. This approach has been applied in urban settings as well. During the US-led occupation of Iraq, the US military discovered that one of the most effective ways to prevent al-Qaeda in Iraq's campaign of suicide and car bombings against Shi'ites was to erect a series of large concrete barriers around targeted neighborhoods. One can also see the use of blockades at the entrance to any federal building or other large, commonly populated structure (e.g., an airport terminal, a train station, or a skyscraper) in most cities across America. In a substantially different environment, but with comparable counterterrorism objectives, the US Transportation Security Administration airport screening and the Federal Bureau of Investigation's No Fly List perform similar functions. Such barriers to movement are obviously significant at the tactical and operational level, but they also reflect a strategic assessment. The use of walls connotes a recognition that certain threats cannot be easily eliminated and must be endured. In this sense, barriers acknowledge that conventional military victory is not a viable option for the foreseeable future.

Settlement and "Capacity Building"

A related stratagem that territorial states commonly employ against barbarians is to settle, trade, educate, and develop the communities in which terrorists find sanctuary. The central concept underlying this strategy is to incentivize the target group to prevent the export of violence from its population by giving it something to lose (e.g., a territory or trading rights) and to enable the group to perform this function by establishing institutional structures that centralize power and vest select individuals with responsibility for policing their people. In this way, the barbarian horde, tribal confederacy, or nomadic clan gradually transforms into something resembling a territorial state that's amenable to political, economic, and military pressure. One of the more brutal examples of this approach was the confinement of the Plains Indians to reservations in the late nineteenth century; another was the incorporation of Arabian raiding tribes into the Saudi state during the early twentieth century. While the following comparison is rarely made, these efforts at pacification bare some fundamental similarities with more recent modern "capacity building" initiatives. The US military made colossal investments in this approach through entities such as the provincial reconstruction teams that it deployed in Afghanistan and Iraq. Other efforts outside of official war zones also fit within this category of activity. For example, the United States has provided radiological detectors to a number of foreign governments for use in their airports and border crossings as part of the National Nuclear Security Administration's Second Line of Defense program. While these monitors help bolster a foreign government's capacity, their principal purpose and the reason why American taxpayers foot the bill is to allow foreign authorities to control threats extant in their territories from becoming external problems.[2]

Employing Specialized Paramilitary Forces

Neither police nor conventional military forces are especially well suited for combating violent barbarians. Typical police forces are manned by local officers who won't deploy outside of their hometowns for an extended period of time. Often the street cop also tends not to possess the military discipline and tactical acumen to effectively challenge highly motivated terrorist networks. Conventional military forces also aren't particularly effective at this task. Large conventional forces are expensive to deploy for significant periods of time, slow to maneuver, and liable to be worn down in mountainous or desert terrain where insurgents are free to employ hit-and-run tactics.

Adapting to this reality, governments throughout history have been compelled to develop special paramilitary, constabulary, and irregular forces to confront violent nomads. Sometimes governments build these types of units by pulling select candidates out of conventional military forces or regular police units. The French fielded the Maréchaussée ("constabulary"), and the marshalcy of France served as the genesis for the French Gendarmerie, a paramilitary force that combined foot- and cavalrymen. The British developed and deployed similar units across their empire, including the Royal Irish Constabulary, Royal Ulster Constabulary, Royal Newfoundland Constabulary, Royal Canadian Mounted Police, Pennsylvania Constabulary, and Jamaica Constabulary Force.

Despite the versatility of these specialized forces, governments still require the kind of unique knowledge that only local populations possess. Consequently, imperial powers have always worked through local proxies and amenable ethnic groups that are accustomed to military operations in terrain that is inhospitable to foreign forces. Army officers in British India referred to such peoples as "martial races"—a concept that complemented Indian culture's Vedic social system, which identified a "warrior" sect among Hinduism's four orders or *varnas*. Among the most well-known of the groups given this label by the British included the Gurkhas, Pashtuns, Scots, and Sikhs. The British also used hybrid forces manned by members of applicable ethnic groups under the command of British officers in order to take advantage of local knowledge while ensuring its utilization on behalf of the empire. For example, in 1907 George Curzon, the viceroy of British India, created the Frontier Corps. The corps integrated seven militia and scout units manned by men from the tribal areas of the Afghanistan border, including the Khyber Rifles, Zhob Militia, Kurram Militia, Tochi Scouts, Chagai Militia, South Waziristan Scouts, and Chitral Scouts. The efficacy of this capability is attested to by the fact that the Frontier Corps endures to this day under the command of the sovereign state of Pakistan, which continues to recruit most of its enlisted men from the tribal areas along its western border.

Punitive Expeditions

The term *punitive expedition* tends to be associated with acts of egregious, immoral, and unnecessary violence; the kind of massacre general George Armstrong Custer committed against defenseless Indian villages. When a punitive expedition is placed in the context of the full range of military options, however, it can also be interpreted as an act of humility that reflects recognition of the limits of military force. The punitive expedition is an alternative to violence on a much larger scale—war waged to destroy an enemy completely. As such, punitive expeditions can be the tool of pragmatic leaders who need to respond to terrorism but accept that the cost of total victory—the pacification of a given territory or the annihilation of an extremist group—is prohibitively high in blood and treasure. Put in more contemporary parlance, and in the language of the administration of president Barack Obama, such conduct might be described as "a time-limited, scope-limited military operation." Governments have conducted these types of operations when their leaders feel compelled to coerce, compel, and deter violent extremists or populations that harbor them. The chief distinguishing feature of such missions is that unlike typical military operations they are conducted without the hope of destroying an enemy's ability to organize violence. The most that the punitive expedition can be expected to accomplish is to degrade a hostile force and buy time until conditions allow for a more permanent resolution.

These four strategies have a solid historical foundation, and each contains lessons for responding to nuclear terrorism. Let us consider a few of these historical events in detail and how they relate to the various threats of the present day.

The Comanche and Warfare on the American Plains

The Comanche warriors of the Southern Great Plains meet many of the criteria associated with a terrorist group. During the eighteenth and nineteenth centuries, these nomadic warriors who never numbered more than five thousand at any given time were the object of tremendous fear on the part of Mexicans, Spaniards, and Texans as well as numerous Native American peoples who were victims of Comanche pillage and plunder. The Comanche were a scattered people composed of widely separated bands that joined together only in common cause against their enemies. Constantly on the move, these warriors rarely occupied the same location twice. Their social hierarchy was based on martial virtue, and wealth was measured in horses rather than fixed estates or land. The Comanche were feared not only for the brutality of their violence—historical accounts suggest that they honored rape, torture, and the vicious extermination of their enemies—but because they commanded all of the advantages of "barbarians" such as mobility, adaptability, nonhierarchical organization, and offensive orientation.

The Comanche had superior mobility; the Spanish brought the horse to North America and introduced the Comanche to the powerful mustang along with bridles and saddles. Quickly thereafter, the Comanche developed the same skills that the Romans of late antiquity observed in the Huns and that the people of central Asia saw among Genghis Khan's Mongol

Horde. They virtually lived on horseback. The superiority of Comanche horsemanship was matched by their deadly bowmanship. Every Comanche boy learned from a young age to hold his seat with his knees on a charging, swerving pony while unleashing a torrent of arrows with pinpoint accuracy. According to contemporary accounts, a mounted Comanche could cross three hundred yards and loosen twenty shafts in the same time a musket-armed man could get off one shot and reload. Their arrowheads were made of flint and later iron and were designed to be small and narrow with barbed edges so that they could not be pulled from a wound without inflicting further damage on the victim. The Comanche also carried fourteen-foot lances, copied from the Spanish conquistadores, for direct assault on horseback. Some wore buffalo-skull war helmets and most used shields made out of bison hide, shaped to present a convex surface and packed in between with furs in a manner that made them able to deflect lances and arrows as well as musket balls shot beyond fifty yards. Under fire a Comanche warrior also was capable of swinging over the far side of his horse and shielding his body from incoming projectiles. The rapidity of their movements was enhanced by a long-distance communication system effectuated through smoke signals and scouting.[3]

The Comanche dominated terrain that was difficult to pacify and subject to central authority. At the height of their power, the Comancheria stretched over six hundred miles from north to south, four hundred miles from east to west across the Southern Great Plains, from the Ninety-Eighth Meridian to the foothills of the Rockies—territory that today includes parts of

Colorado, Kansas, New Mexico, Oklahoma, and Texas. This was high, level country composed of vast limestone plateaus, shallow rivers, and thick prairies. These terrain features were central to their way of life because given the nature of Comanche raiding practices all camps, roads, and settlements within a thousand miles of their area were within their riding range and vulnerable to assault. This land was home to the Apache people before the Comanche drove them entirely off the Plains. In the eighteenth century it was also at the frontier of the Spanish Empire, and during the nineteenth century it was one of the last great barriers to the expansion of Anglo-American power across the continent. Moreover, in those rare instances when the victims of the raids penetrated a Comanche camp, it was extremely challenging for them to distinguish combatant from innocent bystander. The Comanche were a communal people, and women and children were known to participate in the torture of their victims.

For hundreds of years, communities bordering Comancheria lands were ill prepared to defend themselves against these raiders. Farmers and ranchers were scattered across a thinly populated frontier; Anglo-Americans tended to settle as family units and by the mid-eighteenth century they numbered no more than one hundred per thousand square miles. Communication between these families was too slow to allow for common defense against raids or to enable effective hot pursuit. Armed with Kentucky rifles, hand axes, and tomahawks, these families were not accustomed to Plains Indians. The Kentucky rifle was as long as a man's body, cumbersome to reload, and designed for firing from a resting position in a covered location;

it could be used with deadly accuracy in the forests and hill country of the Northeast or even behind strong fortifications, but it was not an effective weapon on horseback or in an open field. Similarly, the hand ax and tomahawk were useful for militia scurrying over rocky hills and through thick brush but stood no chance against the Comanche's fourteen-foot lance coming from a warrior on horseback. The settlers could only fight from fixed, fortified positions. Unable to afford a sizable permanent army, the family unit was often the sole defensive organization confronting Comanche raiding parties.

The Anglo-Americans of Texas eventually adapted to this threat by employing versions of the four approaches identified above. The first major developments took place between 1836 and 1840 when the Texas Legislature authorized the establishment of a special force, a mounted frontier battalion. Composed of "ranging companies," the battalion was filled with young men drawn from the Texas population who had learned to ride from an early age and had an appetite for adventure and a violent honor culture all their own. The Texas Rangers, as they would later be known, were neither normal militia, nor regular army, nor police. Instead they bore many similarities to their Comanche foes. These irregulars eschewed the conventional tactics of the professional Western soldier and at times lived a semibarbarian, seminomadic existence in a manner that enabled the type of raids and ambushes favored by their targets. The Rangers often worked with and through allied Indians, such as Apache and Tonkawa warriors who held common cause against the Comanche. They recognized the need for specialized weaponry, and in 1838 replaced the Kentucky rifle with Samuel Colt's "six-shooter" revolving pistol. The Rangers were never able to entirely defeat the Comanche, but their operations—many of which were as brutal as those of their enemies—effectively managed and mitigated the threat until the broader strategic environment shifted.[4]

The decisive strategic change occurred between 1869 and 1881 when the Comanche were stripped of their mobility. In 1869 the Transcontinental Railroad was completed and the US government opened reservations for the Plains Indians. The railroad brought cattle, an influx of ranchers to herd them, and buffalo hunters carrying .50-caliber Sharp rifles. The American leather market offered lucrative rewards—especially for buffalo skin. And so, while millions of buffalo were seen roaming the Southern Plains in 1869, after 1881 none could be found. At the same time that this essential component of Comanche life was being destroyed, the Plains Indians were being resettled. In 1867, the Treaty of Medicine Lodge was signed in Kansas by Indians of the Southern Plains, including prominent Comanche. The document stipulated that the US government would provide schools, churches, food, and annuities in exchange for the cessation of the Indians' raiding. It further stated that 38.5 million acres, or 60,000 square miles, were to be provided for a reservation. The Quaker administrator of this reservation firmly believed that it was his duty to assist the Comanche transition to civilized life—or what might be called today the modern world.

As it turned out, quite a few Comanche disagreed with him. Bloody raids continued into the early 1870s, which prompted intervention by the US Army in the person of colonel

Ranald S. Mackenzie. For three years, Mackenzie's Anglo and Tonkawa Indian forces failed to capture the Comanche responsible for the assaults, but a turning point came in 1873 when they seized fourteen hundred of the Comanche's horses. The colonel ordered that all the horses his forces didn't take were to be slaughtered. This brought his campaign to a successful conclusion. Cut off from the buffalo and from their means of transportation, the Comanche fighters had no choice but to accept the reservation.

The bloody conflict between the Anglo-Americans and the Comanche is neither a morality tale nor a road map for future policy. The point in its retelling is certainly not to honor the victors or celebrate the destruction of the Comanche; rather, this case study serves to highlight some intractable problems associated with diffuse, tribal combatants and how those problems were addressed by the military establishment. For over a hundred years the Comanche could not be deterred or completely defeated, a trait they share with today's global terrorists. But the Comanche threat could be managed and their raids mitigated by specialized forces and punitive expeditions until they were eventually worn down by the reach and resources of the centralized state.

The Pashtuns and Frontier Warfare in the Mountains

During the same period when Anglo-American settlers were confronting the Comanche across America's Great Plains, the British were struggling with a society composed of some of the most martial mountain warriors in the world. The Pashtuns occupy the mountainous border region comprising eastern

Afghanistan and what is today the westernmost part of Pakistan. Throughout recorded history, the various empires that claimed authority over this territory never exercised control beyond the plains and a few passages through these mountains. Only the Mughals attempted to pacify the hill tribes, and they failed. The Pashtuns are not a nomadic people like the Comanche, but because they have always been protected by the harsh terrain of the Hindu Kush they share the characteristic of being largely immune from conventional military pressure. This trait, along with a tribal culture described by contemporary sources as producing "the most notorious raiders and plunderers in history,"[5] posed the kind of unconventional military challenge that terrorist groups have repeatedly presented throughout history.

In the mid-nineteenth century, the fusion of a radical ideology—Wahhabism of the variety espoused by Taqî ad-Dîn Aḥmad ibn Taymiyya that ultimately informed Osama bin Laden and his ilk—with Pashtun tribalism, fanned the flames of terrorism. Between 1827 and 1828, Syed Ahmad brought to the Pashtuns a message of religious reform and a call to jihad against the infidels that spurred a large group of followers known as the Hindustani Fanatics. Under Ahmad's leadership, the Fanatics launched a series of attacks against Shi'a, Sikhs, and British civilian and military officials. Ahmad's movement and his call to restore the Islamic honor that had been lost with the fall of the Mughal Empire resonated with many Muslims of the Indian Subcontinent and ultimately culminated in the Sepoy or Indian Mutiny of 1857. Indeed, the deadly fusion of Wahhabism with Pashtun warrior culture remains an enduring feature of the landscape to the present time. Today the Pashtun belligerents are known as the Taliban, and the violent jihadists they harbor comprise a number of Islamist militant organizations, including al-Qaeda.[6]

The British were forced to develop a method to manage relations with the Pashtun tribes soon after they occupied six Pashtun-inhabited frontier districts in 1848. The system they utilized relied primarily on the use of "carrots and sticks" through intermediaries who were local notables or men whom the British believed to be notables. The purpose of this system was to superimpose a minimally intrusive political structure over a fragmented population. It was nothing new. The same approach was used by the Sikhs, who never attempted to speak the language of the Pashtuns, and before them by the officials of the Durrani Empire who spoke Persian. Ultimately codified as the Frontier Crimes Regulations (FCR) in 1901, this system granted appointed political agents the authority to administer each of seven agencies in the federally administered tribal areas (FATAs) by referring disputes to tribal councils or local notables called Maliks. When confronted by "hostile or unfriendly" tribesman, agents were authorized to seize "wherever they may be found . . . all or any of the members of such tribe [and] all or any property belonging to them"; they also had discretionary power to expel from any given tribal area a person who "cannot give a satisfactory account of himself." The agents reported to a commissioner who, in turn, served as the primary link between the FATA and the central government.

As befitting this region's name, tribalism was the foundation of this system. As Olaf Caroe, who served as an administrator in the British Indian Political Service, explains it, "All of these systems depend on the existence in the tribal society of a communal sense of responsibility. In any tribe with a living tribalism the outstanding feature is that the tribe as a whole and every member of it, is responsible for the misdeeds of any of its members, just as it and they, are entitled to share in any benefit or advantage secured by any member." Premised on this cultural environment, the FCR permitted the collective punishment of tribe or family members for the crimes of individuals. Punishments were determined not by the modern judicial processes imported by the British but by tribal *jirgas* and local elders. When the crimes of a Pashtun were substantial and extended beyond the FATA, the commissioner would order a punitive expedition against the responsible tribal elements. As Caroe recalls, "the military expedition into tribal territory as a punitive measure was the all-too-frequent panacea for tribal misbehavior." There were no fewer than eleven military operations, ranking as expeditions, in the years succeeding the mutiny (1857–77) and twelve in the years 1877–81. Cognizant of the failure of former empires to pacify the Pashtuns, the British and later the Pakistani authorities refused the temptation to attempt an occupation of the FATA.

Like the Anglo-Americans in Texas, the British also employed a special paramilitary force to confront the threat. As Caroe notes, "Since the trans-border tribes were armed to the teeth . . . it was necessary to build up a force which would be more mobile than regular soldiers and act under the civil authority." In 1851 the British raised such a militia primarily out of elements of the Corps Guides, which were developed in the Peshawar Valley as a part infantry and part cavalry force. Known initially as the Punjab Irregular Force (or "Piffers"), the force recruited from a range of local ethnic and linguistic groups, existed outside of the control of the conventional British Army, and answered exclusively to the chief magistrate of the Punjab. The Piffers ultimately consisted of five cavalry regiments, eleven infantry regiments, and five batteries of artillery.

The punitive expedition was only one method for controlling tribal depredations in the border districts. The political agents could cease the allowances that they paid to Maliks, and they could order blockades and *baramta*. Baramta is a word of central Asian Turkic origin, meaning the seizure of persons, animals, or property belonging to a tribe or individual at fault in order to bring pressure for restitution.[7] Blockades exerted economic pressure by excluding a tribe from markets, land, or grazing in the neighboring district. In 1890, Rudyard Kipling wrote a short story titled "The Head of the District" that tells a tale of a "mad mullah" who incites his tribe to jihad after being enraged by the appointment of a "lowly" Bengali, rather than an Englishman, to be the deputy commissioner of the local district. The deputy commissioner's chief assistant Tallantire curtly responds by saying to the tribal intermediary, "Tell the Mullah if he talks any more fool's talk . . . he takes his men on to certain death, and his tribe to blockade, trespass-fine, and blood-money." If the intermediary failed to neutralize the Mullah, "the baffled and out-generalled tribe would now, just when their food-stock was lowest, be blockaded from any trade with Hindustan until they had sent hostages for good behavior, paid compensation for disturbance, and blood-money at the rate of thirty-six English pounds per head for every villager that they might have slain."[8]

This was obviously a far-from-perfect system. It certainly didn't end Pashtun militancy, which continues to terrorize the Pakistan government today, but it was effective at managing the problem and at mitigating violence. The most significant evidence of this fact is that the Frontier Crimes Regulations, the Piffers, and the Frontier Corps, along with the overall strategy employed by the British, were retained with minimal modification by the sovereign state of Pakistan. America's counterterrorism activities– the war against al-Qaeda waged through unmanned aerial vehicles and informants on the ground—is also largely consistent with a traditional model of punitive expedition even if US action is more discriminating due to advances in intelligence and targeting technologies. Outside the theater of military operations, America's economic sanctions, border controls, and No Fly List represent a contemporary version of the blockade and *baramta*.

America's War against Al-Qaeda and Its Affiliates

More than enough has been written about al-Qaeda and America's war on terrorism, but it is impossible to address the topic of terrorism without considering the largest, most costly, and arguably most dramatic counterterrorism campaign in history. The evolution of US policy over the course of this conflict, from an approach guided by expansive political objectives and effectuated through largely conventional military methods to one focused on limited goals pursued through an economy of force, also reinforces the components of effective counterterrorism highlighted by the previous case studies. The methods and mechanics of US counterterrorism rely on the integration of state-of-the-art technologies, including sophisticated intelligence collection platforms, remotely piloted armed aircraft, and a truly global network of spies, diplomats, military officers, and international partners. Yet America's underlying approach more closely resembles the frontier warfare of the premodern era than the recent wars of the twentieth century. There is a great deal that is old in this new struggle against al-Qaeda. Indeed, the enduring strategies will likely remain critically important if technological advances and geopolitical conditions evolve to the point at which terrorists are able to conduct a nuclear attack.

The genesis of al-Qaeda's war on the United States is fairly well known and can be summarized as follows: Osama bin Laden's terrorist group emerged out of a larger current of Sunni extremism that spread throughout the Islamic world with the failure of Arab secular nationalism and the rise of Islamist governments in Saudi Arabia and Iran. This movement combined the xenophobic intolerance of the Wahhabis of central Arabia with the revolutionary politics of Egypt's Muslim Brotherhood. Viewing current affairs through a paradigm first articulated by seventh-century Muslim jurists who divided the world between the Dar al-Islam (abode of territory of Islam) and the Dar al-Harb (the abode of territory of war) and who held the conviction that the former was destined to overtake the latter, these radicals attributed the stagnation of the Islamic world to the unwillingness of Muslims to wage violent jihad.

This line of thought was nothing new and most prominently associated with Taqî ad-Dîn Aḥmad ibn Taymiyya (1263–1328) and his response to the crusader and Mongol invasions and the spread of Christianity and Suffism. In the 1980s this ideology was given institutional foundation through the militant groups formed to fight the Soviets in Afghanistan and the through an array of global Islamist associations and charities financed by petrodollars from the Persian Gulf. The spark that ignited the conflagration later known as the global war on terrorism was Saddam Hussein's invasion of Kuwait in 1991. The deployment of American soldiers in "the land of the two holy places" outraged bin Laden and prompted his declaration of war against the United States.[9]

Al-Qaeda became a problem of strategic concern not because of its extremist ideology but because it proved capable of organizing mass violence on a scale that had previously been restricted to states and national governments. Like the Comanche, the Pashtuns, and other substate entities, al-Qaeda had extraordinary mobility and used civilians as both targets and shields. Osama bin Laden used the modern media, instant telecommunication, and an open global commercial system to increase the advantages of a barbarian group by orders of magnitude. Just as the Huns invaded Rome on the same road that the Roman legions built to expand their empire, al-Qaeda used the technologies and open systems of the modern world to penetrate and assault the beacons of liberal democracy. It would take some time for the United States to adapt to this new threat, and when it did so its approach bore striking similarities to tried and test counterterrorism methods.

COUNTERTERRORISM AS A WAR OF IDEAS

Under president George W. Bush the United States responded to al-Qaeda's 9/11 attacks by launching a global war aimed at transforming the Islamic world through the promotion of liberal democracy. Many commentators have since charged the administration with radically altering the course of US foreign policy. In truth, the Bush administration looked to its nation's own history as an explanatory framework from which to understand contemporary events and to find strategies to guide its conduct. Societies tend to construct maps of political geography that highlight distinctions that reflect particular values and historical experiences.[10] For example, with the rise of nationalism in the nineteenth century, European society identified the borders of nation-states as the most critical fault lines in the West. At the same time, Europeans often divided the wider world between the "civilized" and "uncivilized"—the West and "the rest." These lines functioned as the key borders that European statesmen considered when crafting foreign policy.[11] With the collapse of Europe's colonial empires in the twentieth century and the emergence of the Soviet Union, the map of the continent became bifurcated between the democratic and the communist. Neither the nineteenth- nor the twentieth-century paradigms fully reflected reality, but they provided structure and made complexities comprehensible. Arguably, they also identified the fault lines that best defined the political geography of contemporary international politics.

The collapse of the Soviet Union and the end of the Cold War sparked a great debate over what type of maps would define world politics in the twenty-first century. Naturally, visions of the future reflected past experience. Many Europeans predicted the next century would experience a continuance of the "national liberation" struggles that had brought an end to their colonial empires. The French-born doctrine *tier mondisme*, which held that non-Western societies and states should not be judged by Western standards, contributed to the European projection that nationalism versus empire (or "hegemony") would define international politics. Looking farther back in history to premodern times, Samuel Huntington argued that the wars of the twenty-first century would be fought along the fault lines of the great civilizations. According to his formulation, culture—which he argued is grounded in religion—would reemerge as the world's most significant political boundary.

Despite the European origins of the United States, Americans have always perceived international politics differently from the inhabitants of the Old World. To Americans, the differences that Europeans emphasized between France, Prussia, and Spain were always less significant than their commonality. Thomas Paine articulated what most Americans, for most of US history, identified as unifying Old World characteristics: "Every spot of the Old World is overrun with oppression. Freedom hath been hunted round the globe. Asia and Africa have long expelled her. Europe regards her like a stranger and England hath given her warning to depart."[12] Americans tend to see the world as divided between freedom and tyranny. "There are but two sorts of men in the world, freemen and slaves," declared John Adams.[13] Traveling a great distance in time, but not particularly far in substance, one can connect Adams's words with those of Harry Truman. At the onset of the Cold War, President Truman proclaimed that "every nation must choose between alternative ways of life," one based on freedom, the other on oppression.[14] Arguably, this worldview was first clearly applied to US foreign policy by James Monroe. In 1823 President Monroe declared: "The political system of [the Holy Alliance] is essentially different in this respect from that of America. This difference proceeds from that which exists in their respective Governments . . . we should consider any attempt on their part to extend their system to any portion of this hemisphere as dangerous to our peace and safety."[15] While Europeans—particularly the British—feared any one nation dominating strategic territory, Monroe's primary fear was the expansion of a political system antithetical to republicanism gaining a foothold in America's backyard. Over a century later, National Security Council report NSC-68 (1950) stated that the primary objective of American strategy was to "foster a world environment in which the American system can survive and flourish."[16] The notion of a clash of political systems has remained the central paradigm structuring Americans' view of world politics. After 9/11 the Bush administration rejected alternative maps of the world in favor of this American paradigm.

This view of the world directly and deeply influenced US counterterrorism policy. While American military forces were fighting their way to Baghdad for the second time, Thomas P. M. Barnett penned *The Pentagon's New Map*, an account of "war and peace in the twenty-first century" but also an actual map he crafted while working in the Office of the Secretary of Defense. Barnett didn't rely primarily on the simple language of "freedom" and "tyranny" to bifurcate the world; instead he divided the world between societies that are "actively integrating into globalization's 'Functioning Core'" and those that remain trapped in its "Non-Integrating Gap." In Barnett's words, those in the Gap are "disconnected from the global economy" and its "rule sets."[17] However the fundamental difference between Barnett's "Functioning Core" and the "Non-Integrating Gap" is the degree of freedom that individuals have to trade, to worship, to participate in politics, and to express themselves.

According to Barnett's paradigm, the glaring fact that the entire Islamic world is encompassed in the Non-Integrating Gap isn't considered particularly noteworthy. Barnett notes that a reviewer pointed this out to him during a radio interview, and he retorted, "The Gap contains all religions, and all religions inside the Gap are more fundamentalist than their counterparts in the Core."[18] This is indeed a peculiar response. After all, the term *fundamentalism* originated from a schism within the American Presbyterian Church that testifies to the significance of religion in American life. Moreover, an Israeli from Tel Aviv or a secular Armenian would certainly take issue with the charge that their societies are more religious than, for example, that of a Jew living in Crown Heights, Brooklyn, or a Southern Baptist living in Mississippi. Barnett's rejection of religion as a relevant factor in his map is palatable for Americans because this view reflects the American paradigm taken to its logical extreme. When one sees society as a collection of autonomous individuals, it is not worth even mentioning religious and cultural differences.

Barnett's map, or the ideas it represented, ultimately proved far more consequential than any of the thousands of maps produced by the Pentagon in the course of America's wars in Iraq and Afghanistan, for it clearly identified the end state—the incorporation of the Islamic world, or at minimum, the most strategic regions of that world into a liberal democratic world order. This end also implicated the means—military occupation, economic assistance, and political institution building. Paul Bremer, the chief US administrator in Iraq after the US-led coalition's invasion, often declared that the post–World War II reconstruction of Germany and Japan would serve as models. As such, this project required massive conventional military power and tremendous economic expenditure. The American people gave it a try. A number of associated US objectives may have been achieved through this venture, but for a variety of reasons, not least of which was that the success of such an enterprise was never in America's control, the larger democratization project ultimately did not succeed.

AN ECONOMY OF FORCE

While American conventional forces were patrolling the streets of Fallujah and the high command was articulating the merits of counterinsurgency, CIA operatives, US Special Forces, Treasury Department officials, law enforcement officers, and the guardians of America's borders were engaged in a different approach to counterterrorism and—for all practical purposes—in an entirely different war. The central and near exclusive focus of these men and women was finding, fixing, and finishing senior terrorist operatives. This mantra—which traces back to the Korean War and lieutenant general Matthew Ridgway's order to "Find them! Fix them! Finish them!"—had the central advantage of simplicity.[19] Their strategy offered no permanent solution to the problem of al-Qaeda or Sunni radicalism; it didn't promise to "drain the swamp." But it did have the benefit of being sustainable. The members of this community who operated abroad—mainly CIA paramilitary teams and joint Special Forces—were small enough in number that they could not entertain the conceit that they would transform foreign societies nor build the foundations of liberal democracy. Protecting the population, a fundamental tenet of effective counterinsurgency strategy, was simply beyond their means. If removing senior terrorists from the battlefield diminished the threat to the locals, that was an ancillary benefit. To the extent that their efforts aimed to alter the foreign political environment, they worked to arm, train, and equip local forces that would serve as America's surrogates in combating al-Qaeda.[20]

In practice if not in explicit word this was the overarching approach to counterterrorism that Barack Obama embraced when he became president. Nearly all of these initiatives began under President George W. Bush, but they became key features of Obama's foreign policy. The armed unmanned aerial vehicle (UAV) had made its debut under Bush's tenure, but the Obama administration ordered its employment against terrorist targets on a heretofore unprecedented scale. This represented a revolution in military affairs as significant as Samuel Colt's six-shooter over a century earlier. It allowed the United States to finally reach out and touch terrorists hidden in isolated mountain villages without enduring the risks associated with deploying boots on the ground. It certainly saved American lives and very likely the lives of innocent civilians in places like Afghanistan, Pakistan, Somalia, and Yemen. Not only does the precision of such surveillance technology allow the United States to wait until targets are outside of areas where a strike could result in significant collateral damage, but the missiles are so accurate that targets can be struck with high confidence of avoiding civilian causalities. In his most explicit remarks on his administration's counterterrorism policy, President Obama noted, "Our efforts must be measured against the history of putting American troops in distant lands among hostile populations. In Vietnam, hundreds of thousands of civilians died in a war where the boundaries of battle were blurred. In Iraq and Afghanistan, despite the extraordinary courage and discipline of our troops, thousands of civilians have been killed."[21] That said, the UAV does not remove the tragedy from war, and the tactic is not so different from the nineteenth-century raids of the Piffers into Waziristan.

In August 2009, President Obama publicly acknowledged that the CIA had killed Tehrik-e-Taliban commander Baitullah Mehsud in a Hellfire missile strike via a UAV. Given Mehsud's responsibility for numerous terrorist attacks, this was indeed an important accomplishment. Yet the *Washington Post* soon thereafter reported that Mehsud was killed only after fifteen prior attempts had resulted in the death of two hundred other individuals.[22] Both President Obama and his most senior counterterrorism adviser, CIA director John Brennan, have been at pains to explain that these strikes are conducted only to remove terrorists from the field of battle and eliminate imminent threats. "We are not seeking vengeance," Brennan has said. "Lethal action is not about punishing terrorists for past crimes."[23] This may well be the case. The British Commissions in the FATA and the Texas Rangers in the Southern Plains were equally certain that their counterraiding effectively removed terrorist threats.

President Obama reflected the mood of many Americans when he publicly stated, "We must be humble in our expectations that we can quickly resolve deep-rooted problems like poverty and sectarian hatred."[24] In keeping with this principle, his administration acted to remove the United States from the war in Iraq and made plans to withdraw US military forces from Afghanistan. These policies were often characterized as "ending wars," but in practical effect they simply removed Americans from conflicts that were—and still remain—far from over. His administration dramatically rescaled America's objectives in the Islamic world. Al-Qaeda affiliates could launch fifty car bombs a month in Iraq, the Taliban could take control over sizable Afghan villages, and 150,000 Syrians could be killed without provoking American military action so long as such violence remained contained. As the president later remarked before the UN General Assembly, "The United States is chastised for meddling in the region, accused of having a hand in all manner of conspiracy; at the same time, the United States is blamed for failing to do enough to solve the region's problems and for showing indifference toward suffering Muslim populations. . . . These contradictory attitudes have a practical impact on the American people's support for our involvement in the region."[25] From Egypt's revolution and coun-terrevolution to the rise of sectarian violence from Lebanon through Syria and Iraq, under President Obama the US gov-ernment has avoided getting pulled deeply into Middle Eastern politics. After all, the president stated his objective in no un-certain terms: "Neither I, nor any President, can promise the total defeat of terror. . . . But if dealt with smartly and propor-tionally, these threats need not rise to the level that we saw on the eve of 9/11."[26]

While commentators have placed tremendous focus on US direct lethal counterterrorism actions, the United States has also relied on traditional security force assistance to bolster the capabilities of foreign forces to combat al-Qaeda and its affili-ates. These foreign forces support government institutions that can be held accountable for preventing the export of terrorism. In 2006, the US Congress granted theDepartment of Defense in section 1206 of the National Defense Authorization Act (NDAA) the first global train-and-equip authority since the passage of the Foreign Assistance Act of 1961, which placed oversight for military assistance with the secretary of state. Under section 1206 the secretary of defense is provided the authority to train and equip foreign military forces specifically for counterterrorism and stability operations. Over the course of section 1206's first seven years (FY2006–FY2012), its fund-ing totaled some $1.78 billion and supported bilateral programs in forty-one countries, fifteen multilateral programs, and addi-tional global human rights initiatives. The largest recipients over that period were Lebanon, Pakistan, the Philippines, and Yemen. At the same time, the US government used a variety of other authorities to bolster foreign institutions to contain terrorism, including section 1208 of the fiscal year 2005 NDAA, an authorization to provide support to "foreign forces, irregular forces, groups, or individuals" that assist or facilitate US forces, including the Defense Counterterrorism Fellowship Program (which funds foreign military officers and defense and security officials to attend US military educational institutions, regional centers, and conferences), the Coalition Support Fund (expended primarily in Iraq and Afghanistan to fund countries assisting in US military operations), and the State Department–executed International Military and Education Training program.[27] These counterterrorism-focused programs aim to foster security conditions in which direct US involvement is unnecessary because local governments have the capacity to kill or capture terrorists on their own.

While American forces took and enabled direct lethal action in foreign lands, officials in Washington, DC, were developing capabilities to isolate and restrict al-Qaeda's mobility by cutting off its finances, intercepting its communications, and putting its operatives on the No Fly List. In 2004, Stuart Levey was sworn in as the first undersecretary for terrorism and financial intelligence within the US Treasury Department. Under his leadership, the Treasury developed a new tool of national power: the targeted financial sanction. By fusing public and private information on global banking, Levey's office helped map global financial networks, identify the chokes points of al-Qaeda's financial flows and threaten those who were enabling terrorism with expulsion from the American financial system. General David Petraeus went so far as to call

Levey "a true American hero" for this accomplishment. President Obama's decision to keep Levey on the US payroll during the first three years of his administration was a clear testament to the value and effectiveness of these efforts. Since 9/11 US efforts through the multinational Financial Action Task Force have helped more than forty countries pass legislation in line with international standards to curb the flow of money to terrorist groups through banks and across borders.[28]

North of Washington DC, at Fort Meade in Maryland, the employees of the National Security Agency took another approach to isolating al-Qaeda's operatives: they developed new signals intelligence platforms and increased the deployment of electronic interceptors at key locations around the globe. In time, the US government was able to listen in on the communication of its enemies even as they took shelter in some of the most remote and inhospitable parts of the planet. Specific communications intercepts were often leaked and reported in the American media, such as a 1998 *Washington Times* article that revealed the monitoring of bin Laden's satellite phone and the interception of communications from Ayman al-Zawahari to Nasser al-Wuhayshi, the head of the Yemen-based al-Qaeda in the Arabian Peninsula.[29] But even al-Qaeda's awareness of these intelligence operations didn't eliminate their strategic significance because they made it that much more difficult for al-Qaeda operatives to communicate. Every time al-Qaeda operatives suspected that the United States was monitoring them, they were forced to develop new, often more expensive and more time-consuming methods for organizing their operations.

The Federal Bureau of Investigation and the Department of Homeland Security also immobilized al-Qaeda by denying terrorists the ability to travel. On September 11, 2001, the FBI had a total of sixteen people deemed "no transport" because they were judged to present a specific known or suspected threat to aviation. By 2012, the number of people on the Terrorist Screening Center's No Fly List grew to over 21,000 names.[30] The United Nations al-Qaeda sanctions regime, established under UN Security Council Resolution 1267, has since been used to impose sanctions on 221 individuals and sixty-three entities providing support to al-Qaeda. Airport screening also became more rigorous in addition to being more restrictive. The US government streamlined processes for requesting that Interpol and other governments monitor and at times prevent the movement of suspected terrorists. While the global transit system remained open and international travel increased, the amount of government oversight grew to unprecedented levels. Like all organizations, groups such as al-Qaeda can only function if their members can freely communicate, transfer money and material, and occasionally meet. Face-to-face gatherings are particularly important because in an environment permeated with collaborators, suspicion and conspiracy theories proliferate when militants cannot verify the loyalty and reliability of their associates. By disrupting these interactions the United States severely degraded the operational capacity of al-Qaeda, its affiliates, and associated forces.

In the aftermath of nuclear terrorism, the foreign and defense policies of the United States would be shaped in no small part by these counterterrorism experiences. The response options available to American decision makers would be based on the counterterrorism tool kit built over the last decade and informed by the enduring lessons of effective response to transnational substate violence. These include the need to develop special forces to meet unique challenges, limit US objectives to realistic achievable goals, isolate the enemy, and promote foreign forces and institutions that can manage security conditions where direct US involvement is expensive and poses unacceptable risks.

CHAPTER FIVE

GLOBAL IMPACT
FIVE DAYS "RIGHT OF BOOM"

"**G**OOD MORNING. I'D LIKE TO BEGIN TODAY'S SHOW BY thanking our viewers for their generous support of last night's telethon on behalf of the residents of Washington, DC. Our hearts and prayers are with the victims and their families. Today we're taking a short break from our ongoing live coverage of the crisis to consider the longer-term implications of the attack on Washington. To explore this topic, we've brought together a panel of experts on international law and international security. Let's begin with a professor from Harvard University. What are you telling your students?"

"Yesterday I began class by instructing my students to each take out their syllabus. And then to tear it up."

"Excuse me, professor, but why did you do that? Isn't an understanding of international law important to understanding the evolution of the current crisis?"

"Indeed it is, but the international laws of last week. The laws that I had planned to teach my class, well, they may still exist in print, but for all practical effect, they are no more. One of the victims of the terrorist attack on Washington was the international security system. We are truly 'wandering between two worlds, one dead, the other powerless to be born.' So, instead of learning about United Nations resolutions, recent treaties, and multilateral agreements, my class is going to open some history books. We are going to read about the political and military affairs of late antiquity, the universal edicts of the medieval Catholic Church, the wars of religion, the treaties that the European imperial powers used to construct the modern system of states, and much more. We are going to search these texts for transformational conflicts that undid, and ultimately reformed, the world order."

"That's an interesting approach. Let's turn to our guest from the Center for an Independent Foreign Policy to hear how she thinks the United States is likely to go about shaping a new international order."

"Thank you, I'd be happy to. I strongly agree with the distinguished professor that the international norms of the past are now defunct. This crisis has forced America's leaders to finally discard the outdated treaties and conventions that have for too long tied the hands of America's diplomats and soldiers. The American people will no longer tolerate having these paper commitments prevent their government from addressing growing dangers. As the late Irving Kristol noted many years ago, 'international law is a fiction abused callously, or ignored ruthlessly, by those nations that, unlike the Western democracies, never took it seriously in the first place.' In the aftermath of nuclear terrorism we can no longer ignore a fact that we've always known. We live in a world without a world community committed to a universal definition of law and civilized behavior. No longer will we see a US foreign policy predicated on this kind of suicidal fantasy."

"That's quite an assertion. What I'm hearing is that the United States will not build a new order but instead take unilateral actions to protect itself amid global chaos. Let's hear what our guest from the Coalition for International Partnerships has to say about that."

"Thanks for the opportunity to comment. I admit that there is a grain of truth in my colleague's prediction, but only a grain. International laws and global norms will be discarded, but they will be replaced by new mechanisms for international cooperation. Even during historical periods distinguished by tremendous isolation and disconnection, there have always been written or unwritten rules of the road that enable international cooperation. But forget history; there is a very simple reason why we should expect to see increased rather than decreased international cooperation: nuclear terrorism is too big a problem to be solved by any one country. Nuclear weapons materials exist all over the world; it's a global problem. The attack on Washington makes this obvious to even the most insular world leader. Our collective vulnerable is now totally apparent. It's only logical and rational for the world's leaders to work together against a threat that puts everyone in danger."

"All right, so here's hoping that enlightened self-interest wins the day. To get more of an international perspective let's give the last word to our guest from Beijing's Institute for International Leadership."

"Thank you. Now, I find the comments of your other guests to be thoughtful, but the paths taken by the United States— either a road characterized by increased unilateralism or by increased cooperation—is far less significant than whether

America ultimately reaches its destination—that is to say, whether America is able to reestablish its strength. The future of the international system will depend less on how the United States responds than on how effective its response proves to be. As your Samuel Huntington understood, 'The West won the world not by the superiority of its ideas or values or religion, but rather by its superiority in applying organized violence. Westerners often forget this fact, non-Westerners never do.' America's double failure, both to defend itself from nuclear attack and to identify the perpetrators, reveals just how weak the country has become. Current international laws and global norms reflect American values and American interests because they were crafted and sustained in large part by American power. If the United States reestablishes its strength unilaterally, with a small foreign coalition or through a grand international alliance, the global system will likely adapt and endure."

"Thank you, and thanks to all of our panelists."

TODAY'S INTERNATIONAL SECURITY SYSTEM

What does the potential for a nuclear attack of limited or uncertain attribution mean for the international security system? How would international politics and the modalities of military action change if such an attacked occurred?

Today's international security structure is defined by nation-states that claim—and are widely recognized as exercising—sovereignty over territory demarcated by internationally acknowledged borders. Each state is responsible for maintaining order within its territory and for preventing disorder from spilling over its borders. The most widely cited basis for this arrangement is the Peace of Westphalia that was established by a series of treaties ending the Thirty Years' War in 1648. The main tenet of the pact was that princes would henceforth have the right to determine the religion of their states—the principle of *cuius region, eius religio*. This marked a departure from the universalism of the Holy Roman Empire and the elevation of the concept of nonintervention in the "sovereign affairs" of particular regimes. Initially such sovereignty was based on princely/family dynasties. With time and the rise of Protestantism, secularism, nationalism, and democracy, sovereignty became associated with a nation of people defined by shared geography. The nation-state is a unique hallmark of modernity; it did not exist for most of human history and it is unlikely to be a permanent condition.

Even today, despite the global spread of nationalism in the nineteenth and twentieth centuries and the legitimization of the concept by forums such as the United Nations, the nation-state framework isn't equally applicable to all peoples and all places. In 1992, Lucien Pye famously described China "as a civilization pretending to be a nation-state."[1] The kingdom of Saudi Arabia is just that—a kingdom united by the power of a particular family, the House of Saud, and legitimated by the religious tenets of Ibn Abdul al-Wahhab. It is not a nation-state. The Kurds comprise a nation, but as of this writing, even with their semiautonomy in northern Iraq they do not possess a state. The nation-state rose to the pinnacle of powerful actors in world affairs because of the confluence of material developments such as Napoleon Bonaparte's *levée en masse* (mass mobilization) and industrialization and the ideology of nationalism. In those places of the world where these material and ideological developments failed to take root, the nation-state framework serves primarily as a facade behind which alternative political structures—the clan, the tribe, the empire, or civilization—really maintain order.

The collapse of the Berlin Wall and the ensuing economic liberalization of the 1990s, along with the terrorist attacks of 9/11, provoked a slew of authors to herald the decline and fall of the nation-state with the rise of "superempowered individuals," multinational corporations, and global terrorism movements that would obscure culpability in the event of a nuclear attack. But reports of the nation-state's demise have proven to be greatly exaggerated. The state resurged in one respect, even as its purview retracted in another. From Iran's successful disruption of "YouTube revolutionaries" to the effective US domestic and international counterterrorism activities, the nation-state has demonstrated that it remains the entity most capable of organizing violence and imposing security. In those places—principally in the Arabic-speaking world—where the state has broken down, security hasn't been imposed by transnational entities. From Tunisia to Libya, Egypt to Lebanon, and into the "Islamic Caliphate" that used to be parts of Syria and Iraq, the immediate alternative to autocratic governments has proven to be chaos rather than peaceful federalization or liberal democracy.

The state has come back with a vengeance, but state sovereignty hasn't emerged from the war on terrorism as strongly. With sovereignty comes responsibility—specifically the responsibility to prevent the export of violence. In the aftermath of 9/11, the United States embarked on a range of military operations within the borders of countries with which it was not at war. As president Barack Obama remarked in a speech at the National Defense University in May 2013,

> Al Qaeda and its affiliates try to gain a foothold in some of the most distant and unforgiving places on Earth. They take refuge in remote tribal regions. They hide in caves and walled compounds. They train in empty deserts and rugged mountains.
>
> In some of these places—such as parts of Somalia and Yemen—the state only has the most tenuous reach into the territory. In other cases, the state lacks the capacity or will to take action.[2]

The administration of president George W. Bush sought to impose order over key terrain, such as Afghanistan and Iraq, through direct action by the United States. When this proved difficult, expensive, and politically unpopular, the Obama administration opted to decrease direct US involvement in foreign lands and counter security threats increasingly through foreign partners. New military technology also propelled this evolution in policy. Unmanned aerial vehicles and new computer network capabilities, which were only beginning to have a strategic impact under the Bush administration, allowed Obama to project power in less expensive and less politically risky ways.

President Obama didn't abandon aggressive unilateral military operations—such as the famous Navy Seal raid against

Osama bin Laden in Pakistan—but his policies reflected the tempering of America's ambitions abroad. Working through partners can't "liberate" Iraqis and Afghans in the manner championed by liberal internationalists or neoconservatives. Nor can an indirect approach offer the prospect of achieving the level of stability that the United States imposed over Germany and Japan after World War II. However, with the US government having successfully prevented another 9/11 scale attack for over a decade, the American people have become increasingly tolerant of a certain amount of chaos in foreign lands. This is especially true in light of the absence of compelling reasons or recent examples that demonstrate that the United States has the strategic acumen, political will, and material resources to establish order in fractured societies.

The fusion of nuclear weapons and terrorism and an attack of limited or no attribution would certainly change this calculus and irrevocably alter the global security system. The kind of nuclear exchange envisioned during the Cold War—state-on-state employment of tactical or strategic nuclear weapons—would also have been unprecedented, but it would have largely conformed to the contemporary international system. One state (e.g., the Soviet Union or the United States) launches an attack on the other, the victim responds in kind, escalation or de-escalation occurs, and that is followed by victory, defeat, or draw. Neither country would have "won" a large scale nuclear war, but the point here is that the main players and their respective moves were consistent with an intensified version of traditional interstate war. In contrast, the potential national response to limited or nonattributable nuclear attack is far less straightforward. Massive retaliation won't only be an unattractive and likely ineffective option; it is unlikely to be an option at all. The public would demand action, but what action could realistically be taken?

What happens after a modern state, which in a globalized economy requires sufficiently transparent borders to enable international commerce, is shown to be incapable of defending its population against truly massive violence? First, undergoverned and chaotic areas of the world would become far less acceptable to global powers. It has become a common custom of politicians and diplomatic officials to proclaim various actions and situations to be "unacceptable." After the attacks of 9/11, many people exclaimed that in a world of global terrorism "insecurity anywhere threatens the United States," but this has been proven to be both unworkable in practice and untrue in reality. Neither the United States nor the type of multilateral alliances that exist today can or need to ensure security everywhere. A WMD attack would increase by orders of magnitude the risk of inaction and consequently would compel the United States to expend blood and treasure around the world in ways that have heretofore been inconceivable. It would also increase the willingness of global powers to infringe on the sovereignty of other nation-states to such a degree that the concept of sovereignty would likely be redefined and international norms irrevocably changed. Sovereignty exists as it currently does because it promotes peace and security; once it ceases to promote these benefits it will lose its legitimacy.

THE STRATEGIC INNOVATIONS OF THE COLD WAR

The Cold War both began and ended with technological revolutions. The first occurred in July 1945 with the weaponization of atomic energy and the coming of the nuclear age. The second innovation was what Daniel Bell has labeled the "information revolution," the sum of advances during the 1980s in rapid electronic computation and telecommunications. Both revolutions were vital to the ultimate defeat of communism and both were preconditions for a world of nuclear terrorism. The nuclear revolution destroyed an international political structure under which the United States could not have prevented communism from spreading to Western Europe. To defend America's allies, principally its European treaty partners, the only force that the United States could field with sufficient credibility was it's massive nuclear arsenal. This proved essential to achieving its main strategic objectives.

In the last decade of the Cold War, a new age—the information age—further strengthened the United States and liberal democracy vis-à-vis the Soviet Union and the communist political system. The information revolution, a product of advances in telecommunications technology and the development of rapid electronic computation, dramatically enhanced American power on multiple fronts of the war: military, economic, and cultural. M. A. Gareev, a former Soviet Army general and deputy chief of general staff, explained the military impact of information technology to a group of Sovietologists in the 1990s; he recalled, "On average we lagged behind [the U.S. in the military balance]. But as far as defense is concerned, we could make up for these deficiencies with other things such as greater quantity and less advanced technologies. . . . The dynamics of R&D [research and development] in the military sector revealed that our greatest weakness was information processing technology."[3] The liberal democratic system, being more open and more economically efficient than the communist system, better utilized and built upon information technology to augment its military arsenal. This comparative advantage forced the Soviets to counter the United States and its allies' qualitative military superiority by spending increasing amounts to maintain a quantitative lead in weapons production. In fact, the chief of the general staff of the Soviet Army, Nikolai V. Ogarkov, and the head of the Soviet KGB, Yuri Andropov, supported premier Mikhail Gorbachev partly because they recognized that the Soviet Union was losing its military edge. Substantial credit for the US victory in the Cold War can therefore be attributed to the administration of president Ronald Reagan's exploitation of the revolution in military affairs and the costs it imposed on the Soviet Union.[4]

While the information revolution's effect on the military balance was certainly important, the economic boom that information technology provided to the liberal economies of the free world arguably proved most decisive. Under the conditions of a mature industrial economy, markets direct the flow of capital to create aggregate wealth a great deal more efficiently than does state planning.[5] In the mid-1980s advances in rapid computation and telecommunications dramatically accelerated this process among America's coalition of liberal democracies.[6] These governments reduced direct controls and taxes on capital movements, liberalized long-standing regulatory constraints on financial services, and expanded relationships with offshore financial havens.[7] In contrast, communist governments attempted to control currencies and investment. Ironically, Karl Marx had anticipated the ultimate victor in this contest when he wrote, "The bourgeoisie, by the rapid improvement of all institutions of production, by the immensely facilitated means of communication, draws all, even the most barbarian, nations into civilization. The cheap prices of its commodities are the heavy artillery with which it batters down all Chinese walls. . . . It compels all nations, on pain of extinction, to adopt the bourgeois mode of production."[8] New technologies accelerated this process by decreasing transportation costs and creating economies of scale greater than were possible in even the largest national market; the consequence was the unification of much of the noncommunist world in a single integrated market. The 1980s witnessed a steep decline in the relative economic power of the Soviet Union and communist states. While centrally planned economies could compete with market economies in the age of coal, steel, and heavy manufacturing, they could not follow their capitalist adversaries into the information age.[9]

Information technology not only served to enhance US military and economic power but also projected American popular culture into the enemy camp. In the words of Joseph S. Nye, who championed the saliency of soft power, "Long before the Berlin Wall fell in 1989, it had been pierced by television and movies."[10] At the beginning of the Cold War, American radio, television, and cinema helped Americans shape the preferences of others through co-optation rather than coercion. By the 1980s, information technology made American entertainment almost a ubiquitous characteristic of the global environment. In her study of East Germany, Mary Fulbrook illustrates how the availability of Western European television in Eastern Europe demonstrated the stark contrast between the free world and the Soviet empire, and ultimately helped to delegitimize the communist system among the citizens of the Warsaw Pact.[11] As succinctly put by Walter Russell Mead, "Elvis Presley, Walt Disney, and Marilyn Monroe did as much to carry out the American Cold War project as John Foster Dulles and C. Douglas Dillon."[12]

THE TRANSFORMATION OF THE STATE

In the twentieth century the nation-state became the preeminent social, economic, and political institution because it was best able to satisfy the two primary functions of a state. Max Weber identified these as the ability to organize violence more efficiently than alternative political systems and the capacity to institutionalize justice.[13] The nation-state came to fulfill these roles because of structural change (industrialization) and ideological change (nationalism), which coalesced to challenge the ability of the prior state system—multinational empires—to satisfy these requirements. Industrial technology promoted a new form of organized violence based on massive mobilization of people and materials. The institutions of the multinational empires were unsuited to this type of organization. Only a nation-state could provide the centralized bureaucracy needed to structure the mass mobilizations that organized violence in the modern age. (Even after the development of nuclear weapons, nation-states remained the dominant feature of international politics because only advanced industrial economies could produce nuclear weapons and such economies required the centralized governments of the nation-state.) The nation-state fulfilled the second function of a state—the institutionalization of justice—because it defined identity. Justice is intrinsically connected to identity, which is why multinational empires recognized different systems of justice for different ethnic and religious communities. In contrast, nation-states instituted one system of justice founded on civic fraternity among people living within common territorial boundaries. In the modern era, identity based on shared geography was reinforced by institutions such as the factory, the centralized government bureaucracy, the public school system, and universal military conscription.[14]

By the late twentieth century the structural changes set in motion by the strategic innovations of the Cold War began to challenge the nation-state's ability to secure its citizens and institutionalize justice. All revolutions destroy defining structures of a previous era. The information revolution was no different. The limitations imposed by distance and geography were fundamental to the social, economic, and political structure of the nation-state. In 1995 Frances Cairncross, senior editor of the *Economist*, pointed out that information technology destroys distance, insamuch as distance serves as a barrier to communication.[15] Decades earlier, scholars such as Daniel Bell accurately predicted that information technology would grind down the institutions of the modern era through deindustrialization.[16] In 1997, William Julius Wilson confirmed, "Today's close interaction between technology and international competition has eroded the basic institutions of the mass production system."[17] Just as there was a correlation between the development of industrial economies and the rise of centralized governments, there is a correlation between their disintegration. In 1937 the eminent sociologist William Ogburn correctly predicted that industrial technology would result in greater political centralization because the industrial economy required it. More recently Joseph S. Nye has suggested that while "the twentieth century saw a predominance of the centripetal forces predicted by Ogburn, the twenty-first may see a greater role of centrifugal forces."[18]

The "death of distance" and the disintegration of industrial age institutions put substantial strain on identities based on shared geography. When large concentrations of people worked in urban factories, people identified with those in regional proximity. "Factory owners lived in the city and were all forced to interact at some level with the working class. Their children attended public schools [and] their wives shopped at the local department stores," notes Elizabeth McLean Petras.[19] Information technology allows individuals to be economically productive outside of urban centers. It also provides the means for people to construct "virtual communities" that don't take account of geography. As the National Intelligence Council (NIC) anticipates, "Growing connectivity . . . will be accompanied by the proliferation of transnational virtual communities of interest. . . . Groups based on common religious, cultural, ethnic or other affiliations may be torn between their national loyalties and other identities. The potential is considerable for such groups to drive national and even global political decision-making on a wide range of issues normally the purview of governments."[20] As geography becomes less significant in shaping human social and economic interaction, other sources of identity take on greater prominence.

There is a direct correlation between the disintegration of national borders and the renewed prominence of religious identity in global politics. There is a historical symmetry in this dynamic considering that the system of sovereign states was established for the primary purpose of ending the wars of religion. In the early twenty-first century, religion is filling a vacuum left by the failure of state politics to explain, moderate, or accommodate the forces unleashed by the information revolution. In fact, today's religious revival might well be an inevitable outgrowth of the modernizations of the twentieth century. "Modernization," Samuel Huntington explains, "generates feelings of alienation and anomie as traditional bonds and social relations are broken and leads to crisis of identity to which religion provides an answer."[21] Expanding on this trend, the NIC predicts that "the primacy of ethnic and religious identities will provide followers with a ready-made community that serves as a 'social safety net' in times of need."[22]

Religion is not the only form of transnational identity that is reinvigorated by the information revolution. As Nye explains, "In some postindustrial counties, cosmopolitan identities such as 'global citizen' or 'Custodian of Planet Earth' are beginning to emerge."[23] The journalist and world traveler Robert Kaplan sees the strengthening of a "global cosmopolitan elite" that identifies with no country and has no stake in any national community. He notes that the information era may usher in a new world order, but it is reviving an old class structure: "Information technology will certainly bring the middle classes of Asia and the rest of the world closer together, but they will become like the aristocrats of medieval Europe, who had more in common with each other than with their own peasant populations. Traditional state forms will not forever survive such crosscutting loyalties."[24] Transnational contacts across geopolitical boundaries were typical in the feudal era, but gradually became constrained by the rise of the centralized nation-state.[25] Given the dynamics produced by the information revolution, the twenty-first century may bear certain similarities to late antiquity, when the processes that eventually culminated in feudal society first began to undermine the institutions of the Roman Empire.

Despite the strains that transnational identities place on the nation-state's ability to institutionalize justice, a more serious threat to the state system comes from "superempowered" transnational organizations, entities that are increasingly assuming functions previously limited to national governments. As Nye noted in 2004, "Thirty years ago, instantaneous global communication was sufficiently expensive that it was restricted to large entities with big budgets like governments, multinational corporations, or the Roman Catholic Church. Today the Internet makes global communications virtually free for anyone with access to a modem."[26] To communicate is to organize, and to organize is to empower. International political power is becoming increasingly diffuse, moving away from national governments to global nongovernmental organizations and transnational corporations. By utilizing information technology, twenty-first-century journalists have become, in Robert Kaplan's words, "the grand inquisitors of the age," shattering reputations and significantly affecting domestic and international politics. He points out that the consolidation of major media outlets combined with the increasing intensity of the audiovisual experience, through innovations like big-screen television, "has created a new realm of authority akin to the emergence of a superpower with similarly profound geopolitical consequences."[27]

While the increasing influence of transnational identities and the growing power of transnational entities are troubling, the revolution in military affairs may be the most threatening dynamic unleashed by the information revolution.[28] It is a process that challenges the nation-state's ability to monopolize massive violence.[29] "Bandits, robbers, guerrillas, gangs have always been part of the domestic security environment," Phillip Bobbitt explains. "What is new is their access to mechanized weapons . . . the mobilization of the industrial capacity of a nation is irrelevant to such threats; the fielding of vast tank armies and fleets of airplanes is as clumsy as a bear trying to fend off bees."[30] In the 1990s Thomas Friedman predicted that political and economic democratization would inevitably lead to the "democratization of technology," which would transfer the instruments of mass violence into the hands of private individuals and nongovernmental organizations.[31] This reality was made devastatingly apparent on September 11, 2001. More American civilians were killed on that day than on any other in the history of the republic. Yet the destruction was carried out by nineteen men initially armed only with box cutters. Such asymmetry of power is truly unprecedented.

The confluence of information technology and nonattributable nuclear weapons would place additional strain on the nation-state system. At the start of the nuclear age, few expected the great powers to permanently monopolize the production of atomic weapons. Albert Einstein famously remarked, "There are atoms in all countries."[32] Yet few foresaw a future in which the manipulation of atoms became the prerogative of nonstate actors or the proliferation of nuclear weapons would become so widespread that a nuclear strike could take place with limited attribution. In light of these developments, the quintessential "realist," Henry Kissinger, confirmed the dissolution of the international security model that he spent his entire professional life defending. In a *Newsweek* article penned in 2004 Kissinger explained that because weapons were relatively small and technology moved slowly during the twentieth century, threats to the international order could generally be averted by awaiting actual aggression. Today, in contrast, "in a world of privatized terror and proliferating weapons of mass destruction, the balance can be upset and survival threatened by developments entirely within the borders of a sovereign state."[3] In the first decade of the twenty-first century, the theoretical possibility of a nuclear detonation carried out by nonstate actors convinced many Americans to support what was in part a preventive war against Iraq. Limited attribution of nuclear weapons will heighten the willingness of

states to cross international borders and accelerate the conflation of preventive war with preemptive military action.

A "NEW NORMAL"

The US military has been so heavily involved in lethal
counterterrorism activities abroad that it is easy to forget that
this is an anomaly within an international security system structured around nation-states and national sovereignty. The Charter of the United Nations embraces the principle of "sovereign
equality" and requires that member states "settle their international disputes in a peaceful manner" and "refrain in their
international relations from the threat or use of force against
the territorial integrity or political independence of any state."
This is a nearly blanket prohibition on coercive action inside
the borders of foreign states. Chapter VII of the UN Charter
outlines only two exceptions. The first is "any threat to the
peace, breach of the peace, or act of aggression," which permits
"action by air, sea, or land forces as may be necessary to maintain or restore international peace and security." Since the
United Nations never acquired the standing army envisioned
by its charter, in practice this language means that the UN Security Council can pass a resolution authorizing member states
to use force to carry out its mandates. The second exception to
the prohibition on coercive action is self-defense: article 51 of
the charter states that "Nothing in the present Charter shall
impair the inherent right of individual or collective self-defense
if an armed attack occurs against a Member of the United Nations, until the Security Council has taken the measures nec-

essary to maintain international peace and security." Legitimate acts of self-defense aren't precisely defined and therefore can be interpreted quite broadly. Traditionally, however, self-defense hasn't been interpreted to allow for persistent military action inside of countries whose governments aren't engaged in armed hostilities.[34]

Citing the dictates of the Peace of Westphalia and the UN Charter isn't meant to suggest that lethal intervention in the affairs of sovereign countries from outside states is anything new. Indeed, the age of European empire and the heyday of colonialism took place well after the establishment of the Westphalia system. Nor did the UN Charter forestall the deployment of US military power across the globe and American involvement in an array of small wars and unconventional conflicts during the Cold War. Yet America's post-9/11 counterterrorism activities are distinct in at least one important respect: the US government now publicly acknowledges lethal operations in foreign countries with which it is not at war.

These operations are conducted under the authority granted to the US military in title 10 of the United States Code rather than title 50, which governs US intelligence activities. This is an important distinction, because it differentiates clandestine actions from covert operations. Clandestine actions are hidden and intended to be secret, but if uncovered the US government does not deny them. In contrast, covert actions are deniable. The US military is granted the authority to conduct clandestine actions, but it is not granted covert action authority by the president.[35] This is due in part to a desire to protect the military's reputation from being tarnished by the shadowy world of espionage. In the words of admiral Vern Clark, "The line that exists [between covert and overt] is part of our good standing in the world. We have carefully tried to keep the military out of the covert world. . . . The covert side has appropriately resided within the CIA. We want the citizens, when they look at men and women wearing the cloth of the nation, to know that is who they are."[36] Because of the nature of American society and the structure of the US government, covert actions that are significant rarely remain out of the public domain for very long, especially if these actions substantially affect international or domestic politics. Yet even when these actions are made public, the ability to deny them remains important.

While it may seem counterintuitive, covert action authority can help bolster the shaky edifice of international law. It is one thing to violate the sovereignty of a foreign country and another thing to do so and boast about it in public. The former may actually help maintain international law through actions that prevent terrorism and preempt war, both of which are also illegal and have more dire consequences; the latter undermines the international security system by promoting a norm that's not meant to be normal. In other words, covert action authority allows the president of the United States to violate international law for the greater good of international peace and stability. This isn't hypocrisy; it is practical reality. There is no Hobbesian Leviathan to enforce international laws; international security is maintained by a combination of balance of power, established norms and traditions, and shared values and common interests. Publicizing actions that, however merited, challenge national sovereignty diminishes respect for the international security system enshrined in the UN Charter.

This is the reason that the US government's decision to undertake lethal counterterrorism actions (under title 10) via the Defense Department rather than the CIA is so significant. This kind of direct action was almost exclusively the domain of the CIA prior to 9/11. The magnitude of that event shifted popular perceptions and political dynamics to such a degree that it suddenly became acceptable for the US government to acknowledge that it was killing people in countries with which it is not at war. This represents not just a major shift in US policy but also a significant change in the international security system. And it is unlikely to be the only such shift during the twenty-first century.

STRIKING FIRST GOES MAINSTREAM

A nuclear attack that's not attributable or only minimally attributable would cause a much larger change in international security norms than the 9/11 attacks and the subsequent global war on terrorism. One plausible scenario is that such an event would propel a dramatic expansion in the use of clandestine coercive instruments and military countermeasures. Just as lethal counterterrorism operations became a publicly recognized norm of American statecraft after 9/11, after a "nuclear 9/11" the United States, along with like-minded countries, could aggressively target nodes along the various pathways to nuclear weapons. This pathway would include nuclear research, processing, weaponization, infrastructure development, scientific training, and the transit of sensitive materials. A range of active countermeasures could be used to target each of these nodes. Minimally intrusive and less risky policies may include more restrictive barriers to goods at customs sites and new restrictions along global transit routes. On the high side of the spectrum of conflict, active countermeasures could include confiscation of nuclear-related materials and sabotage of nuclear weapons capabilities. Such coercive instruments of counterproliferation could become as typical tools of foreign policy as economic sanctions and Predator strikes are today against terrorist targets.

Interdiction Operations

International lawyers have not traditionally interpreted the transfer of strategic weapons, militarily related components, or special nuclear materials as a "threat to the peace," as articulated in the UN Charter. Yet there is precedent for the United States treating this type of activity as sufficient grounds for a naval quarantine—an "act of war" of limited intensity. The blockade is a time-tested tactic of statecraft, and it was the principal instrument that president John F. Kennedy used to respond to the Cuban Missile Crisis. Part of Kennedy's order articulated the rationale for preemptive action: "We no longer live in a world where only the actual firing of weapons represents sufficient challenge to a nation's security to constitute maximum peril. Nuclear weapons are so destructive and ballistic missiles are so swift, that any substantial increased possibility of their use or any sudden change in their deployment may well be regarded as a definitive threat to peace."[37] On May

30, 2009, secretary of defense Robert Gates made a similar assertion in which he also highlighted weapons-usable nuclear material: "The transfer of nuclear weapons or material by North Korea to states or non-state entities would be considered a grave threat to the United States and our allies."[38] Notably, neither statement mentions the transfer of nuclear weapons technology or the provision of nuclear expertise. In 2008, the absence of this specificity in US policy might have led North Korean government officials to believe that they could help Syria construct a clandestine plutonium-producing nuclear reactor without provoking American intervention.

In the aftermath of a "nuclear 9/11," governments may choose to employ blockades and interdictions on a regular basis. Customary international law prohibits searches and seizures on the high seas under most circumstances; the right to stop and board vessels under the protection of a foreign nation's flag on the high seas is limited to situations in which there are reasonable grounds for suspecting that the ship is engaged in piracy, the slave trade, certain instances of unauthorized broadcasting, or when the ship is without nationality or refusing to display its flag.[39] This law is the product of history more than abstract legal theory and as such can evolve over time. In a postnuclear terrorism environment, it is reasonable to assume that such customary laws would be the slave to new security necessities. In this case, interceptions along global trade routes in the maritime, air, and ground domains could take a range of forms. They include increased inspections at border crossings by local authorities, frequent "hail and queries" and inspections of suspect vessels in international waters, the violent disablement of noncompliant ships, and even forced landings of suspect aircraft. Nuclear weapons–related cargo en route to suspect parties could be confiscated, returned to the senders, or destroyed on the spot. Hostile parties could be imprisoned or compelled to return to their countries of origin. Economic blockades in the form of financial sanctions and travel restrictions could also be imposed on potential nuclear proliferators as a form of interdiction.

The persistent application of these tools would be highly disruptive and provocative. On a very basic level, the increased checkpoints, inspections, and interdictions of people and materials in transit that could be demanded after a nuclear strike would significantly impede trade and global exchange. Today the American people tacitly accept the saturation of US markets with certain illegal drugs because the limited size of the drug shipments needed to satisfy American customers and the ease with which they can be concealed in transit makes draconian inspections the only way of halting them at the border. Given the choice between open borders and effective drug enforcement, Americans choose the former. When it comes to nuclear weapons and their associated trade-offs it is likely that they will make a different choice. And in a world with nonattributable nuclear weapons this will be a choice faced by all countries. A single nuclear terrorist attack presents an existential threat to small states like Israel and the United Kingdom that don't have the continental depth available to China, Russia, and the United States. City-states like Singapore and the United Arab Emirates, for whom trade is their lifeblood, would face an especially stark choice if confronted with the decision to impose heighted security barriers. The prospect of military escalation among countries would also increase once "the global commons" became fair game for coercive activity.

Following the People

Unprecedented scrutiny of goods and materials would likely be matched by additional barriers to individual travel and the curtailment of individual privacies. There could be pressure to apply the "big data" surveillance-collection systems that have been used to identify potential terrorists since 9/11 to mapping various human-centric pathways to nuclear weapons. Individuals with academic training in the physical sciences could be required to regularly report to government agencies on their activities. New scrutiny and security screening could be applied to metallurgists and miners involved in sensitive metal extraction. Academic training in related fields could be restricted to individuals with security clearances or those who agree to submit to periodic monitoring and evaluation. The "rendering" of al-Qaeda fighters associated with the war on terrorism could be expanded to include key personnel at work on suspect nuclear weapons programs. Retired general Stanley McChrystal's 2012 autobiography explains how the manhunt became a central Defense Department mission under his leadership and documents how the military built an extraordinarily effective system to this end—the "find, fix, finish, exploit, analyze, disseminate" the F3EAD cycle. In extreme cases governments may grant capture or kill authority for military forces against "high value targets" participating in vital aspects of nuclear weapons programs. Due to the inherent dual-use nature of

most nuclear-related work, it would be extremely difficult—
more so than in the fight against conventional terrorism—to
distinguish between legitimate civilian work and malicious activity. If this scenario came to pass a very large number of innocent people would be ensnared in government security nets.

Sabotage

Traditionally, low-intensity military operations have been
synonymous with Special Operations forces, direct action, and
unconventional warfare. Sabotage is a subcomponent within
this type of military activity and involves the use of clandestine
operatives to damage or destroy installations, supplies, and
strategic components. The use of sabotage against nuclear
weapons programs is far from new. In 1943 Norwegian sabo-
teurs working with the British Special Operations Executive
successfully raided Adolf Hitler's heavy water plant at Vemork,
Norway, and demolished the Nazis' main source of deuterium
oxide, depriving them of fuel for their weapons program.[40] Future sabotage efforts could very well include these types of traditional military activities, but they are high on the escalation
ladder and would be far from the first choice of most statesmen. Alternatively, countries could seek to deploy new technologies that have smaller attribution signatures and are less
likely to provoke violent reaction.

Cyberoperations may be the wave of the future with respect to low-risk and low-intensity forms of state coercion. As
specifically applied to nuclear targets, the general objective of
offensive cyberoperations could be the physical disablement of
nuclear weapons development, production, storage, and deliv-

ery systems. Possibly the most famous alleged operation aimed at sabotaging a nuclear weapons program is the Operation Olympic Games program known as Stuxnet. The basic story of this suspected sabotage campaign is detailed in a series of *New York Times* articles by David Sanger and in his book *Confront and Conceal*. According to Sanger, in 2006 the United States and Israeli governments began collaboration on a major sabotage effort to disrupt and delay Iran's nuclear centrifuge program. The first step in this effort was to design a "beacon" computer program that could be covertly installed into the Natanz nuclear enrichment plant, which would then infiltrate and map the supervisory control and data systems; the beacon would then transmit the details of the design configuration back to the United States. With this information, Israeli and American programs proceeded to design a computer worm capable of taking control of critical functions in the plant in a manner that disrupted enrichment activities without alerting Iranian scientists to its presence. In the summer of 2010, the worm escaped Natanz and spread to the Internet, where it was soon identified by computer security companies. Eventually Stuxnet's function and target were deduced through a combination of suspected leaks and inductive reasoning based on the location of the worm (Symantec noted in August 2010 that 60 percent of the infected computers worldwide were in Iran[41]) and the fact that worm's components were focused exclusively on the type of Siemens systems suited to Iran's centrifuge program.[42] The ultimate effectiveness of Stuxnet is contentious, according to the *New York Times*. Some claim it delayed Iran's nuclear program by one to two years, while others suggest that politics and the media's infatuation with the novelty of the technology led reporters to significantly overstate its strategic effect. In any event, the most consequential effect of Operation Olympic Games may ultimately be that that it revealed to the whole world the possibilities of offensive cyberoperations.

A New World

If the Stuxnet virus was the product of Hollywood screenwriters, the movie would likely end at this point of the story, but in the real world its consequences continue to be felt. The Islamic Republic of Iran has struck back within the parameters of its national interest. The Quds Force and its partners in Lebanese Hezbollah continue to strike Israeli targets through terrorism. In a new twist, during 2012 some thirty thousand computers of Saudi Aramco were crippled by a computer virus sent by the government of Iran, according to press reports.[43] Given the limited strategic effects of these attacks it is easy to dismiss them as evidence of Iranian weakness, but time will tell. Unlike the capacity to field massive industrial scale militaries, the ability to use low-intensity coercive instruments is relatively widespread. Once the shield of "sovereign equality" is removed and the exclusive claim to the monopolization of coercive action within a country is no longer widely respected, state and substate actors will have a range of disruptive techniques and technologies at their disposal.

A world in which these activities go mainstream would be unstable and substantially more anarchic than the one we inhabit today. With the weakening of state sovereignty, the diplomatic protections granted to government personnel in oversees embassies erodes. We've already seen this occur over the last few decades as groups like al-Qaeda ignore this major tenet of the international legal protections and strike Americans stationed in vulnerable diplomatic posts. As President Obama declared in his 2013 speech at the National Defense University, the United States has used coercive action within foreign countries where the central government lacks capacity to police its territory. This is a slippery slope: it is only a small step for foreign governments to respond that they cannot be held responsible for security in territory in which even the United States has asserted it lacks the ability to maintain order. After all, culpability cannot exist without capability. The frequent violation of national sovereignty leads to a condition in which governments no longer feel required to fulfill the basic requirement of the international security system: preventing the export of violence from their territory. In a world of frontiers rather than borders,[44] the United States and other global powers will face the prospect of regularly suffering causalities among their diplomatic core and corporations will face increased threats to their overseas staff. Governments and businesses would thus have to accept frequent causalities as the cost of actively engaging in the wider world or severely curtail their traditional levels of involvement abroad.

Over the last decade, terrorism has garnered the greatest attention among various forms of low-intensity conflict, but cyberattacks are the more prevalent and will likely be a more strategically significant instrument of coercion during the twenty-first century. According to publicly available reports, the Chinese are already the world's foremost experts on cyber-hacking and espionage operations. In the Department of Defense's 2013 report to the US Congress on China's military capabilities, the Pentagon acknowledged what has been public knowledge for some time: "China is using its computer network exploitation (CNE) capability to support intelligence collection against the U.S. diplomatic, economic, and defense industrial base sectors that support U.S. national defense programs."[45] Moreover, these attacks haven't been limited to political or military targets. Iain Lobban, director of Britain's Government Communications Headquarters, acknowledged that foreign backers were stealing business secrets on an industrial scale: "People are going after intellectual property and then seeking to translate it into national gain. We started a couple of years ago thinking this was going to be very much about the defence sector but really it is any intellectual property that can be harvested."[46]

So far the objective of these cyberoperations appears to be restricted to exfiltration of information, but the same capabilities can be applied to offensive operations. In 2012, the greatest number of high-profile cyberattacks was attributed to Iran and North Korea. Iran's attack on Saudi Aramco failed to halt oil production, and the North Korean attack on South Korea's banking and media companies didn't cause any long-term damage.[47] These types of cyberattacks are disruptive but not debilitating. Future attacks may be far more consequential. According to the Defense Department's annual report to Congress on China, "Cyberwarfare capabilities could serve Chinese military operations in three key areas. First and foremost, they allow data collection for intelligence and computer network attack purposes. Second, they can be employed to constrain an adversary's actions or slow response time by targeting network-based logistics, communications, and commercial activities. . . . Third, they can serve as a force multiplier when coupled with kinetic attacks during times of crisis or conflict."[48] Private analysts have explained in greater detail the specifics of offensive cyberattacks. For example, it may be possible for such attacks to disrupt, degrade, or even destroy pipelines, power grids, communication systems, financial processes, business record-keeping and supply-chain operations, airlines, railroads, and databases of all types, from sensitive medical records to bank statements.[49] Today's industrial-scale computer network exploitation could lead to computer network sabotage with consequences commensurate to the reach of today's information age technologies.

Arguably the greatest virtue of an international security system structured around the borders of sovereign states is that it clearly defines acts of aggression. The movement of military forces across internationally recognized borders is the common definition of "a threat to the peace." Red lines are fairly clear. This is a relative characterization rather than an absolute one. The Cuban Missile Crisis is a prime example of the room for miscommunication and the incongruity of nuclear weapons within this framework. But it is also true that the risk of escalation between competing powers would be substantially higher if coercive counterproliferation were to become the norm. If nuclear terrorism convinces officials that they need to position overt or clandestine forces in foreign states to prevent follow-on attacks, then red lines become blurred. The distinction between acts of aggression and acts of self-defense would be opaque and miscommunication highly probable. Moreover, low-intensity coercive counterproliferation does not offer a comprehensive solution to the threat of nonattributable nuclear attacks. Like the alleged Stuxnet attack, such actions are only likely to serve as delaying functions to buy time and push back a major conflict. Sometimes this is the best option available. Problem solving can be a hubristic temptation when problem management is the only prudent policy. An alternative scenario is also possible, however, in the aftermath of nuclear terrorism: the internationalization of nuclear materials through a system of collective security.

A NEW COLLECTIVE SECURITY

"It is a disease of the soul to be in love with impossible things," wrote Walter Lippmann. All too often officials succumb to this ailment and propose grand international agreements that disregard Thucydides's observation that humankind is driven by fear, honor, and interest. History has not been kind to proponents of proposals such as the 1928 Kellogg-Briand Pact (officially the General Treaty for Renunciation of War as an Instrument of National Policy). Yet, it is possible that nuclear terrorism would fundamentally transform perceptions regarding the meaning of national and international security. A greater willingness to infringe on other countries' sovereignty could be matched by new openness to the partial surrender of sovereignty. In keeping with Thomas Hobbes's concept of the individual and the state, which attributes the willingness of individuals to surrender their natural rights to escape a condition of all against all, governments may be willing to surrender some or all of their nuclear related materials.

At the dawn of the nuclear age, the Danish physicist Niels Bohr proposed international stewardship of fissile materials. This idea matured into the concept on the part of the administration of president Harry S. Truman's of an international agency called the Atomic Development Authority, which would own all fissile materials, have access to the world's uranium and thorium despots, and release small amounts to individual nations for peaceful production of nuclear energy. The initiative died a quick death, but the idea survived, and while it was never implemented, the notion has been a consistent—if silent—presence at the world's nuclear diplomacy forums. A time may come when it gets a seat at the table. In the aftermath of nuclear terrorism, initiatives that are politically infeasible today would get renewed consideration. These include proposals for more restrictive nuclear materials control, enforced transparency of nuclear weapons programs, and even multilateral stewardship of nuclear weapons.

Nuclear Lockdown

Within current political constraints and in the absence of the kind of political will that would be necessary to subject nuclear materials to international control, officials from the scientific, diplomatic, and defense communities have done what they can to secure the world's nuclear materials. Since the 1970s these officials have successfully decreased the number of locations where nuclear weapons and weapons-usable nuclear material exist. They have developed and shared material security procedures and established UN resolutions and other international conventions focused on nuclear security and the criminalization of nuclear materials smuggling. These efforts have decreased the production of weapons-usable material through the promotion of safer nuclear power options; consolidated, secured, and eliminated stocks of weapons-usable nuclear materials; and spread awareness of the problem through multilateral summits and bilateral meetings. In April 2009 President Obama called on the international community to unite behind an effort "to secure all vulnerable nuclear material around the world in four years." Soon thereafter this effort was endorsed by the UN Security Council through Resolution 1887 and by the leaders of more than fifty countries at the subsequent Nuclear Security Summits held in Washington, DC, and Seoul.

While the Obama administration's initiative has achieved undeniable successes, it represents a continuation of the patchwork of conventions and treaties that have constituted the central focus of nonproliferation efforts for decades. In the 1980s the Convention on the Physical Protection of Nuclear Materials (CPPNM) went into effect. The CPPNM criminalizes nuclear theft and smuggling and gives all parties jurisdiction to prosecute such crimes; its 2005 amendment extends its coverage to materials in domestic use, in storage, and in transport. Its requirements are, however, very general and don't identify specific standards for effective materials security.[50] Similarly, the UN Security Council in 2004 adopted Resolution 1540 requiring every state with nuclear weapons or "related materials" to provide "appropriate effective" security and accounting for them, but again the language doesn't specify the essential elements of an effective security structure. In 2006, president George W. Bush and Russian premier Vladimir Putin launched the Global Initiative to Combat Nuclear Terrorism, which expresses a voluntary commitment of members to "improve accounting, control and physical protection systems for nuclear and other radioactive materials and substances."[51] A year later the International Convention on the Suppression of Acts of Nuclear Terrorism (ICSANT) entered into force, requiring parties to "make every effort to adopt appropriate measures to ensure the physical protection of radioactive materials." This is yet another much heralded document that doesn't specify necessary conditions for effective materials security.[52]

The reason for these elisions is simple. Countries don't want to make commitments that require concrete actions, funding, and the regulation of domestic industries. Nor do they want to open their actions or nonactions to scrutiny by making specific pledges. In the absence of any compelling reason to believe national governments will be held responsible for lost or stolen nuclear materials, there is limited incentive for government leaders to spend political and financial capital achieving a gold standard of nuclear security. The closest thing to a global nuclear security standard that exists is the 2011 International Atomic Energy Agency's recommendations on physical protection, which are purely advisory.[53] Moreover, with respect to conventions and treaties, the actual signatories, rather than the *number* of signatories, matters a great deal in terms of effectiveness. The majority of countries that possess nuclear weapons have not ratified either ICSANT or the CPPNM 2005 amendment, including France, Israel, North Korea, Pakistan, or the United States; sixteen states that possess weapons-useable nuclear material have not joined ICSANT; five states from the same group have never ratified the Convention on Physical Protection; and fifteen of these states have not ratified the amendment to the CPPNM.[54]

These efforts may represent the very best that can be done in the current international political environment, but in the aftermath of nuclear terrorism the victimized nation and probably the dominant voices in the global community will demand a new approach. At various instances throughout history massive violence has concentrated the minds of political elites on common threats, compelled disparate polities to join arms to fight for shared objectives, and birthed new institutions. The grand alliance of the Second World War—actually called the United Nations—that prosecuted the war against Nazi Germany was solidified by fear of fascism and was one example of cooperation compelled by exigent circumstances. Like the Second World War, a nuclear terrorist attack would be a transformative event of such magnitude that new institutions could emerge from the rubble. Under this scenario, an institution empowered to secure nuclear materials could be viable. Indeed, the building blocks of such an edifice already exist in the form of the International Atomic Energy Agency (IAEA) and to a lesser extent in the alphabet soup of initiatives, forums, and committees focused on counterproliferation and nuclear security. Today these entities have no sovereign authority or coercive power, but this could change.

After a nuclear terrorist attack, a coalition of willing states could emerge that provides political, financial, and military force to empower a multinational entity—a nuclear security agency—dedicated to nuclear materials security. Scholars and legal experts could put forward an argument that nuclear terrorism nullifies the concept of national sovereignty over special nuclear materials. It is conceivable that such an agency could be declared sovereign over all such material. Obviously, in the absence of a force to compel this outcome such a statement would be no more than rhetoric. But at the political level, a coalition of global powers could use various forms of persuasion (popular protest and public messaging) and coercion (economic and military power) to force national governments to cooperate with the new institution. The arrangement could resemble the UN's military action during the Korean War in which the multinational entity provided a joint command and was technically in charge but the military forces of contributing nations provided the real power. Similarly, in the case of a multinational nuclear security agency, a coalition of like-minded nations could serve as the "cannons behind the curtain."

The parameters of the entity's authority would be scoped along a spectrum based on the dynamics of the political situation, but its essential mandate would be locking up the world's nuclear materials. Current unclassified estimates suggest that nuclear weapons are located in over a hundred sites across fourteen countries, which include the nine nuclear weapons states and five other countries where US nuclear weapons are stored. Thirty-two countries contain weapons-usable nuclear materials that are stored in hundreds of locations.[55] The proposed nuclear security agency's intermediate objectives could include consolidating the location of weapons-usable nuclear materials into a limited number of locations over which the entity would provide on-site security; setting standards and testing the performance of security structures; establishing and managing personnel-screening procedures for individuals with access to sensitive nuclear weapons-related technology; and managing the phasing out of civilian use of highly enriched uranium.

Another responsibility of such an agency could be to develop and manage an official database containing reference signatures and data from worldwide sources of nuclear material for the purposes of helping to establish attribution. Some databases exist now, but a number of critical countries have not cooperated in providing the necessary samples. In 2006, Michael May (the former director of the Lawrence Livermore National Laboratory), Raymond Jeanloz (the chair of the National Academy of Sciences' Committee on International Security and Arms Control) and Jay Davis (the former director of the Defense Threat Reduction Agency) called for the establishment of "an international data bank of known nuclear explosive materials."[56] The international cooperation, transparency, and (in some cases) political top cover associated with a multinational organization could promote greater participation as well as increase confidence in an attribution process.

Countries that refused to cooperate would open themselves up to a presumption of guilt and complicity in nuclear terrorism. The United States has a long-standing "negative security assurance" by which it declares that it "will not use or threaten to use nuclear weapons against non-nuclear weapons states that are a party to the NPT (Non-Proliferation Treaty) and in compliance with their nuclear non-proliferation obligations."[57] Following a nuclear terrorist attack, world leaders could push for a new international legal norm that places non-cooperative countries in a "zone of suspicion and vulnerability." As such, this new regime would shift the burden of proof on noncooperative states and justify retaliation in the absence of airtight evidence.

Nuclear Forensics

Responsibility for a clandestinely conducted nuclear attack will never be as apparent as it would be in the case of a nuclear weapon delivered by missile, submarine or aircraft, but actions can be taken to disperse some of the fog of uncertainty. The debris near a nuclear blast site contains physical, chemical, isotopic, and elemental data containing clues to the nature and history of the weapon. The physical characteristics, such as the texture, size, and shape of solid objects, and the particle size distribution of powder samples are often unique to a given manufacturing process. The chemical composition, which is essentially the association of unique molecular compounds, can be indicative of a particular reprocessing operation. Elemental signatures identify the nuclear material, and minor trace elements or residues provide information about the fabrication process. The isotopic signatures, which show fission or neutron-capture products, may be the most informative. According to the IAEA, their half-life can be used to determine when the parent isolate was last chemically separated from its decay products—how old it is—and "serve as a fingerprint for the type and operating conditions of a given reactor."[58]

Even the best nuclear forensics won't be perfectly reliable, and in the aftermath of an attack politics will certainly be a factor in interpreting the results. After all, what's the legal standard for massive retaliation? Is 85 percent certainty of origin sufficient to justify retaliation in kind? Is 99.5 percent? The inherent ambiguity of isotopic analysis could also be compounded by deliberate misdirection. Material could be purposefully laced with substances of different chemical or isotopic composition to disguise the nature of the primary element. Such tactics could even be part of an effort to frame a third party. Arguably no institution is more focused on this issue than the US Department of Energy's national laboratories, and according to scientists at the Lawrence Livermore Laboratory, "Nuclear forensics will always be limited by the diagnostic information inherent in the interdicted material. . . . Some nuclear materials inherently have isotopic or chemical characteristics that serve as unequivocal markers of specific sources, production processes, or transit routes. Other nuclear materials do not."[59] Moreover, as frequently dramatized by Hollywood, there is always the potential for error and therefore the option to claim sabotage in the chain of custody at the blast site. Certainly the chaos of a nuclear attack site affords the possibility for contaminating data samples and the planting of false evidence. In this opaque environment, the credibility of any nuclear forensics efforts will be heavily colored by international politics.

Who Controls the Nuclear Weapons?

The greatest obstacle to a collective security arrangement would be the disposition and control of the world's nuclear weapons. One conceivable option is for a coalition of the world's nuclear powers to retain their nuclear weapons capabilities while acting to impose security over nuclear materials in other countries and/or forcefully disarming nuclear weapons states of proliferation concern. This approach would involve extreme risks depending on the target countries and could even trigger governments to employ nuclear weapons during a confrontation, but it is a conceivable course of action in the aftermath of a nuclear terrorist event. In one sense it also would represent a change in magnitude—rather than kind—from established policy, which is essentially aimed at preventing the acquisition of nuclear weapons by states that do not yet have them. A more limited response, but one within this framework, would entail the use of military, economic, and diplomatic tools, possibly under the banner of a nuclear security agency, to impose security over nuclear materials rather than through the current voluntary approach that relies on sovereign governments. Obviously imposing the authority of such a proposed agency on nonnuclear weapons states would be a global campaign with major risks, but one less dangerous than attempting to disarm nuclear weapons powers.

Alternatively or concomitantly, nuclear weapons states could surrender their arsenals to the control of such an international agency. A framework could be developed through which the entity would manage nuclear weapons under the condition that they be deployable and available for use for the purpose of national self-defense. The command and control relationships would obviously require tailoring for each country given the unique function of nuclear weapons in different governments' military planning (e.g., the role of America's nuclear weapons in US war plans is fundamentally different from the function of nukes in Pakistan's national defense). Having an independent agency ensure the material security of nuclear weapons that are aimed at each other would be awkward, but it is not entirely inconceivable. After all, countries have willingly relinquished nuclear weapons, dismantled nuclear weapons programs, and chosen not to atomically arm themselves despite possession of all the necessary ingredients (e.g., Argentina, Belarus, Brazil, Japan, Kazakhstan, Libya, South Africa, South Korea, Sweden, Taiwan, and Ukraine). Turning to a multinational agency to manage the ultimate military deterrent would be unprecedented, but less intuitive security frameworks have existed (e.g., mutually assured destruction). The likelihood of such a scenario would also increase if the world's military powers sought to make nuclear weapons obsolete by developing alternative weapons of equal or greater destructive capacity (biological weapons appear to be the most likely candidate). In that case, however, nuclear powers might agree to dismantle their atomic arsenals entirely. That's nearly unfathomable today, but "right of boom" this kind of evolution could suddenly become conceivable.

CHAPTER SIX

THE RED LINE
FIFTEEN DAYS "RIGHT OF BOOM"

THE PRESIDENT AND HIS CHIEF OF STAFF ARE SITTING ALONE in the Oval Office.

"Eight sites. They tell me that the nuclear material used in the attack probably came from one of eight identified sites."

"That's good news, Mr. President. It gives us the ability to respond."

"Does it? The secretary of defense just handed me a strike plan. It proposes launching as many as eight nuclear missiles. He is waiting for my order."

The chief of staff is already aware of the plan. The Pentagon has been pushing him to get the president to make a decision.

"Mr. President, we need to reestablish deterrence. That requires a proportional response. The American people paid for a nuclear arsenal for just this purpose."

Only minutes earlier the president ended a meeting with his pastor. He was reminded that God agreed to spare the city of Sodom for the sake of ten righteous people. How many innocent people would die if he gave the order? Thousands? How many of the guilty? Maybe none. Would it even eliminate the threat? Or would it just provoke a larger war?

The president closes his eyes. "My highest duty is to ensure the security of the American people. I know that. But I don't know if this is how to do it."

"If we launch our nuclear weapons, won't that just convince nuclear weapons states to build more weapons, leading to the production of even more nuclear material? Won't it provoke countries without nukes to seek a nuclear deterrent? Will it increase the chance that another president in the not too distant future will be stuck in the same situation I'm in today? And that may not be the worse possibility; some of my advisers think that the country we're striking is going to be forced to respond in kind, in which case I've got a second major strike plan here."

The president gets out of his chair and shuffles to his desk.

"Seen this? It's a plan to basically wipe out a country's entire military and industrial capacity along with tens of millions of people."

"That's a contingency plan, Mr. President. The intelligence community has moderate to high confidence that we won't get into that type of situation."

"Yes, I know. You know what else I know? I know it's possible that even after unleashing an unprecedented level of violence, after literally bombing a country back to the Stone Age, there could still be a bunker in some remote outpost with enough nuclear material to destroy multiple American cities. So tell me again, what can we hope to accomplish with this?"

There is a long pause.

"And even if we succeed, and the threat is eliminated, what will the world think of us, of the American people?"

"Mr. President, what will they think of us if we *don't* succeed?"

Morality, Legitimacy, and Credibility

In 2001, CIA director George Tenet flew to Islamabad and told Pakistani president Pervez Musharraf, "You cannot imagine the outrage there would be in my country if it were learned that Pakistan is coddling scientists who are helping Bin Laden acquire a nuclear weapon. Should such a device ever be used, the full fury of the American people would be focused on whoever helped al-Qa'ida in its cause."[1] One wonders what was going through Musharraf's mind at that moment and in subsequent instances of reflection on Tenet's warning. Offended by such a direct accusation, a piqued pride might have come forth; a scintilla of fear likely also bubbled up. But Musharraf was probably also a little curious. What exactly is the "full fury of the American people," he may have wondered, and how would the United States possibly know who to direct it against? In the years that followed Tenet's meeting with Musharraf, the United States would endure its longest war ever in neighboring Afghanistan. Across and along the Afghanistan-Pakistan border, American soldiers fought against an enemy that enjoyed the active support of parts of the Pakistani government. A slew of American officials followed Tenet's path into the corridors of Pakistani power to issue warnings of equal or lesser diplomatic subtlety. The United States would act against those with the blood of America's sons and daughters on their hands! Or would it?

There is obviously a difference between words and deeds,

threats and action, principles and pragmatism. Each has a distinct place in international politics, but a nation's credibility is respected only as long as the gap between them isn't excessively wide. Threats, warnings, and planning assumptions that aren't informed by real-world limitations can do more harm than good both abroad and at home. Just as the United States faced constraints in responding to Pakistani support for the Afghan Taliban, its response options to a nuclear attack of uncertain attribution would be circumscribed by a variety of factors. These include not only innumerable military and intelligence limitations but also political, economic, and cultural constraints. Time would also play a powerful role. Popular support for aggressive military actions tends to be highest immediately following an attack and diminishes over time as the appearance of normalcy returns. It is also more challenging to establish a united front against a common threat when the identity of the aggressors is uncertain and a topic susceptible to public debate. In the run up to the Second World War, approximately 80 percent of Americans opposed military support to the Allies before the Japanese attack on Pearl Harbor in 1941. Even after the attack, the public was divided on the level of US involvement. Imagine the conflict and consternation that would ensue if all that could be pointed to in identifying those responsible for a terrorist attack were fragments of intelligence reports. "Trust us" wouldn't be enough to maintain strong and enduring public commitment to a robust US military response.

Warnings, threats, and public declarations that aren't informed by the realities that constrain US action in the event of limited attributable nuclear terrorism pose significant risks. For example, reliance on an assumption that might have been valid during the Cold War, such as the notion that massive nuclear retaliation is a realistic and viable option, provides little incentive to develop alternative and more flexible response capabilities. Such false or anachronistic assumptions can promote complacency; they can also produce results that confuse foreign audiences about the content and location of American "red lines." Ill-conceived words can give the impression that the United States is bluffing and incapable of effective retaliation. It is therefore worth considering in some detail the options that are really available to government leaders in the days after a nuclear terrorist event.

Declaratory Policy

Declaratory policy, manifested through publicly articulated warnings and threats, signals the willingness of a country to act in response to perceived threats and is a critical element of a country's deterrence posture. The central choice facing those who develop such statements is between clarity and ambiguity. Clarity has the advantage of helping to eliminate uncertainty by clearly conveying red lines (i.e., proscribed actions) and by shifting onto an adversary the liability attached to a "last clear chance" of avoiding escalation. However, clarity diminishes flexibility by staking a nation's reputation on fulfilling specific commitments. Clarity can also circumscribe the extent of an adversary's conduct targeted for deterrence based on the logic of "that which is not prohibited is permitted." Alternatively, calculated ambiguity provides maximum flexibility for policy makers, but the heightened uncertainty can encourage adversaries to take probing actions to test the limits of tolerable conduct.

The official declaratory policy of the United States is articulated in the 2010 Nuclear Posture Review. It states, "The [United States] will hold fully accountable any state, terrorist group, or other non-state actor that supports or enables terrorist efforts to obtain or use weapons of mass destruction, whether by facilitating, financing, or providing expertise or safe haven for such efforts."[2] While this statement identifies general types of proscribed conduct, it is deliberately ambiguous with respect to response options. In contrast, it is far less specific than president John F. Kennedy's threat to order "a full retaliatory response" if Cuban-based nuclear-tipped missiles were launched against the United States. It also does not specify proliferation activity short of the transfer of an actual weapon or nuclear materials (e.g., it does not address shipping Nuclear Supplies Group–controlled aluminum tubes, transferring fully assembled centrifuges, or building a nuclear reactor for a foreign government). Senior US officials have gone into more detail in statements directed at particular countries of proliferation concern. In 2009, secretary of defense Robert Gates used the platform provided by the annual Shangri-Law Dialogue in Singapore to declare, "The transfer of nuclear weapons or material by North Korea to states or non-state entities would be considered a grave threat to the United States and our allies. And we would hold North Korea fully accountable for the consequences of such action."[3] His statement does not specifically address North Korean transfers of nuclear technology (such as the technical assistance provided to Syria), but it does include reference to both nuclear weapons and materials directed at either state or nonstate entities. Yet among the subtle but significant omissions from this statement, and from the language in the Nuclear Posture Review, is reference to transfer through negligence. While a US senator, vice president Joseph Biden stated in May 2007, "We must make clear in advance that we will hold accountable any country that contributes to a terrorist nuclear attack, whether by directly aiding would-be terrorists or willfully neglecting its responsibility to secure the nuclear weapons or weapons-usable material within its borders."[4] However, this position did not become the official policy as reflected in the Nuclear Posture Review.

What exactly does "hold fully accountable" mean? More important, what do adversaries and allies who read and hear those words think they mean? As noted, the credibility of military threats rests on at least four basic factors: capability, interest, reputation, and risk propensity. The United States has the greatest military capabilities on the planet and possibly in the history of the world, but because the use of capabilities accrues costs, credibility requires that the US government convey that its interests are of such importance that it will bear costs and accept risks to defend them. Reputation includes the whole range of historical and cultural considerations unique to a country and its armed forces. For example, the willingness to suffer can be a more strategically significant quality than the ability to organize violence. It was a character trait that the North Vietnamese possessed in greater supply than their American adversaries during the 1970s, and it proved decisive in the Vietnam War. Reputation also involves the issue of values and conceptions of justice. The credibility of military threats rests in significant part on their perceived morality—their "legitimacy." Especially in the absence of a total war that presents an existential threat to society, military action is constrained by popular values and cultural norms. What's realistic in the context of America's unique history and culture? What kind of responses would the dominant voices in American society consider to be legitimate?

Capability

What are the capabilities that the United States has available to hold adversaries "fully accountable"? A comprehensive response to this question requires consideration of the temporal dimension. In other words, US military capabilities the day after a nuclear terrorist attack are not going to be the same as they will be six months later. To demonstrate this point, one can recall that when the Second World War began with the German invasion of Poland in September 1939, the US Army ranked seventeenth among armies of the world in size and combat power, just behind Romania. When the Japanese attacked Pearl Harbor in December 1941, only one American division was on full wartime footing.[5] If there is any single factor that has most contributed to past US military successes, it is the country's great industrial and technological capacity. When these sectors are put on a wartime footing, new capabilities are born. But this process takes time—more so than in the past, when the United States possessed a large and more independent military industrial base. And the political necessity to respond immediately after a nuclear attack won't provide a great deal of time. This means that the US response will most likely be determined by the capabilities available the day after the attack.

In the days immediately following a nuclear attack on America, the government could launch air and missile strikes with a variety of conventional and unconventional (nuclear) payloads. The US Air Force's Global Strike Command, head-quartered at Barksdale Air Force Base in Louisiana is responsible for the nation's three intercontinental ballistic missile wings, the two B-52 Stratofortress heavy bomber wings, and the B-2 Spirit long-range stealth bomber wing. It provides combat-ready forces on continuous, around-the-clock alert for global strike operations.[6] In the event of a nuclear attack of uncertain or limited attribution, the president could order this command to strike a range of preselected targets (i.e., "the usual suspects"). The American people would demand that something be done to reestablish US deterrence, and global strike could be used to meet the immediate domestic political requirement. However, given the lack of intelligence at that point in time, these strikes would almost certainly serve a symbolic political function rather than degrade the responsible party's nuclear terrorism capabilities. The size and scale of a punitive expedition would be left to the judgment of the commander in chief.

As weeks pass, the US government could posture additional elements of national power to surge existing capabilities and prepare for an escalating conflict. Much of the FBI could be put on overtime and lay out a dragnet to catch all possible leads; the US Treasury Department could impose targeted sanctions against suspect individuals and entities. The intelligence community could redirect collection platforms and order case officers to increase their risk tolerance in recruiting human assets; the Department of State could engage foreign capitals and present "carrots and sticks" to foreign governments in order to encourage information sharing and diplomatic support. The US military could ready forces for contingency operations based on preestablished plans and could begin to develop new war plans.

The American people would exert popular pressure for their government to take action proportionate to the unprecedented destruction inflicted on the homeland. At the same time, there would be bureaucratic and institutional pressure to ensure that the actions taken were consistent with the processes, procedures, and plans already in place. The president would be presented with a range—though not a wide range—of additional military options, including Special Operations forces raids, massive air strike campaigns, and employment of large-scale conventional ground forces. The military would be capable of carrying out these actions relatively well, but what *can* be done and what *should* be done aren't necessarily the same thing. It is unlikely that any of these actions would actually address the threat of follow-on nuclear terrorism or "hold fully accountable" all of those responsible for the attack.

Interests

Effectively responding to the nuclear attack would obviously be of vital national interest, but it would not be the nation's only interest. Arguably, the last time that the United States truly devoted all instruments of national power to a war effort was during the Second World War and this was a unique situation for reasons unassociated with geopolitics. Occurring during the Great Depression, America's World War II military mobilization complemented rather than competed with economic growth and industrial development and therefore served interests beyond the nation's defense policies. After an event of nuclear terrorism, economic growth would remain a vital interest and one that could conflict with US military response options. A steep rise in military spending could provide a short-term stimulus to the economy but could also pose long-term threats, especially if coupled with existing fiscal deficits and the projected rise in medical and entitlement costs.

Trade relations and the need to maintain the free flow of goods and services would also be a central consideration. The nuclear threat network could include nodes inside major trading partners such as European Union member states. Companies based in Europe were intimately involved in the network of Abduel Qadeer Khan, and such companies could again be used to purchase sensitive nuclear enrichment components and specialized explosive materials. Following the attack, the US government would demand that the European Union and national governments finally put an end to these types of transfers. Yet the United States has been making these requests for years and it is not clear that a threat even after a nuclear terrorist attack would produce more effective action. In any event, the government would face tremendous pressure to avoid aggressive responses against noncompliant countries that would jeopardize trade relations.

While developing policies to "hold fully accountable" the

perpetrators of the attack, the president of the United States would also think twice before ordering actions that could lead to war with a major military power. American maneuver room would be severely curtailed if the nuclear threat network emanated from Russian or Chinese territory. The United States would need to very carefully weigh policies that crossed Chinese and Russian red lines; while a fifteen-kiloton nuclear detonation in the heart of the US capital is a genuine catastrophe, it pales in comparison to a nuclear war that involves the arsenals of these global powers. Even if escalation with these countries didn't reach a nuclear threshold, their conventional forces could inflict severe damage on US installations abroad and even target the American homeland. Despite maintaining more significant military advantages, the United States would also have a strong interest in avoiding escalation with North Korea and Pakistan. While the damage they could inflict on US interests isn't commensurate with the capabilities of the Russians or Chinese, these countries also have extensive military power at their disposal.

Reputation

The United States continues to be widely viewed as a superpower that will use military force when its vital interests are threatened. This perception is grounded not only in recent events but also comes from a long history of aggressive military action. As Robert Kagan explains in his book *Dangerous Nation*, there is and may always have been a marked gap in American self-perception of their nation's involvement in international affairs and the perceptions of others.[7] Before and after the

American Revolution, *isolated*, *separate*, *nonentangled*, and *neutral* were words that Americans commonly used to describe their nation in contradistinction to the imperialism of the European empires. This tradition still echoes in America's collective consciousness today. Self-perceived American disinterest in international affairs is also exacerbated by historical bipolarity. The history of the United States is punctuated by periods of acute pessimism about the efficacy of American power. These periods typically come after wars that end unsatisfactorily (e.g., the Philippine-American War, World War I, the Vietnam War, and the Second Iraq War).

Yet, in reality, the United States has consistently projected force abroad. Every single generation of Americans has gone to war since the birth of the republic. They have fought in major conflicts: the War of Independence, the War of 1812, the Mexican-American War, the Civil War, the Spanish-American War, World War I, World War II, the Korean War, the Vietnam War, the 1991 Persian Gulf War, and the post-9/11 global war on terrorism including the major campaigns in Afghanistan and Iraq. They've also regularly fought small wars. From the punitive campaigns against the Barbary pirates memorialized in the US Marine Corps anthem ("to the shores of Tripoli") to today's Special Forces operations against Somali pirates, the US military has been constantly engaged in low-intensity conflicts. Between 1800 and 1934, the US Marines staged 180 landings abroad; the US Navy sent forces into China to rescue besieged American in Peking during the Boxer Rebellion of 1900. President Theodore Roosevelt dispatched a navy fleet to Morocco in 1904 to compel bandits to release a kidnapped American expatriate. The same president Woodrow Wilson who crafted the Fourteen Points and the League of Nations ordered the occupation of the Dominican Republic and Haiti in 1915, a military expedition into Mexico to kill or capture Pancho Villa in 1916 and committed 15,000 soldiers to Siberia and northern Russia in 1918 to protect American interests against the Bolsheviks. During the course of the Cold War, American military forces were deployed to thousands of locations across the globe; the pace of these deployments only accelerated after the fall of the Berlin Wall. In the decade between the collapse of the Soviet Union and the collapse of the Twin Towers, US military force was employed repeatedly in Bosnia, Haiti, Kosovo, and Somalia, among other places.[8]

Yet as Wall Street's investment bankers warn, past performance does not guarantee future outcomes. And a general reputation for military power doesn't provide a clear guide to America's likely conduct in response to nuclear terrorism. While the US military has been very active abroad, a tradition of eschewing entangling alliances and the transitory nature of democratic politics has limited American commitment to long-term deployments and has hampered nation building. An adversary might conclude from this history that America's response to nuclear terrorism would resemble an angry and blinded giant: stumbling, destructive, and dangerous.

Just War and the American Tradition

One of the unique characteristics of nuclear terrorism is the asymmetry between the number of people required to commit an act and the number of people harmed by that act:

it is conceivable that fewer than a hundred people could build and deploy a bomb that kills or wounds hundreds of thousands. While technology has always created asymmetries in warfare, historically it has taken the mobilization of a significant segment of a population to threaten a large segment of another population. The aberration presented by the prospect of limited attributable nuclear terrorism poses a very serious question with regard to conducting a just and legitimate response: What happens to the innocent civilians caught between the perpetrators and the victims?

Americans have waged war at the highest level of intensity to defend themselves and their way of life. From the devastating tactics of the wars against the Indians to general William Tecumseh Sherman's sacking of Atlanta during the Civil War to the firebombing of Germany and Japan during World War II, the US military has ruthlessly pursued its enemies. American bombers killed more than 900,000 Japanese civilians during the last five months of World War II. This number excludes the estimated 127,150 additional deaths caused by the nuclear attacks on Hiroshima and Nagasaki.[9] These figures represent over five times the combat deaths American forces suffered in the entire duration of that war.[10] American action during the Korean War directly contributed to the death of nearly one million North Korean civilians—more than 10 percent of the population. The United States dropped nearly three times as much explosive power in Vietnam as it used during the entire Second World War. An estimated 365,000 Vietnamese civilians perished during this conflict, a ratio of eight Vietnamese deaths for every slain American soldier. American military strategy has persistently resulted in heavy casualties among an enemy's civilian population. In recognition of president and former general Andrew Jackson's actions, Walter Russell Mead characterizes this as America's "Jacksonian tradition."[11]

"If the people raise a howl against my barbarity and cruelty," General Sherman retorted to critics of his scorched-earth tactics, "I will answer that war is war," stating additionally that "war is cruelty, and you cannot refine it."[12] The view that Sherman expressed in these words holds that war has its own natural logic that is not amenable to moral or cultural restraints. This position is most consistent with total wars and wars of attrition in which the belligerents are motivated by desperation. Yet during more limited conflicts, morality and concepts of "just war" have restrained violence and constrained the use of military force. Examples range from the near abolition of the gun in fifteenth-century Japan, to stigmatization of chemical weapons in the aftermath of World War I, to contemporary opposition to land mines and the taboo over biological warfare. History is filled with cases in which various societies imposed normative restrictions on the use of force against noncombatants.

One of the most widely accepted principals of restraint is the concept of *proportionality in attack*. As the International Committee of the Red Cross articulates in its book of rules of customary international humanitarian law, "Launching an attack which may be expected to cause incidental loss of civilian life, injury to civilians, damage to civilian objects, or combination thereof, which would be excessive in relation to the concrete and direct military advantage anticipated, is prohibited."[13] This definition differs from some popular notions of proportionality that hold that the concept proscribes a symmetry and equality of destruction. However, reflecting a more realistic concept of war, the principle that the Red Cross cites holds that the level of destruction must be justified by the anticipated military advantage. This complements other ethical traditions such as those associated with the Hebrew Bible, Greco-Roman philosophy, and Saint Augustine and the medieval Christian church. Examples include the requirement that wars should only be fought by those who are acting for the sake of heaven, the protection of food trees during siege, some amelioration of the status of female captives, the requirement to make an offer of peace for terms of condition to any city that is besieged, and the condition that there should be a reasonable prospect of achieving the positive aims of a military activity.[14]

While the United States may be the most dangerous military power in history, at times it has also been one of the most restrained. The US government has repeatedly chosen not to unleash the full destructive power of its armed forces even in conditions where American soldiers faced the prospect of stalemate or defeat. From Harry S. Truman's decision not to employ the atomic bomb during the Korean War, to Richard Nixon's efforts to deescalate the Vietnam War, to George W. Bush's choice to order a population-centric counterinsurgency strategy in Iraq, the US military has accepted failure at various levels of war rather than resort to actions that would cause large-scale civilian casualties. The United States has not only *not* used its nuclear arsenal in any of many wars its wars since 1945 but has also eschewed brutal tactics frequently employed by other militaries. When the Soviet Army "cleared" towns during its occupation of Afghanistan in the early 1980s, this meant the forced eviction of entire populations and often the destruction of their homes and industries. When the Pakistani Army conducted counterinsurgency operations in the Federally Administered Tribal Areas in 2009, it drove over a million people out of their homes. The Syrian government of Bashir al-Assad has employed Scud missiles, mass artillery, and death squads in its attempts to put down a domestic insurgency and in the process destroyed cities and displaced millions of people.

Often when confronted by the comparison between these tactics and those of the American military, commentators with an axe to grind suggest that the difference is due to America's superior technology and resources. According to their thinking, if other governments had the capabilities at the US president's disposal their leaders wouldn't resort to such brutality. Yet this line of reasoning cannot explain why the United States hasn't resorted to these tactics when its high-end capabilities have been proven ineffective. In 2004, when confronted by attacks emanating from the Iraqi city of Fallujah, the US Marine Corps could have positioned artillery outside the city and leveled it; such an approach is common practice in many of the world's militaries. Instead the marines went block by block to retake the city, a place in which the United States had no economic or political aspirations. Moreover, honorable conduct and the recognition of human rights have repeatedly been of equal or greater concern as military efficacy in battle to senior US government officials. During the 1991 Persian Gulf War, a US F-117 aircraft bombed the Al-Firdos bunker in Baghdad, an installation that American war planners believed to contain a command and control center but which was found to be a bomb shelter for civilian dependents of Iraqi government officials. The air strike killed approximately two to three hundred civilians. Immediately after the disaster, US officials declared Baghdad off limits to further air strikes, and minimal targets were struck in the city for the remainder of the war.[15] The notion that the United States was restrained by "the international community" and global public opinion bears some truth. However, considering that other nations whose governments are equally vulnerable to international condemnation have nevertheless used such tactics, the restraint of the US military is historically remarkable.

Limited Military Options

This raises the question of martial restraint. How would moral considerations and cultural norms regarding the legitimacy of military actions shape the scope and range of military options available to the US president in the aftermath of a nuclear attack of limited or no attribution? The most immediately executable response that the president would have at his or her disposable would be punitive missile or air strikes. In all likelihood these strikes would be aimed at the military and industrial sites of an adversarial government. While large segments of the American public would be looking for a show of force, the US government would still face pressure from a public seeking righteous retribution to justify its target set. Specifically, the cultural norms of American society would compel the government to offer a plausible explanation of how the strikes would effectively prevent follow-on attacks and punish those who had committed the terrorist act.

A nuclear detonation with no clear "return address" could make this an all-but-impossible requirement to meet. American officials would not be able to prove that the government under threat of retaliation ordered the attack or even had the capability to prevent it. In the event that the president decided that the benefit of releasing classified intelligence information about the attack superseded the need to protect sources and methods, the raw intelligence still could not be held up as airtight evidence. It certainly wouldn't convince those inclined to oppose US military action, especially in the aftermath of the major intelligence failure that was used to justify the US-led war to topple Saddam Hussein in 2003. Moreover, American officials would find it difficult to justify air strikes on the grounds of strategic effectiveness; such strikes might weaken the targeted government by demonstrating its inability to protect its country. Alternatively, limited strikes could incite the population to "rally around the flag" and grant additional powers to the head of state and his regime. Even if air strikes weakened the state, the effect could be to provide a more permissive environment for terrorists to operate. Unable to plausibly claim that those killed in US strikes were linked to the terrorist attack and unable to effectively degrade the nuclear capabilities of the transnational network, the US government would be hard pressed to conduct punitive strikes if those strikes did not satisfy the public's standards for legitimate military action.

The United States would face similar challenges in justifying a major military campaign aimed at dismantling a state's nuclear weapons–related programs through air power. Depending on the nuclear threat network, the locations that facilitated and/or contributed to the terrorist attack could be dispersed across multiple countries. Many of these could be dual-use facilities with primarily civilian functions. A major bombing campaign could be conducted against these sites, but to what effect? Large numbers of innocent civilians would likely be harmed and the security of nuclear-related materials would likely be further compromised. Blowing up nuclear facilities could cause significant radiological contamination over an expansive area. It would be impossible to know if all dangerous materials had been rendered unusable without a presence on the ground. And, having severely damaged these sites, there would be no protection to prevent theft of remaining sensitive materials.

Americans have invaded countries for lesser offenses than nuclear terrorism, but in most conceivable scenarios a ground war would be a high-risk venture with limited prospects of eliminating the threat. It is conceivable, depending on the nature of the regime in question, that US military forces could invade a country and forcefully take control over nuclear related sites and facilities. These forces could then destroy enrichment facilities, plutonium reactors, reprocessing sites, and other resources that present a threat. Depending on the size of uranium deposits, it may even be possible to extract fissile material from that country over an extended period of time. All of this, however, would be unprecedented. There is little in the modern American tradition that would suggest that the United States is interested in or particularly adept at maintaining a long-term occupation in a foreign land. Moreover, fissile material is a global commodity. It is simply not practical for the United States to occupy by force all of the world's nuclear-related sites or seize all of the world's fissile material. This goes beyond American cultural proclivities to the practical limitations of political and military power in the contemporary era.

For decades, the phrase "hold fully accountable" has been a favored signaling device of American officials seeking to alert adversaries and assure allies, but it is a warning that lacks credibility. Only Pervez Musharraf can know his own thoughts after hearing George Tenet's warning in 2001, but as an educated and informed observer of world affairs he no doubt reflected on the limitations of the American "superpower." It is even possible that at that moment his appraisal of American power was more accurate than Tenet's. Yet even if Musharraf doubted the ability of the United States to carry out Tenet's threat, he probably presumed that the US government could still cause a lot of problems for him and his country. This may be the reason he did eventually make some concessions, though Pakistan never came close to meeting all of Tenet's demands. While the US government and the American people ultimately became resigned to Pakistani intransigence, that outcome would be far less acceptable in the days after the detonation of a nuclear bomb on American soil.

CONCLUSION
TWENTY-THREE DAYS "RIGHT OF BOOM"

"**M**R. PRESIDENT, YOU ARE LIVE IN THREE . . . TWO . . . one . . ."

"Hours ago the US armed forces, with the support of our friends and allies, launched a series of strikes against nuclear weapons–related facilities that posed a threat to international peace and security. Tactical nuclear weapons were employed against a number of hardened and deeply buried targets. As president and the commander in chief, with the advice of my cabinet and the consent of Congress, I ordered these operations in response to the terrorist attack on Washington, DC. The unprecedented horror inflicted on our nation's capital demanded that we take unprecedented action; our military response is appropriate, proportional, and consistent with both my duty to defend the American people and our international legal obligations. The use of nuclear weapons was limited in scale and scope to minimize civilian causalities while achieving necessary military effects.

"To the many of you who are horrified by the return of nuclear warfare, take comfort in knowing that the civilized world is able to bring force to bear against this new barbarism. To those who are fearful for the future, find assurance in your gov-

ernment's capacity to focus that force. This is only the beginning of a long campaign, but we will not unnecessarily escalate
the current conflict. We do not seek war with foreign governments or their citizens, but will continue to take aim at the
nodes of nuclear threat networks—individuals, organizations,
and facilities—that enable nuclear terrorism and the clandestine use of weapons of mass destruction. No one should doubt
our will and ability to exercise our right to self-defense. Nor
should anyone believe that America is alone in combating this
threat. We will bring to bear all instruments of our nation's
power, including our military, economic, and diplomatic partnerships with our international friends and allies. The perpetrators of the attack on Washington will be brought to justice,
but our most vital objective is to ensure that no one is ever able
to repeat what they did. This will be a long struggle, but we will
not rest until a new international order has been formed and
the world's nuclear materials have been permanently secured."

The president rises and walks past his aides to exit the
room. He believes in what he has said. He is also aware and
deeply distressed by what he left unsaid. Soon government
leaders from around the world will meet in small rooms to discuss how to respond to the United States. They will consider
ways of cooperating with US officials and accommodating the
exercise of American power. At the same time, many will explore strategies for obstructing and opposing US policy. The
outcome of these deliberations will be tremendously consequential. The president has shown his cards and played his
hand, but he doesn't know how it will all stack up. And like so
much that has happened, the outcome is out of his control.

TODAY'S REALITY

Long ago the secret of designing a nuclear weapon ceased to be a secret, and for some time the industrial processes necessary to construct a bomb have been available to most governments. The central bulwark that has prevented individuals and substate groups from building and detonating a nuclear bomb has been the scarcity and security of special nuclear material. Yet, today "nascent nukes"—the facilities for producing nuclear materials—are expanding in countries that harbor violent extremists, some of which have a history of supporting terrorist groups. Despite decades of commendable initiatives by the United States and other governments, including president Barack Obama's recent promotion of "global nuclear lockdown," the world's specialized nuclear materials are not secure. As a result, it is increasingly plausible for a group of people to develop and employ a nuclear weapon without an evidentiary chain implicating a national government. This is unprecedented, and it is a fundamentally new dynamic in international security affairs. It combines the threat presented by nuclear war in the twentieth century with the age-old threat posed by terrorists who have nothing to lose and territorial authorities who refuse to restrain them. The actions of the United States and world powers after a nuclear terrorism event are unknowable, but the range of options they will confront is not inconceivable. They will be an extension of past policies. The history reviewed in this book highlights policies and actions that have proven effective against nuclear weapons and nonnuclear terrorism as distinct phenomena because the most effective response to nuclear terrorism incorporates lessons from both experiences.

RETALIATION: THE DAYS AND WEEKS
"RIGHT OF BOOM"

In the hours and days following a nuclear attack on American soil, the most immediate task before the president and the National Security Council would be tending to the battered psychological condition of the nation. This may seem like an incidental concern compared with managing the material damage inflicted by a nuclear blast, but the emotions and expectations of the American people would be the primary force driving the political and military decisions of the US government. Fear and panic would be widespread, just as they were following Japan's attack on Pearl Harbor and after al-Qaeda's attacks on 9/11. Ambiguity about the perpetrators of the attack would exacerbate both the emotional and physical trauma. People would expect—and public officials would be on high alert for—follow-on attacks. There would be a significant risk of vigilantism and mob violence. Uncertainty would retard global markets for at least a short period and paralyze American economic growth. Rumors and false reports would keep the public off balance for some time. To steady the ship of state, the administration would take action to reestablish the public's confidence in the capability of the US government to impose order and security. Tremendous political pressure would exist to reassure the public through the projection and demonstration of American power. In this fractious environment and in the fog of fragmentary information, the risk of misapplying US power would be extraordinarily high.

The politics of the day would favor risking impetuous action over being perceived to be excessively cautious. American history is replete with instances of ill-conceived military responses launched in the heat of moments of such vulnerability. As such, the central challenge of America's elected officials would be to channel public fear, and the force of the US military, in a pragmatic direction within the parameters set by demands of the American public. Prudent policy would be that which not only satisfied immediate political and psychological needs but also preserved longer-term strategic interests. For example, there would be segments of the American population and members of the political establishment pushing to strike out at foreign governments that US security would be better served by cooperating with. In the days and weeks ahead, the world would surely witness the ferocity of US retaliation. Yet, if undertaken wisely, such retaliation would occur in a way that ultimately set the conditions for reconstruction of a reformed international security system—the creation of new security arrangements capable of managing the unique dangers presented by nuclear terrorism.

A presidential address would be among the very first actions of the US government. It would be a message made by a commander in chief leading his people toward war. Despite the opacity surrounding the terrorist attack, the president would almost certainly identify an enemy; this would be a political necessity. Despite the anonymity of the perpetrators, the range of plausible suspects would not be infinite. If the president were well advised, he or she would narrowly define the enemy; it would be an individual or an entity linked to terrorism and nuclear weapons, and a target that could be struck without risking unnecessary and potentially catastrophic escalation. It would make sense to focus US retaliation against suspects with a history of malign activity that could be manageably confronted. In other words, the enemy would be defined in a way that wouldn't lead the American people down a path toward nuclear war with a country like Russia or China. Wise US policy also wouldn't preclude bilateral and multinational cooperation that could eventually be essential to improving the security of the world's nuclear weapons–related materials.

While the president communicated American resolve to the public and the world, the US Department of Defense would be developing a major strike plan based on existing capabilities and generating concepts of military operations. Just as president Franklin Delano Roosevelt ordered an air raid into Tokyo on April 18, 1942—the "Doolittle Raid"—knowing that it wouldn't inflict any significant damage of the Japanese war machine, the US president in our scenario would likely be compelled to order military strikes that would have negligible effects on the threat of nuclear terrorism. These could include the visible destruction of command and control centers, Special Forces raids against known terrorist leaders, and the arrest of terrorism and proliferation suspects. If a nexus existed with adversarial foreign governments, US air strikes could target symbols of regimes that have aided terrorists, such as the headquarters of the Iranian Republican Guard or the palaces of the supreme leader of North Korea. Conventional military targets like airfields and weapons factories would likely be on the strike list. Even if the US government concluded that reestablishing deterrence required the employment of tactical nuclear weapons, these actions would do little to measurably diminish the nuclear terrorist threat in the short term.

Bombing nuclear-related sites would pose additional risks but would likely also be considered. Most plausible scenarios envisioning the employment of conventional munitions against a nuclear reactor entail widespread nuclear fallout. Strikes against uranium enrichment sites could also spew radioactive materials for miles, depending on the nature of the ordinance and the layout of the targeted facility. Moreover, damaging nuclear storage sites would expose nuclear weapons–related components and increase the risk of loss or theft of special nuclear materials. This essential conundrum—the strength in a state's weakness—would be a central concern of both defense officials and diplomats. Striking a government that is firmly in control of its nuclear weapons infrastructure poses less risks from a nuclear security perspective than inflicting damage on a government that has limited capacity to secure its nuclear materials. The recent situation regarding Syria's chemical weapons clearly demonstrates this dilemma. In the absence of Bashar al-Assad's security forces there would have been nothing to prevent Syria's chemical weapons from falling into the hands of non-state actors, such as a terrorist group, a regional militia, or smugglers in search of profit. Consequently, while US bombs would certainly fall on foreign facilities in the weeks after a nuclear terrorist attack, in truth they would be aimed at a psychological target with a political purpose: increasing the morale of the American people, reassuring friends and allies, and relieving popular pressure to escalate to a higher and more dangerous level of violence.

Alongside American missiles and warships, the United States would hopefully push forward a framework to both its friends and enemies that laid out a vision for how the conflict should end. This message, and the diplomatic actions in support of it, would be both more complicated and more important than the concomitant military strikes because it would communicate paths toward achieving resolution without provoking nuclear escalation and threatening a "total war." For reasons of domestic and international politics, someone would need to be held publicly accountable for the terrorist attack. The US message would identify whom this should be and with whom the US government would be willing to work in order to achieve that outcome. The crux of diplomacy would be a negotiation over the individuals and entities that would be punished for the trauma inflicted on America. Just as the United States made demands on Iran, Pakistan, and the Taliban after 9/11, such as the cessation of support for al-Qaeda and assistance in attempting to capture Osama bin Laden, American officials would issue entreaties alongside threats in order to construct a coalition of foreign partners. The specifics would be based on the particulars of the situation, but this diplomatic effort would have at least two critical phases. The first would articulate immediate tasks needed to meet urgent political, military, and economic necessities such as military basing, over flight rights, intelligence cooperation, and public support for US policy. The second phase would express the range of long-term changes needed in nuclear security practices, international law, and cooperation against nonstate actors. Hopefully, global powers would quickly accept the need to accommodate and adapt to the new realities presented by a postnuclear terrorism environment.

RECONSTRUCTION—EMPLOYING THE PAST TO INFORM THE FUTURE

The initial response phase—at minimum a dramatic show of force, and possibly the outbreak of a major conventional war—would not establish the conditions to prevent future nonattributable nuclear attacks. The ingredients for a bomb are simply too easily available and the mechanics of doing so is 1940s technology. Cataclysmic wars tend to begin with the development of new technologies of violence and end only when new political arrangements are established that are capable of managing that technology. Nuclear terrorism would likewise demand alterations in the global security system, the generation of new national defense capabilities, and the acceptance of new norms of international behavior. Institutionalizing these changes would be the second major phase of the US response; it would likely begin months after the attack and would take years. The initial military response—and act of destruction, however necessary—would be far easier than this delicate process of construction. In determining how best to build this global framework, its architects would be well served by considering the lessons of the Cold War's nuclear brinkmanship and the enduring features of effective counterterrorism.

Red Lines

One of the central and most applicable lessons of the nuclear standoff between the United States and Soviet Union is the supreme importance of identifying and communicating actions that constitute a threat to the peace—a government's "red lines." During the Cold War, these lines were typically international borders and they were literally crossed when armies marched over them. To shine a bright light on this trip wire, the US government built alliances, formulated treaties, and entered mutual defense pacts focused on strengthening internationally recognized borders. The proliferation of nuclear weapons across borders was a significant issue but did not rise to the same level of concern that the movement of foreign militaries did. Consequently, despite US policies and numerous international efforts to highlight the threat possessed by nuclear terrorism, neither international law nor US defense policy was developed to communicate red lines associated with this threat with the same clarity that exists regarding the movement of armies across international borders. This situation has persisted despite an increase in military actions aimed at the threat of the proliferation of weapons of mass destruction. These include Israel's attack on Iraq's nuclear reactor in 1981 and the US-led invasion of Iraq in 2003, as well as threatened military actions such as the US response to Syria's chemical weapons use in 2012 and the recent standoff over Iran's nuclear program.

In the absence of international norms or unilateral declarations that identify nuclear activities that pose "a threat to the peace," it is difficult for governments to understand what they cannot do and what they need to do in order to avoid military escalation. This was evident through the Syrian government's repeated use of chemical weapons against rebels in a campaign that culminated in a mass attack that killed over a thousand people in August 2013. Despite a declaration by President Obama the previous year indicating that the use of chemical weapons would cross a red line, Assad's government did not expect that its actions would prompt the United States to threaten air strikes. Similar confusion existed in 2006 when North Koreans chose to provide Syria with nuclear weapons engineers to help construct a reactor for producing plutonium; the North Koreans probably didn't expect this assistance to trigger a military strike from Israel. More broadly, a range of countries from Europe to east Asia have made the implicit decision not to crack down on proliferators of nuclear weapons–related components because their inaction isn't clearly identified as a threat to peace for which they will be held accountable. In the aftermath of a nuclear terrorist attack, American and like-minded world leaders would be compelled to identify a range of nuclear-related activities, from research to funding to enrichment, as "threats to the peace," red lines, and *casus belli* that have the potential to provoke unilateral or multilateral coercive—and possibly violent—action.

Scalable Capabilities for Flexible Responses

The Cold War's nuclear brinkmanship demonstrated that red lines are only as meaningful as the capability for force that stands behind them. The challenge presented in the 1960s by nuclear weapons parity and the issue of "suicide or surrender" showed that managing escalation and responding to threats short of a total war require scalable options—a range of capabilities and plans. The assumption that the United States would respond to nuclear terrorism through massive retaliation lacks plausibility in the same way that during the Cold War threats to use atomic weapons against indirect Soviet expansion in the third world lacked credibility. President John F. Kennedy's administration met this challenge through a buildup of conventional forces, the development of the Special Forces, and the maintenance of a nuclear triad. The complexity of the nuclear terrorism threat requires an even wider range of capabilities. While it is conceivable for nuclear missiles to be used to retaliate against nuclear missiles, nuclear terrorism cannot be used to counter nuclear terrorism. Just as the US Congress authorized force broadly after 9/11 to encompass retaliation against the entire terrorist network—"those nations, organizations, or persons"—responsible for the attacks, in the aftermath of nuclear terrorism the American people will demand action against global nuclear threat networks. To effectively carry out such a campaign, the United States would require scalable military and nonmilitary capabilities to target nodes along the nuclear threat pathway: capabilities to conduct missions ranging from halting the sale of dual use components through legal and diplomatic processes, to freezing funds of weapons proliferators, to isolating and immobilizing terrorist groups, to improving security practices at nuclear materials storage sites, to coercive interdictions on the high seas, to seizing and securing nuclear weapons sites, and even to destroying nuclear weapons arsenals.

Just as threats from bandits and barbarians in the premodern era caused settled societies to create innovative strategies and irregular capabilities, the threat of nuclear terrorism demands new types of forces and institutions. In today's current political environment, public officials are focused on seemingly more urgent issues than nuclear terrorism, and this constrains the nature and scale of new initiatives. In the months and years after a nuclear terrorist attack, expansive actions would take place at both the national and international levels. The US government could establish a national entity whose exclusive mission would be to develop, train, and equip forces along with crafting strategies, tactics, and techniques for managing the threat of nuclear terrorism. In one sense, this entity would face an entirely new mission: not to destroy a foreign military or retaliate against the industrial capacity of a nation but to target global nuclear threat networks.

The components of this type of entity already exist across multiple US government agencies including the Departments of Defense, State, Energy, and Homeland Security, the Federal Bureau of Investigation, and various sectors of the intelligence community. The purpose of the new entity would be to create a unity of effort that leverages all elements of national power in a way that develops a credible capability for the US government to dismantle foreign nuclear weapons programs, secure nuclear materials, and prevent nuclear proliferation. Given the enduring lessons of effective counterterrorism, this entity would likely develop expertise in isolating and immobilizing malign networks through low-intensity paramilitary operations, including special operations, law enforcement, cyberoperations, sabotage, and the use of foreign partnerships. The entity would operate in the mission space below major military strike planning and large-scale combat operations but above traditional covert action and law enforcement. Just as the US military conducted public tests of nuclear weapons during the Cold War, this entity could demonstrate that the government is prepared and capable of responding to nuclear terrorism by conducting exercises. Some of the elements of these demonstrations could include military interdictions, neutralizing nuclear devices, freezing foreign assets, isolating enemy individuals and immobilizing networks, and destroying nuclear weapons–related facilities in a way that limits collateral damage and is therefore a politically plausible option.

Defense Pacts and the Promotion of New International Security Norms

In the months and years after a nuclear terrorism event, the United States would also draw on another of its traditional approaches to addressing WMD threats: bilateral and multilateral diplomacy. Just as the administrations of presidents Harry S. Truman and Dwight D. Eisenhower shaped international institutions and defense arrangements in the early years of the Cold War to contain the threat of communism, the US government could promote new legal arrangements aimed at the threat of nuclear terrorism. A necessary first step would be to establish new mutual defense pacts. These commitments would publicly identify red lines and lend credibility to warnings by individual governments to hold accountable people who enable nuclear terrorism through action or inaction. These formal defense agreements could be bolstered by multilateral exercises that highlight combined response capabilities. Exercises would promote the legitimacy of aggressive actions that could be used to disrupt the pathways toward a nuclear weapons capability and encourage acceptance of these practices as a new international norm of behavior. The ultimate goal would be to re-form and redraft core components of international law to allow for increased nuclear materials security, but bilateral agreements would be the most realistic and effective starting point.

While the United States and like-minded countries would promote offensive measures to address nuclear terrorism, they would also likely act to improve defensive measures through increasing the capacity of national authorities to control malign activities within their sovereign territory. Since 9/11, much of US foreign capacity building has been focused on countering terrorism, but less visible and smaller scale efforts have been aimed at securing nuclear materials. After the trauma of a nuclear terrorism event, additional money and effort could be placed on not only creating but also enforcing a "gold standard" for nuclear materials security. Comprehensive collective security initiatives would be politically feasible for the first time. Aspects of President Truman's vision of an international structure to control nuclear energy could become a reality. Greater international control of special nuclear materials would be a likely proposal. Increasing the authority of the International Atomic Energy Agency or a newly created international entity would likely have new supporters. Officials from such an organization could be granted authority to conduct more intrusive inspections and empowered with punitive authority to issues fines and seize poorly secured nuclear materials. New political pressure might also compel governments to reduce and consolidate their nuclear weapons stockpiles. The absolute sovereignty that governments have exercised over these weapons may become viewed as a dangerous anachronism and replaced with more transparent arrangements.

Just as the West had to fight the Soviet bloc to set the terms of the international system following the Second World War, there would be opposition and competition at the political level. The United States would have to build a coalition to set the terms of discourse and promote new standards for responsible international conduct. One conceivable approach would be to model nuclear international legal norms on US "negative security assurance," which exempts countries that are party to the Non-Proliferation Treaty and in compliance with nonproliferation obligations from US nuclear threats. As such, a coalition of like-minded nations could declare that those countries who refuse to participate in new nuclear materials security arrangements would occupy "a zone of suspicion and vulnerability" in which they would be presumed guilty and a legitimate target for retaliation following nuclear terrorism even in the absence of proof of complicity. If this became the "new normal," it would reflect the evolution of the Peace of Westphalia framework into a new order more capable of managing the unique threats associated with nuclear terrorism.

A NEW ORDER EMERGES FROM THE RUBBLE

A nuclear detonation with no home address in an American city would confront the president of the United States with unprecedented decisions amid an unparalleled level of uncertainty. In the days immediately following the attack, the requirements of deterrence and domestic politics would almost certainly provoke a series of US air strikes against token targets, but this could only be the beginning of a far more complicated project. To prevent follow-on nuclear terrorism, a range of actions would be required to disrupt nuclear threat networks around the globe. This campaign would include building the capacities of sovereign states to control threats within their territories while simultaneously undertaking clandestine, covert, and sometimes kinetic operations within foreign countries. Americans and their international partners would be entering uncharted territory, but we can hope that they would do so carrying tools developed during previous conflicts and keeping in mind lessons from the past. Recognizing that history never repeats itself, it can still be a useful guide for understanding an unsettling but all too possible future.

NOTES

Introduction

1. Parker F. Jones, "Goldsboro Revisited: Account of Hydrogen Bomb Near-Disaster over North Carolina—Declassified Document." *Guardian*, 21 September 2013, *http://www.theguardian .com /world/interactive/2013/sep/20/goldsboro-revisited-declassified -document.*

2. Shirley Kan, "China and Proliferation of Weapons of Mass Destruction and Missiles: Policy Issues," *Congressional Research Service*, 11 March 2013; Dinah Deckstein and Matthias Scheep, "Parts for Tehran's Nuclear Program: Was Siemens Involved in Dubious Trade?" *Der Spiegel*, 9 August 2010; Cathrin Gilbert, Holger Stark, and Andreas Ulrich, "Nuclear Technology for Iran: German Investigators Uncover Illegal Exports," *Der Spiegel*, 1 October 2012.

3. Jakub Grygiel, "To Survive, Decentralize! The Barbarian Threat and State Decentralization," *Orbis* 55, no. 4 (2011): 663-684

4. David Sanger, *Confront and Conceal: Obama's Secret Wars and Surprising Use of American Power* (New York: Broadway, 2012).

5. David Albright and Christina Walrond, *North Korea's Estimated Stocks of Plutonium and Weapons-Grade Uranium*, Institute for Science and International Security, 16 August 2012, *http://isis-online.org/uploads/isis-reports/documents/dprk*

_fissile_material_production_16Aug2012.pdf; Julian Ryall, "North Korea Could Have Fuel for 48 Nuclear Weapons by 2015," *Telegraph*, 20 August 2012, *http://www.telegraph.co.uk/news /worldnews/asia/northkorea/9487574/North-Korea-could-have -fuel-for-48-nuclear-weapons-by-2015.html.*

6. "Illicit Trafficking in Weapons-Useable Nuclear Material: Still More Questions Than Answers," Center for Nonproliferation Studies, 11 December 2011, *http://www.nti.org/analysis/articles /illicit-trafficking-weapons-useable-nuclear-material-still-more -questions-answers/.*

7. Feroz Khan, *Eating Grass: The Making of the Pakistani Bomb* (Stanford, CA: Stanford Security Studies, 2012).

8. David Albright, "The Rocky Path to a Long-Term Settlement with Iran," *Washington Post*, 25 November 2013.

9. David Albright, *Testimony of David Albright before the Senate Committee on Foreign Relations on Reversing Iran's Nuclear Program: Understanding Iran's Nuclear Program and Technically Assessing Negotiating Positions*, *http://isis-online.org/uploads /isis-reports/documents/Testimony_Albright_senate_foreign _relations_committee_oct_2_2013.pdf.*

Chapter One: The Persistent Danger

1. Paul Bracken, *Fire in the East: The Rise of Asian Military Power and the Second Nuclear Age* (New York: HarperCollins) 2.

2. US Department of Homeland Security, *National Capital Region: Key Response Planning Factors for the Aftermath of Nuclear Terrorism*, November 2011, *http://blogs.fas.org/secrecy/2012 /03/ncr_nuclear/.*

3. John McPhee, *The Curve of Binding Energy* (New York: Farrar, Straus and Giroux, 1973), 4.

4. Thomas C. Reed and Danny B. Stillman, *The Nuclear Express: A Political History of the Bomb and Its Proliferation* (Minneapolis: Zenith, 2009), 4.

5. *Letter from Albert Einstein to President Franklin Delano Roosevelt about the possible construction of nuclear bombs*, 2 August 1939, *http://www.pbs.org/wgbh/americanexperience/features /primary-resources/truman-ein39/?flavour=mobile*

6. Ibid., 13.

7. *Report of the Committee on Political and Social Problems, Manhattan Project "Metallurgical Laboratory," University of Chicago, June 11, 1945 (The Franck Report)*, *http://www.dannen .com/decision/franck.html*.

8. Reed and Stillman, *The Nuclear Express*, 69, 87, 96; Marian Holmes, "Spies Who Spilled Atomic Bomb Secrets," *Smithsonian*, 20 April 2009, *http://www.smithsonianmag.com/history-archaeology /Spies-Who-Spilled-Atomic-Bomb-Secrets.html*; Wisconsin Project on Nuclear Arms Control, "Israel's Nuclear Weapon's Capability," *Risk Report* 2, no. 4 (1996), *http://www.wisconsinproject .org/countries/israel/nuke.html*; Binyamin Pinkus and Moshe Tlamim, "Atomic Power to Israel's Rescue: French-Israeli Nuclear Cooperation, 1949–1957," *Israel Studies* 7, no. 1 (2002): 104–38.

9. Dwight D. Eisenhower, *Address by Mr. Dwight D. Eisenhower, President of the United States of America, to the 470th Plenary Meeting of the United Nations General Assembly*, 8 December 1953, *http://www.iaea.org/About/atomsforpeace_speech.html*.

10. Wisconsin Project on Nuclear Arms Control, "Israel's Nuclear Weapon's Capability: An Overview," *Risk Report* 2, no. 4 (1996), *http://www.wisconsinproject.org/countries/israel/nuke.html*; Binyamin Pinkus and Moshe Tlamim, "Atomic Power to Israel's Rescue: French-Israeli Nuclear Cooperation, 1949–1957," *Israel Studies* 7, no. 1 (2002): 104–38.

11. Reed and Stillman, *The Nuclear* Express, 118.

12. According to the Congressional Research Service, a declassified U.S. Special National Intelligence Estimate as far back as 1974 stated that Israel possessed nuclear weapons. Congressional

Research Service, "Nuclear Weapons R&D Organizations in Nine Nations," 1 May 2013, 6, *http://fas.org/sgp/crs/nuke/R40439.pdf*

13. Karsten Frey, *India's Nuclear Bomb and National Security* (New York: Routledge, 2006), 63.

14. Khan, *Eating Grass*, 7.

15. US Central Intelligence Agency, Directorate of Intelligence, "Prospects for Further Proliferation of Nuclear Weapons," 2 October 1974, Digital National Security Archive, *http://nsarchive.chadwyck.com.*

16. Wisconsin Project on Nuclear Arms Control, "South Africa's Nuclear Autopsy," *Risk Report* 2, no. 1 (1996), http://www.wisconsinproject.org/countries/safrica/autopsy.html.

17. Dwight D. Eisenhower, *Address before the General Assembly of the United Nations on Peaceful Uses of Atomic Energy, New York City,* 8 December 1953, *http://www.presidency.ucsb.edu/ws/index.php?pid=9774&st=atomic&st1=.*

18. Harry S. Truman, *Special Message to Congress on Atomic Energy,* 3 October 1945, *http://www.presidency.ucsb.edu/ws/index.php?pid=12327.*

19. Alice Kimball Smith, *A Peril and a Hope: The Scientists' Movement in America, 1945–47* (Cambridge, MA: MIT Press, 1965).

20. "The Bomb Is No Secret," *New Republic,* 8 October 1945, cited in David Kasier, "The Atomic Secret in Red Hands? American Suspicions of Theoretical Physicists during the Early Cold War," *Representations* 90, no. 1 (2005): 28–60, *http://web.mit.edu/dikaiser/www/Kaiser.RedTheorists.pdf.*

21. Rebecca Press Schwartz, "The Making of the History of the Atomic Bomb: The Smyth Report and the Historiography of the Manhattan Project" (PhD diss., Princeton University, in preparation), 67.

22. Michael Gordin, *Red Cloud at Dawn: Truman, Stalin and the End of the Atomic Monopoly* (New York: Farrar, Straus and Giroux, 2009), 97.

23. Schwartz, "The Making of the History of the Atomic Bomb," 93.

24. Ibid., 114.

25. Ibid., 98.

26. David Kaiser, "The Atomic Secret in Red Hands?" 36.

27. Harry S. Truman, *The President's News Conference Following the Signing of a Joint Declaration on Atomic Energy*, 15 November 1945, *http://www.presidency.ucsb.edu/ws/index.php?pid=12290*.

28. Gordin, *Red Cloud at Dawn*, 75, 93, 103–5.

29. Khidhir Hamza, *Saddam's Bombmaker: The Daring Escape of the Man Who Built Iraq's Secret Weapon* (New York: Simon and Schuster, 2000), 69, 91–104.

30. John McPhee, "The Curve Of Binding Energy," *New Yorker*, 3 December 1973, 115–16, *http://www.newyorker.com/magazine/1973/12/03/i-the-curve-of-binding-energy*; Robert Serber, *The Los Alamos Primer: The First Lectures on How to Build an Atomic Bomb* (Berkeley: University of California Press, 1992); David Hawkins, Edith C. Truslow, and Ralph Carlisle Smith, *The Los Alamos Project* (n.p.: Los Alamos Scientific Laboratory of the University of California, 1961), *http://books.google.com/books/about/Manhattan_District_History_Project_Y_the.html?id=AI1cQQAACAAJ*.

31. Albert Narath, Department of Energy, *Report of the Fundamental Classification Policy Review Group*, 15 January 1997, *http://www.fas.org/sgp/library/repfcprg.html#I16*.

32. Kaiser, "The Atomic Secret in Red Hands?" 35.

33. W. J. Frank, *Summary Report of the Nth County Experiment*, March 1967, *http://www.gwu.edu/~nsarchiv/news/20030701/nth-country.pdf*.

34. Oliver Burkeman, "How Two Students Built an A-Bomb," *Guardian*, 23 June 2003, *http://www.guardian.co.uk/world/2003/jun/24/usa.science*.

35. Kaiser, "The Atomic Secret in Red Hands?" 34.

36. Howard Morland, "The Holocaust Bomb: a Question of Time," 15 November 1999, *http://www.fas.org/sgp/eprint /morland.html.*

37. Lars-Erik De Geer, "The Radioactive Signature of the Hydrogen Bomb," *Science and Global Security* 2 (1992): pp. 351–63, *http://www.princeton.edu/sgs/publications/sgs/pdf/2_4DeGeer.pdf*; A. DeVolpi, G. E. Marsh, T. A. Postol, and G. S. Stanford, *Born Secret: The H-Bomb, the Progressive Case and National Security* (New York: Pergamon, 1981).

38. *Early Atomic Energy Commission Studies Show Concern over Gas Centrifuge Proliferation Risk*, National Security Archive Electronic Briefing Book no. 385, 23 July 2012, *http://www .gwu.edu/~nsarchiv/nukevault/ebb385/.*; S.A. Levin, D. E. Hatch, and E. Von Halle, *Production of Enriched Uranium for Nuclear Weapons by Nations X, Y, and Z by Means of the Gas Centrifuge Process*, 26 February 1960 (Washington, DC: US Department of Energy).

39. *Agreements between the United States and the United Kingdom and between the United States, the United Kingdom, and Belgium Regarding the Acquisition and Control of Uranium*, 13 February 1944, *http://digicoll.library.wisc.edu/cgi-bin/FRUS /FRUS-idx?type=turn&entity=FRUS.FRUS1944v02.p1036&id =FRUS.FRUS1944v02&isize=text.*

40. Zbynek Zeman and Rainer Karlsch, *Uranium Matters: Central European Uranium in International Politics, 1900–1960* (Budapest, Hungary: Central European University Press, 2008), 20–21.

41. Jonathan E. Helmreich, *Gathering Rare Ores: The Diplomacy of Uranium Acquisition, 1943–1954* (Princeton, NJ: Princeton University Press, 1986).

42. Richard G. Hewlett and Oscar E. Anderson, *The New World, 1939–1946: A History of the United States Atomic Energy Commission*, vol. 1 (Berkeley: University of California Press,

1990), 326; Lawrence S. Wittner, *One World or None: A History of the World Nuclear Disarmament Movement through 1953* (Stanford, CA: Stanford University Press, 1993); Robert J. Oppenheimer, "Niels Bohr and Atomic Weapons," *New York Review of Books,* 17 December 1964, 6-8.

43. Harry S. Truman, *Special Message to Congress on Atomic Energy,* 3 October 1945, *http://www.presidency.ucsb.edu/ws/index.php?pid=12327.*

44. Harry S. Truman: "The President's News Conference Following the Signing of a Joint Declaration on Atomic Energy," 15 November 1945, *The American Presidency Project. http://www.presidency.ucsb.edu/ws/?pid=12290.*

45. *The Acheson-Lilienthal Report: Report on the International Control of Atomic Energy,* 16 March 1946, *http://www.learnworld.com/ZNW/LWText.Acheson-Lilienthal.html.*

46. US Department of State, Office of the Historian, "The Acheson-Lilienthal & Baruch Plans, 1946," *http://history.state.gov/milestones/1945-1952/BaruchPlans.*

47. Lauren Barbour, "Appendix 1: Fissile Material Cutoff Treaty: A Chronology," http://isis-online.org/uploads/books/documents/Appendix%201%2012-26.pdf; Joseph L. Nogee, *Soviet Policy towards International Control of Atomic Energy* (Notre Dame, IN: University of Notre Dame Press, 1961), 136.

48. Peter Lavoy, "The Enduring Effects of Atoms For Peace," December 2003, *http://www.armscontrol.org/act/2003_12/Lavoy#notes17.*

49. US Government Accountability Office, *Nuclear Nonproliferation: U.S. Agencies Have Limited Ability to Account for, Monitor, and Evaluate the Security of U.S. Nuclear Material Overseas,* GAO-11-920, September 2011, *http://www.gao.gov/new.items/d11920.pdf.*

50. *Uranium 2007: Resources, Production and Demand OECD-Nuclear Energy Agency and IAEA 2008* (Paris: OECD

Nuclear Energy Agency, 2008); World Nuclear Association, "Uranium Mining Overview," May 2012, *http://www.world-nuclear.org /info/Nuclear-Fuel-Cycle/Mining-of-Uranium/Uranium-Mining -Overview/*.

51. WISE Uranium Project, "Uranium Enrichment Facilities," *http://www.wise-uranium.org/efac.html#ENR*.

52. International Panel on Fissile Materials, *Global Fissile Material Report 2011*, 2011, *http://fissilematerials.org/library /gfmr11.pdf*; "US Sent Plutonium to 39 Countries," *Independent*, 7 February 1996, *http://www.independent.co.uk/news/world/us -sent-plutonium-to-39-countries-1317719.html*.

53. BlatantWorld.com, "Countries with the Most Nuclear Power Reactors in the World," 11 June 2010, *http://www.blatantworld .com/feature/the_world/most_nuclear_power_reactors.html*; Institute for Science and International Security, "Table A1: Cumulative Plutonium Discharges from Civilian Nuclear Power Reactors," *http://www.isis-online.org/publications/puwatch/taba1.html*.

Chapter Two: The New Threats

1. Graham Allison, "The Cuban Missile Crisis at 50," *Foreign Affairs*, July–August 2012, http://www.foreignaffairs.com/articles/137679/graham-allison/the-cuban-missile-crisis-at-50.

2. "North Korea's May Nuclear Test Few Kilotons: U.S.," Reuters, 15 June 2009, *http://www.reuters.com/article/2009/06/15 /us-korea-north-usa-idUSTRE55E5BA20090615*.

3. David Sanger and Choe Sang-Hun, "North Korea Confirms It Conducted 3rd Nuclear Test," *New York Times*, 11 February 2013, *http://www.nytimes.com/2013/02/12/world/asia/north-korea -nuclear-test.html?pagewanted=all&_r=0*.

4. David Sanger, "U.S. Confronts Consequences of Underestimating North Korean Leader," *New York Times*, 24 April 2014, *http://www.nytimes.com/2014/04/25/world/asia/wrong-guesses -about-north-korea-leave-us-struggling-to-adjust.html?_r=0*.

5. Balazs Szalontai and Sergey Radchenko, *North Korea's Efforts to Acquire Nuclear Technology and Nuclear Weapons: Evidence from Russian and Hungarian Archives*, Woodrow Wilson International Center for Scholars Working Paper 53, August 2006, *http://www.wilsoncenter.org/sites/default/files/WP53_web_final.pdf*.

6. Institute for Science and International Security, "North Korea," *http://isis-online.org/country-pages/northkorea*.

7. Siegfried S. Hecker and William Liou, "Dangerous Dealings: North Korea's Nuclear Capabilities and the Threat of Export to Iran," *Arms Control Today* 37, no. 2 (2007): 6–11.

8. Mark Fitzpatrick, *Nuclear Black Markets: Pakistan, A. Q. Khan and the Rise and Fall of a Proliferation Network* (London: International Institute for Strategic Studies, 2007).

9. Khan, *Eating Grass*, 360, 368.

10. David Sanger, "North Koreans Unveil New Plant for Nuclear Use," *New York Times*, 20 November 2010, *http://www.nytimes.com/2010/11/21/world/asia/21intel.html?pagewanted=all*.

11. Albright and Walrond, "North Korea's Estimated Stocks"; Julian Ryall, "North Korea Could Have Fuel for 48 Nuclear Weapons by 2015," *Telegraph*, 20 August 2012, *http://www.telegraph.co.uk/news/worldnews/asia/northkorea/9487574/North-Korea-could-have-fuel-for-48-nuclear-weapons-by-2015.html*.

12. Associated Press, "Diagram Suggests Iran Working on Bomb," *USA Today*, 28 November 2012.

13. Channel News Asia, "Iran modifies Arak reactor over nuclear concerns," 27 August 2014, *http://www.channelnewsasia.com/news/world/iran-modifies-arak/1332744.html*

14. David Albright, Christina Walrond, and Andrea Stricker, *ISIS Analysis of IAEA Iran Safeguards Report*, 14 November 2013, *http://isis-online.org/uploads/isis-reports/documents/ISIS_Analysis_IAEA_Safeguards_Report_14November2013-final.pdf*; David Albright and Christina Walrond, *Iran's Critical Capability in 2014*, 17 July 2013, *http://isis-online.org/uploads/isis-reports*

/documents/Iran_critical_capability_17July2013.pdf; William C. Witt, Christina Walrond, David Albright, and Houston Wood, *Iran's Evolving Breakout Potential*, 8 October 2012, *http://isis-online .org/uploads/isisreports/documents/Irans_Evolving_Breakout _Potential.pdf*.

15. Graham Allison, "Red Lines in the Sand," *Foreign Policy*, 11 October 2012, *http://www.foreignpolicy.com/articles/2012 /10/11/red_lines_in_the_sand*.

16. Ronen Bergman, "Will Israel Attack Iran?" *New York Times*, 25 January 2012, *http://www.nytimes.com/2012/01/29 s/magazine/will-israel-attack-iran.html?pagewanted=all&_r=0*.

17. Maseh Zarif, "The Iranian Nuclear Program: Timelines, Data, and Estimates V4.1," October 2012, *http://www.slideshare .net/CriticalThreats/iran-nuclear-timeline-ver-41?ref=http://www .irantracker.org/nuclear-program/zarif-timelines-data-estimates -october-29-2012#btnNext*.

18. Bergman, "Will Israel Attack Iran?"

19. On the issue of time and distance, see: Ibid.

20. Douglas Birch, "Letting Go of 'Loose Nukes,'" *Foreign Policy*, 31 October 2012, *http://www.foreignpolicy.com/articles /2012/10/31/letting_go_of_loose_nukes?page=0,0*.

21. Center for Nonproliferation Studies, "Illicit Trafficking in Weapons-Useable Nuclear Material: Still More Questions Than Answers," 11 December 2011, *http://www.nti.org/analysis/articles /illicit-trafficking-weapons-useable-nuclear-material-still-more -questions-answers/*.

22. Sharon Wilke, "Rolf Mowatt-Larssen Named Senior Fellow at Harvard Kennedy School's Belfer Center," press release, Harvard University Belfer Center for Science and International Affairs, 2 December 2008, *http://belfercenter.ksg.harvard.edu /publication/18704/rolf_mowattlarssen_named_senior_fellow_at _harvard_kennedy_schools_belfer_center.html*.

23. Rolf Mowatt-Larssen, "Nuclear Security in Pakistan,"

Arms Control Today, July–August 2009, *http://www.armscontrol
.org/print/3724.*

24. William Langewiesche, "The Wrath of Khan," *Atlantic*, 1
November 2005, *http://www.theatlantic.com/magazine/archive
/2005/11/the-wrath-of-khan/304333/.*

25. Khan, *Eating Grass*, 368.

26. Ibid., 366–69.

27. Ibid., 361–62.

28. Ron Suskind, *The One Percent Doctrine* (New York:
Simon and Schuster, 2006), 70; George Tenet, *At the Center of
the Storm* (New York: HarperCollins, 2008), 264.

29. See Robert M. Gates, *Duty* (New York: Knopf, 2014), as
cited by Anwar Iqbal, *Dawn,* "Gates says he never thought of Pakistan as an ally," 11 January 2014, *http://www.dawn.com/news
/1079709*

30. Pew Research Global Attitudes Project, "Pakistani Public
Opinion Ever More Critical of U.S." 27 June 2012, *http://www
.pewglobal.org/2012/06/27/pakistani-public-opinion-ever-more
-critical-of-u-s/.*

31. Bruce Riedel, "Pakistan and the Bomb," *Wall Street Journal*, 30 May 2009.

32. Jeffery Goldberg and March Ambinder, "The Ally from
Hell," *Atlantic*, 28 October 2011, *http://www.theatlantic.com
/magazine/archive/2011/12/the-ally-from-hell/308730/.*

33. Khan, *Eating Grass*, 375.

34. Riedel, "Pakistan and the Bomb."

35. Goldberg and Ambinder, "The Ally from Hell."

36. Stephen P. Cohen, "Pakistan's Road to Disintegration,"
6 January 2011, *http://www.cfr.org/pakistan/pakistans-road
-disintegration/p23744.*

37. David Sanger and Eric Schmitt, "Pakistani Nuclear Arms
Pose Challenge to U.S. Policy," *New York Times*, 31 January 2011.

38. Khan, *Eating Grass*, 353.

39. John McPhee, *The Curve of Binding Energy* (New York: Farrar, Straus and Giroux, 1973), 18.

40. Khan, *Eating Grass*, 387; Paul Kerr and Mary Beth Nikitin, "Pakistan's Nuclear Weapons: Proliferation and Security Issues," Congressional Research Service, 19 March 2013.

41. Kerr and Nikitin, "Pakistan's Nuclear Weapons: Proliferation and Security Issues."

42 Khan, *Eating Grass*, 388.

43. Rodney Jones, *Foreign Policy*, "Pakistan's nuclear Poker bet," 27 May 2011, *http://southasia.foreignpolicy.com/posts/2011/05/27/pakistans_nuclear_poker_bet*

44. Khan, *Eating Grass*, 385.

45. Goldberg, "The Ally from Hell."

46. Kerr and Nikitin, "Pakistan's Nuclear Weapons: Proliferation and Security Issues."

47. Khan, *Eating Grass*, 15.

48. Ibid., 397.

49. Goldberg, "The Ally from Hell."

50. Tenet, *At the Center of the Storm*, 275.

51. David Albright and Christina Walrond, *Civil Separated Plutonium in the IFCIRC/549 States—Taking Stock*, 17 September 2010, *http://isis-online.org/isis-reports/detail/civil-separated-plutonium-in-the-infcirc-549-states-taking-stock/*.

52. Colin Kahl, Melissa Dalton, Matthew Irvine, *Atomic Kingdom, If Iran Builds the Bomb, Will Saudi Arabia Be Next?* (Center for New American Security, February 2013).

53. Shirley Kan, "China and Proliferation of Weapons of Mass Destruction and Missiles: Policy Issues," *Congressional Research Service*, 11 March 2013; Dinah Deckstein and Matthias Scheep, "Parts for Tehran's Nuclear Program: Was Siemens Involved in Dubious Trade?" *Der Spiegel*, 9 August 2010; Cathrin Gilbert, Holger Stark, and Andreas Ulrich, "Nuclear Technology for Iran: German Investigators Uncover Illegal Exports," *Der Spiegel*, 1 October 2012

55. Albert Narath, *Report of the Fundamental Classification Policy Review Group*, US Department of Energy, 15 January 1997, *http://www.fas.org/sgp/library/repfcprg.html#I16.*

Chapter Three: The Lessons of Nuclear Deterrence

1. Thomas Schelling, "An Astonishing 60 years: The Legacy of Hiroshima," *Proceedings of the National Academy of Sciences of the United States of America* 103, no. 16 (2006), *http://www.pnas.org/content/103/16/6089.full#xref-ref-1-1.*

2. Bernard Brodie, "Strategy Hits a Dead End," *Harper's Magazine*, October 1955.

3. John Gaddis, *We Now Know: Rethinking Cold War History* (Oxford: Oxford University Press, 1998) 71–74.

4. The North Atlantic Treaty, Washington D.C., 4 April 1949, *http://www.nato.int/cps/en/natolive/official_texts_17120.htm*

5. Southeast Asia Collective Defense Treaty (Manila Pact), 8 September 1954, *http://avalon.law.yale.edu/20th_century /usmu 003.asp.*

6. John Foster Dulles, "Speech before the Council of Foreign Relations," 12 January 1954, *http://www.freerepublic.com /focus /f-news/1556858/posts.*

7. George Bundy, *Danger and Survival: Choices about the Bomb in the First Fifty Years* (New York: Random House, 1988), 248.

8. James Shepley, "How Dulles Averted War," *Life*, XL (January 16, 1956), 78.

9. Dwight D. Eisenhower, *The President's News Conference*, 16 March 1955, *http://www.presidency.ucsb.edu/ws/?pid=10434 #axzz2hFFBeaCG.*

10. Dean Acheson, "Wishing Won't Hold Berlin," *Saturday Evening Post*, March 7, 1959.

11. John F. Kennedy, "Diplomacy and Defense: A Test of National Maturity," November 16, 1961. *http://millercenter.org /president/speeches/speech-3369*

12. Ibid.

13. John F. Kennedy, "Radio and Television Report to the American People on the Berlin Crisis," 25 July 1961. *http://www .jfklibrary.org/Research/Research-Aids/JFK-Speeches/Berlin -Crisis_19610725.aspx*

14. John F. Kennedy, "Special Message to Congress on Urgent National Needs," 25 May 1961, *http://www.presidency.ucsb.edu /ws/?pid=8151*

15. Peter Paret, Gordon Craig, and Felix Gilbert, *Makers of Modern Strategy* (Princeton, NJ: Princeton University Press, 1986), 758.

16. *Public Papers of the Presidents of the United States: Richard Nixon, 1970,* pp. 116-190.

17. Bernard Brodie, *The Absolute Weapon* (New York: Harcourt Brace Jovanovich, 1972), 76–77.

18. David Alan Rosenburg, "The Origins of Overkill: Nuclear Weapons and American Strategy, 1945-1960," *International Security* 7, no. 4 (1983): 14.

19. David Holloway, *Stalin and the Bomb—The Soviet Union and Atomic Energy 1939–1956* (New Haven, CT: Yale University Press, 1994), 229.

20. Gian P. Gentile, "Planning for Preventive War, 1945–1950," *Joint Force Quarterly*, Spring 2000, *http://www.comw.org /qdr/fulltext/00gentile.pdf.*

21. Rosenberg, "The Origins of Overkill," 46.

22. Ibid., 30.

23. David Kunsman and Douglas Lawson, *A Primer on U.S. Strategic Nuclear Policy*, Sandia National Laboratories report SAND2001-0053, 2001, *http://prod.sandia.gov/techlib/access-control .cgi/2001/010053.pdf.*

24. Stephen Schwartz, "The Costs of U.S. Nuclear Weapons," 1 October 2008, *http://www.nti.org/analysis/articles/costs-us-nuclear -weapons/.*

25. "'The Berlin Crisis,' Research Project 17, Department of State, ca. 1948, President's Secretary's Files, Truman Papers," *http://www.trumanlibrary.org/whistlestop/study_collections /berlin_airlift/large/documents/index.php?pagenumber=9& documentid=49&documentdate=1948-00-00&studycollectionid =Berlin&groupid=*.

26. Seymour Hersh, *The Samson Option* (New York: Random House, 1991); William B. Quandt, "How Far Will Israel Go?" *Washington Post Book World*, November 1991, as cited in Elbridge Colby, Avner Cohen, William McCants, Bradley Morris William Rosenau, *The Israeli 'Nuclear Alert' of 1973: Deterrence and Signaling in Crisis*, April 2013 (Washington: Center of Naval Analysis), 27; Avner Cohen, "Nuclear Arms in Crisis Under Secrecy: Israel and the Lessons of the 1967 and 1973 Wars," in *Planning the Unthinkable: How New Nuclear Powers Will Use Nuclear, Biological, and Chemical Weapons, ed.* Peter R. Lavoy, Scott Sagan, James Wirtz (Ithaca, NY: Cornell University Press, 2000), 117–24.

27. Avner Cohen and William Burr, "Israel Crosses the Threshold," *Bulletin of the Atomic Scientists*, May/June 2006, 22–30.

28. William Burr and Jeffrey Kimball, eds., "Nixon White House Considered Nuclear Options against Vietnam, Declassified Documents Reveal," 31 July 2006, *http://www.gwu.edu/~nsarchiv /NSAEBB/NSAEBB195/*.

29. "Nixon Proposed Using A-Bomb in Vietnam War," *New York Times*, 1 October 2002, *http://www.nytimes.com/2002 /03/01 /world/nixon-proposed-using-a-bomb-in-vietnam-war.html*.

30. Nina Tannenwald, "Nuclear Weapons and the Vietnam War," *Journal of Strategic Studies* 29, no. 3 (2006): 675–722, *http://www.watsoninstitute.org/pub/vietnam_weapons.pdf*.

Chapter Four: The Lessons of Countering Terrorism

1. Alex Schmid and A. J. Jongman, *Political Terrorism* (New York: Transaction, 2005), 5.

2. "U.S. to Deploy Radiation Sensors in Mongolia," 24 October 2007, *http://www.nti.org/gsn/article/us-to-deploy-radiation-sensors-in-mongolia/*; National Nuclear Security Administration, "Second Line of Defense Program," *http://nnsa.energy.gov/aboutus/ourprograms/nonproliferation/programoffices/international materialprotectionandcooperation/se.*

3. T. R. Fehrenbach, *Comanches: The History of a People* (New York: Anchor, 1974) 112–15.

4. Ibid., 299–304; Pekka Hämäläainen, *The Comanche Empire* (New Haven, CT: Yale University Press, 2008), 270; Ernest Wallace, *The Comanches: Lords of the Southern Plains* (Norman: University of Oklahoma Press, 1952); S. C. Gwynne, *Empire of the Summer Moon: Quanah Parker and the Rise and Fall of the Comanches* (New York: Scribner's, 2011); Rupert Richardson, *The Comanche Barrier to South Plains Settlement: A Century and a Half of Savage Resistance to the Advancing White Frontier* (New York: Arthur H. Clarke, 1993); Sally Lodge, *Native American People: The Comanche* (Vero Beach, FL: Rourke, 1992).

5. Olaf Caroe, *The Pathans* (London: Macmillan, 1958), 347–348

6. Tribal Analysis Center, *Mad Mullahs, Opportunists, and Family Connections: The Violent Pashtun Cycle*, November 2008, *http://www.tribalanalysiscenter.com/PDF-TAC/Mad%20 Mullahs.pdf.*

7. Olaf Caroe, *The Pathans* (London: Macmillan, 1958), 348–50.

8. Rudyard Kipling "The Head of District" *Macmillan's Magazine* 33, January 1890, *http://www.readbookonline.net/readOnLine /2422/.*

9. Benjamin Schwartz, "America's Struggle against the Wahhabi/Neo-Salafi Movement," *Orbis* 51, no. 1 (2007) 107-128.

10. Alexander Wendt, "Anarchy Is What States Make of It," *International Organization* 46, no. 2 (1992): 391–425.

11. James Blaut, *The Colonizer's Model of the World: Geographical Diffusion and Eurocentric History* (New York: Guildford, 1993).

12. Bernard Bailyn, *The Ideological Origins of the American Revolution* (Cambridge, MA: Belknap Press of Harvard University Press, 1967), 143.

13. Walter A. McDougall, *Promised Land, Crusader State: The American Encounter with the World since 1776* (Boston: Houghton Mifflin, 1997), 20.

14. Harry S. Truman, "Truman Doctrine," 12 March 1947, *http://avalon.law.yale.edu/20th_century/trudoc.asp*.

15. James Monroe, "Monroe Doctrine," 2 December 1823, *http://avalon.law.yale.edu/19th_century/monroe.asp*.

16. NSC-68, quoted in Ernest May, ed., *American Cold War Strategy: Interpreting NSC-68* (New York: St Martin's Press, 1993), 40.

17. Thomas P. M. Barnett, *The Pentagon's New Map: War and Peace in the Twenty-First Century* (New York: G. P. Putnam's Sons, 2004), 8.

18. Ibid., 187.

19. Carter Malkasian, *The Korean War* (New York: Rosen, 2009), 36.

20. For a good overview of this topic see: Aki Peritz and Eric Rosenbach's *Find, Fix, Finish: Inside the Counterterrorism Campaigns that Killed bin laden and Devasted Al Qaeda* (New York: PublicAffairs, 2012).

21. Barack Obama, "Remarks of the President at the National Defense University," 23 May 2013, *http://www.whitehouse.gov/the-press-office/2013/05/23/remarks-president-national-defense-university*.

22. Joby Warrick, Josh Partlow, and Haw Nawaz Khan, "A Psychological Blow to Pakistani Taliban," *Washington Post*, 8 August 2009.

23. John Brennan, "The Ethics of Efficacy of the President's Counterterrorism Strategy," 30 April 2012, *http://www.cfr.org /counterterrorism/brennans-speech-counterterrorism-april-2012 /p28100.*

24. Barak Obama, "Remarks by the President at the National Defense University," Fort McNair, Washington, D.C. 23 May 2013, *http://www.whitehouse.gov/the-press-office/2013/05/23 /remarks-president-national-defense-university*

25. Barak Obama, "Remarks by President Obama in Address to the United Nations General Assembly," United Nations, New York, 24 September 2013, *http://www.whitehouse.gov/the-press -office/2013/09/24/remarks-president-obama-address-united -nations-general-assembly.*

26. Barack Obama, "Remarks by the President at the National Defense University,"

27. Nina Serafino, *Security Assistance Reform: "Section 1206" Background and Issues for Congress*, Congressional Research Service, 19 April 2013, *http://www.fas.org/sgp/crs/natsec /RS22855.pdf.*

28. Lisa Monaco, "Remarks as Prepared for Delivery by Assistant to the President for Homeland Security and Counterterrorism Lisa Monaco," 19 November 2013, *http://www.whitehouse .gov/the-press-office/2013/11/19/remarks-prepared-delivery -assistant-president-homeland-security-and-coun.*

29. David Rosenbaum, "Bush Account of a Leak's Impact Has Support," *New York Times*, 20 December 2005, *http://www .nytimes.com/2005/12/20/politics/20fact.html.*; Eric Schmitt and Michael Schmidt, "Qaeda Plot Leak Has Undermined U.S. Intelligence," *New York Times*, 29 September 2013, *http://www .nytimes.com/2013/09/30/us/qaeda-plot-leak-has-undermined -us-intelligence.html?pagewanted=all.*

30. "21,000 people now on U.S. no fly list, official says." *CNN News*, 2 February 2012, *http://www.cnn.com/2012/02/02/us/no -fly-list/index.html*

Chapter Five: The Global Impact

1. Lucian W. Pye, "China: Erratic State, Frustrated Society" *Foreign Affairs* 69, no. 4 (Fall 1990).

2. Barack Obama, "Remarks by the President at the National Defense University."

3. Michael Ellman and Vladimir Kontorovich, *The Destruction of the Soviet Economic System: An Insiders' History* (Armonk, NY: M. E. Sharpe, 1998), 60.

4. James Kurth, "Global Threats and American Strategies: From Communism in 1955 to Islamism in 2005," *Orbis* 49, no. 4 (2005): 640.

5. Francis Fukuyama, *The End of History and the Last Man* (New York: Simon and Schuster, 1992), 91.

6. Daniel Yergin and Joseph Stanislaw, *The Commanding Heights: The Battle for the World Economy* (New York: Simon and Schuster, 2002), 137.

7. Philip Bobbitt, *The Shield of Achilles: War, Peace, and the Course of History* (New York: Knopf, 2002), 220.

8. Karl Marx and Friedrich Engels, *The Marx-Engels Reader*, ed. Robert C. Tucker (New York: Norton, 1978), 477; Bobbitt, *The Shield of Achilles*, 220.

9. Fukuyama, *The End of History and the Last Man*, 92–93.

10. Joseph S. Nye, *Soft Power: The Means to Success in World Politics* (New York: PublicAffairs, 2004), 49.

11. Mary Fulbrook, *The Divided Nation: A History of Germany, 1918–1990* (New York: Oxford University Press, 1992), 296, quoted in Bobbitt, *The Shield of Achilles*, 220.

12. Walter Russell Mead, *Power, Terror, Peace, and War: America's Grand Strategy in a World at Risk* (New York: Knopf, 2004), 38.

13. Max Weber, *Economy and Society: An Outline of Interpretive Sociology* (Berkeley: University of California Press, 1978), 904–8, quoted in Bobbitt, *The Shield of Achilles*, xxii.

14. James Kurth, "The Post-Modern State," *National Interest* 28 (1992): 29.

15. Frances Cairncross, "The Death of Distance," *Economist*, 30 September 1995, 26.

16. See Daniel Bell, *The Coming of Post-Industrial Society: A Venture in Social Forecasting* (New York: Basic Books, 1973).

17. William J. Wilson, *When Work Disappears: The World of the New Urban Poor* (New York: Vintage, 1997), 151.

18. Joseph S. Nye, *The Paradox of American Power: Why the World's Only Superpower Can't Go It Alone* (Oxford: Oxford University Press, 2002), 44–45.

19. Elizabeth McLean Petras, *From Paternalism to Patronage to Pillage: Chester, PA., a Chronicle of the Embedded Consciousness of Place in the Second Most Economically Depressed City in the U.S.*, 1991, 5, *https://moodle.swarthmore.edu/plugin file.php /7948/mod_resource/content/0/Course_Documents /Situating_Literacy_Research/Petras__E.M.__From_Patronage_ to_Pillage__Chester__PA_/EDUC151_DA_Petras_Patern.pdf*.

20. National Intelligence Council, *Mapping the Global Future: Report of the National Intelligence Council's 2020 Project* (Washington, DC: GPO, 2004), 77.

21. Samuel P. Huntington, *The Clash of Civilizations and the Remaking of World Order* (New York: Simon and Schuster, 1996), 76.

22. US National Intelligence Council, *Mapping the Global Future*, 79.

23. Nye, *The Paradox of American Power*, 59.

24. Robert D. Kaplan, "Technology as Magnifier of Good and Evil," *Forbes*, 2 December 1996, 51–53.

25. Nye, *The Paradox of American Power*, 54.

26. Nye, *Soft Power*, 22.

27. Robert D. Kaplan, "The Media and Medievalism," *Policy Review* 128 (2004): 47–58.

28. Andrew F. Krepinevich, "Cavalry to Computer: The Pattern of Military Revolutions," *National Interest* 37 (1994): 30, offers a popular definition of a military revolution: "What is a Military Revolution? It is what occurs when the application of new technologies into a significant number of military systems combines with innovative operational concepts and organizational adaptations in a way that fundamentally alters the character and conduct of conflict. It does so by producing a dramatic increase—often an order of magnitude or greater—in the combat potential and military effectiveness of armed forces."

29. On the challenge to the nation-state, see Richard N. Rosecrance, *The Rise of the Virtual State: Wealth and Power in the Coming Century* (New York: Basic Books, 1999); Robert D. Kaplan, *The Coming Anarchy: Shattering the Dreams of the Post Cold War* (New York: Vintage, 2001); Thomas L. Friedman, *The Lexus and the Olive Tree* (New York: Farrar, Straus and Giroux, 1999); Robert Cooper, *The Breaking of Nations: Order and Chaos in the Twenty-First Century* (New York: Atlantic Monthly Press, 2003); Bobbitt, *The Shield of Achilles*; and Martin L. Van Creveld, *The Rise and Decline of the State* (Cambridge: Cambridge University Press, 1999).

30. Bobbitt, *The Shield of Achilles*, 219.

31. See Friedman, *The Lexus and the Olive Tree*.

32. Bracken, *Fire in the East*, 98.

33. Henry A. Kissinger, "America's Assignment," *Newsweek*, 8 November 2004, *http://www.henryakissinger.com/articles/nw 110404.html*.

34. Charter of the United Nations, signed on 26 June 1945, San Francisco, *http://www.un.org/en/documents/charter/*

35. See Mark Lowenthal, *Intelligence: From Secrets to Policy* (Washington DC: CQPress), 165.

36. Vern Clark, quoted in Andru E. Wall, "Demystifying the Title 10–Title 50 Debate: Distinguishing Military Operations, Intelligence Activities & Covert Action," *Harvard National Security*

Journal 3 (2012), 89n6, *http://harvardnsj.org/wp-content/uploads/2012/01/Vol.-3_Wall1.pdf.*

37. John F. Kennedy, Address on the Cuban Missile Crisis, 22 October 1962, *https://www.britannica.com/presidents/article-9116923.*

38. Julian Barnes, *Los Angeles Times*, "Gates Draws the Line on North Korea's nuclear program," 30 May 2009, *http://articles.latimes.com/2009/may/30/world/fg-us-korea30.*

39. See United Nations Convention on the Law of the Sea, 1982, 21 ILM (1982), 1261. UNCLOS was adopted on 10 December 1982 and entered into force on 16 November 1994. It has been signed by 157 states and ratified by 148 states. India signed it on 29 June 1995.

40 "Norwegian Heavy Water Sabotage," Wikipedia.org, *http://en.wikipedia.org/wiki/Norwegian_heavy_water_sabotage.*

41. William MacLean, "Update 2—Cyber Attack Appears to Target Iran-Tech Firms," 24 September 2010, *http://www.reuters.com/article/2010/09/24/security-cyber-iran-idUSLDE68N1OI20100924.*

42. "How a Secret Cyberwar Program Worked," *http://www.nytimes.com/interactive/2012/06/01/world/middleeast/how-a-secret-cyberwar-program-worked.html?_r=0.*

43. Nicole Perlroth, "In Cyberattack on Saudi Firm, U.S. Sees Iran Firing Back," *New York Times*, 23 October 2012, *http://www.nytimes.com/2012/10/24/business/global/cyberattack-on-saudi-oil-firm-disquiets-us.html?pagewanted=all&_r=0*

44. See Robert Kaplan, *The Revenge of Geography* (New York: Random House, 2012).

45. Office of the Secretary of Defense, *Annual Report to Congress: Military and Security Developments Involving the People's Republic of China 2013, http://www.defense.gov/pubs/2013_china_report_final.pdf*

46. Edward Smith, "Britain: Cyber-Attacks on 'Industrial Scale' Steal Business Secrets," *International Business Times*, 1 July 2013, *http://www.ibtimes.co.uk/articles/485054/20130701/prism-nsa-gchq-china-cyber-attack-espionage.htm#.*

47. Choe Sang-Hun, "Computer Networks in South Korea Are Paralyzed in Cyberattacks," *New York Times*, 20 May 2013, *http://www.nytimes.com/2013/03/21/world/asia/south-korea-computer-network-crashes.html*.

48. Office of the Secretary of Defense, *Annual Report to Congress: Military and Security Developments Involving the People's Republic of China 2013*, *http://www.defense.gov/pubs/2013_China_Report_FINAL.pdf*.

49. Robert Samuelson, "Beware the Internet and the Danger of Cyberattacks," *Washington Post*, 30 June 2013, *http://www.washingtonpost.com/opinions/robert-samuelson-of-internet-threats-and-cyberattacks/2013/06/30/df7bd42e-e1a9-11e2-a1le-c2ea876a8f30_story.html?hpid=z5*.

50. International Atomic Energy Agency, *Nuclear Security—Measures to Protect against Nuclear Terrorism: Amendment to the Convention on the Physical Protection of Nuclear Material*, *http://www.iaea.org/About/Policy/GC/GC49/Documents/gc49inf-6.pdf*.

51. Igor Khripunov and Dmitriy Nikonov, eds., *Legal Framework for Strengthening Nuclear Security and Combating Nuclear Terrorism* (Amsterdam: IOS, 2010), 163.

52. General Assembly of the United Nations, *International Convention for the Suppression of Acts of Nuclear Terrorism*, A/RES/59/290, 6, *http://www.un.org/ga/search/view_doc.asp?symbol=A/Res/59/290*.

53. International Atomic Energy Agency, *Nuclear Security Recommendations on Physical Protection of Nuclear Material and Nuclear Facilities*," INFCIRC/225/Revision 5, *http://www-pub.iaea.org/MTCD/publications/PDF/Pub1481_web.pdf*.

54. Matthew Bunn, Eben Harrell, and Martin Malin, *Progress on Securing Nuclear Weapons and Materials: The Four-Year Effort and Beyond*, March 2012, *http://www.nuclearsummit.org/files/security_progress_report_2_482949862.pdf*.

55. Ibid.; Robert S. Norris and Hans M. Kristensen, "Nuclear

Notebook: Worldwide Deployments of Nuclear Weapons, 2009," *Bulletin of the Atomic Scientists*, November–December 2009, *http://bos.sagepub.com/content/65/6/86.full*. See also Nuclear Threat Initiative, "NTI Nuclear Materials Security Index: Building a Framework for Assurance, Accountability, and Action, *http://www.ntiindex.org/*; and International Panel on Fissile Materials, *Global Fissile Material Report 2011*.

56. Michael May, Jay Davis, and Raymond Jeanloz, "Preparing for the Worst," *Nature*, October 2006, 907–8.

57. US Department of Defense, *Nuclear Posture Review*, April 2010, 12, *http://www.defense.gov/npr/docs/2010 Nuclear Posture Review Report.pdf*.

58. International Atomic Energy Agency, *Nuclear Forensics Support*, IAEA Nuclear Security Series no. 2, 2006, *http://www-pub.iaea.org/MTCD/Publications/PDF/Pub1241_web.pdf*.

59. M. J. Kristo, D. K. Smith, S. Niemeyer, and B. G. Dudder, *Model Action Plan for Nuclear Forensics and Nuclear Attribution*, UCRL-TR-202675, 8, *https://e-reports-ext.llnl.gov/pdf/305453.pdf*.

Chapter Six : The Red Line: Fifteen Days

1. Tenet, *At the Center of the Storm*, 226.

2. US Department of Defense, *Nuclear Posture Review*.

3. Robert Gates, remarks delivered at the Shangri-La Dialogue, May 30, 2009 as cited in Julian Barnes, *Los Angeles Times*, "Gates Draws the Line on North Korea's nuclear program," 30 May 2009, *http://articles.latimes.com/2009/may/30/world/fg-us-korea30*

4. Joe Biden, "CSI:Nukes" *Wall Street Journal*, 4 June 2007, *http://online.wsj.com/news/articles/SB118092079691823346*.

5. Rick Atkinson, "Ten Things Every American Student Should Know about Our Army in World War II," *Foreign Policy* 14, no. 15 (2009), *http://www.fpri.org/articles/2009/05/ten-things-every-american-student-should-know-about-our-army-world-war-ii*.

6. Karen Parrish, "Panetta Takes Strategy, Budget Message

to Troops," 17 February 2012, *http://www.defense.gov/News /NewsArticle .aspx?ID=67246.*

7. Robert Kagan, *Dangerous Nation* (New York: Vintage, 2007).

8. Max Boot, *The Savage Wars of Peace* (New York: Basic Books, 2002).

9. Ibid., 25–27.

10. Michael Clodfelter, *Warfare and Armed Conflicts: A Statistical Reference to Casualty and Other Figures, 1500–2000* (Jefferson, NC: McFarland, 2002).

11. Walter Russell Mead, *Special Providence* (New York: Knopf, 2004), 218–19.

12. William Sherman, Letter to Atlanta, 12 September 1864, *http://thehistoricpresent.wordpress.com/2012/04/25/shermans -letter-to-atlanta-what-did-he-say/.*

13. Protocol Additional to the Geneva Conventions of 12 August 1949, and relating to the Protection of Victims of International Conflicts (Protocol I), 8 June 1977, *http://www.icrc.org/ihl /WebART/470-750065.*

14. Howard M. Hensel, ed., *The Legitimate Use of Military Force: The Just War Tradition and the Customary Law of Armed Conflict* (Aldershot, Hampshire, England: Ashgate, 2008).

15. Ward Thomas, *The Ethics of Destruction: Norms and Force in International Relations* (Ithaca, NY: Cornell University Press, 2001).

ACKNOWLEDGMENTS

This book was made possible by the insight and assistance of numerous friends and mentors, many of whom would prefer to remain nameless. A special thanks to Michael Carlisle and William Callahan, who took a risk on a first time author and whose advocacy was essential. Of course my wife deserves the greatest appreciation. In addition to her moral support for this project, she provided me the time and space to write while working a full time job and taking care of our two young boys.

INDEX

1973 Israel-Arab War, 108–10
2010 Nuclear Posture Review, 11, 204, 205
24, 3

Acheson-Lilienthal Report, 47–48
Acheson, Dean G.: on America's defensive perimeter, 85; and material proliferation, 47; and red lines, 85; and "Wishing Won't Hold Berlin," 92
Adams, John, 142
Afghan Taliban, 71, 135
Ahmad, Syed, 134
al-Assad, Bashar: and chemical weapons, 18, 231; and nuclear program, 13; tactics of, 216
al-Fadl, Jamal, on bin Laden nuclear procurement, 78
Al-Firdos bunker, 216
al-Masri, Abd al-Aziz, 79
al-Qaeda: and America's war against, 138–40, 149–52; and antecedents of, 12, 135; and Benazir Bhutto, 72; and Mahmood, 69–70; and Majid, 70; and mass violence, 140; and mobility, 140; and nation states, 10, 185; and nuclear procurement, 78–79; and Pakistan, 16; and technology, 140; and terrorism, 121; and US counterterrorism, 10, 11, 118, 123, 138, 141, 150; and US national security community, 13
al-Wahhab, Ibn Abdul, and Saudi Arabia, 159
al-Wuhayshi, Nasser, 151
al-Zawahari, Ayman, 79, 151
Allison, Graham, and *Nuclear Terrorism: The Ultimate Preventable Catastrophe*, 14; and Three No doctrine, 13–15, 24, 56, 60, 67, 79
American Civil Liberties Union, and American nuclear weapons program, 44
Andropov, Yuri, 165
Apache, 130, 131
Arak heavy water reactor, 16, 62, 63
Armed Forces Special Weapons Project, 37
Arrow antiballistic missile system, 77
Atlantic, and Jeffrey Goldberg, 73, 76
atom: composition of, 25
atomic bomb: materials of, 45; procurement of, 31, 32, 34
Atomic Development Authority (ADA), 48, 189
Atomic Energy Administration, 39

atomic scientists movement, 36

Atoms for Peace program, 32, 34; and DPRK, 57; and Iran's nuclear program, 60; and material containment, 49, 50, 51; and Tehran, 61

Auer uranium processing plant, 46

Australia, New Zealand, and United States Security Treaty (ANZUS), 87

Aviation Technology Research Institute, 27

B-2 Spirit, 207

B-29 Super Fortress, 98, 104

B-52 Stratofortress, 207

Babur cruise missile, 77

Baghdad Pact, 88, 89

Ballistic Missile Early Warning System, 101

Barak, Ehud: and critical threshold, 65; and Iranian capability, 64

baramta, 137, 138

"barbarians," definition of, 121

Barksdale Air Force Base, 207

Barnett, Thomas P. M., 144, and *The Pentagon's New Map*, 143–45

Baruch Plan, 48–49

Baruch, Bernard, 48–49

BBC China, 12, 69

Bell, Daniel, 164, 168

Berlin Airlift, 105

Berlin Blockade, 99-100, 103–6

Bhatti, Shahbaz, 72

Bhutto, Benazir, 72

Bhutto, Zulfigar Ali, 33

Biden, Joseph, 205

bin Laden, Osama: and war against US, 140; and nuclear device, 70, 78, 79, 201; and technology, 140

"binding energy," 24, 25

blockade, as tactic of statecraft, 178–81

Bobbitt, Phillip, on weapons access, 172

Bohr, Niels, 46, 189

Bonaparte, Napoleon, 159

Bracken, Paul, 6, 21

Bremer, Paul, 145

Brennan, John, 147–48

Britain, and nuclear option in Ireland, 112

Brodie, and deterrence, 84, 96; and "Strategy Hits a Dead End," 83

Broiler, 99, 100

Brown, Gordon, and IAEA on Iran, 62

Bulletin of the Atomic Scientists, 39, 44

Burke, Arleigh, 101

Bush, George W.: and 9/11, 141, 143; and Global Initiative to Combat Nuclear Terrorism, 191; on nuclear weapons and terrorists, 78; and war on terror, 146, 161

Bushehr power reactor, 16

Cairncross, Frances, 168

Caroe, Olaf, 135, 136

Carter, Jimmy, 95

Central Treaty Organization (CENTO), 88

Chagai Militia, 126

Chalk River, and French bomb, 30

Charter of the United Nations, 86, 174

Chashma, 75

Cheney, Dick, 24

China: and cyberwarfare, 186; and Lucien Pye, 159; and New De-

fense Technical Accord, 31;
and Syria, 18
Chitral Scouts, 126
Churchill, Winston, and nuclear
weapons information, 42
Clancy, Tom: *The Sum of All Fears*,
3
Clandestine Service, 68
Clark, Vern, 176
Clay, Lucius, 105
Clooney, George, 3
Coalition Support Fund, 150
Cohen, Lona, 30
Cohen, Stephen, 73
Cold Start doctrine, 74, 75
Cold War, and strategic innovation,
164
Colt's "six-shooter," 132, 146
Comanche, 128–33
Combined Development Trust, 45,
46
Committee on International Secu-
rity and Arms Control, 194
Confront and Conceal (Sanger),
183
Congressional Research Service, 77
Convention on the Physical Protec-
tion of Nuclear Materials
(CPPNM), 190, 192
Corps Guides, 136
"counterforce," 94
counterproliferation, 10, 12, 178,
187, 188, 192
counterterrorism: America and al-
Qaeda, 138–40; new national
entity, creation of, 233–34; and
national sovereignty, 174–77;
and Barack Obama, 146–47;
strategies of, 122–40, 149–50;
as war of ideas, 141–45
"countervalue," 94
critical mass, 27

CTR program, 67
Cuban Missile Crisis, 55, 106–8,
178, 187
cuius region, eius religio, 159
Curve of Binding Energy, The
(McPhee), 24
Curzon, George, 126
Custer, George Armstrong, 127
cyberoperations, 182–86

Dangerous Nation (Kagan), 210
Dar al-Harb, 139
Dar al-Islam, 139
Davis, Jay, 194
Day, Sam, 44
Dayan, Moshe, 108
declaratory policy, 8, 11, 95–96,
102, 203–6; and John Foster
Dulles, 89; and Eisenhower
administration, 91; and
Kennedy administration, 92
Defense Counterterrorism Fellow-
ship Program, 150
Defense Threat Reduction Agency,
194
"deliberate escalation," 94
Department of Homeland Security,
152
DGZs, 100
Dien Bien Phu: and France, 31,
and SEATO, 87
"direct defense," 94
Distant Early Warning Line, 101
Dobson, Dave, 42
"Doolittle Raid," 226
DPRK. *See* North Korea
Duck Hook, 111
Dulles, John Foster, 89–90, 91
Durrani Empire, 135

Economist, on information technology, 168

Einstein, Albert: and fission, 25; on nuclear proliferation, 173; and letter to Roosevelt, 26

Eisenhower, Dwight D.: and declaratory policy, 91; and Lawrence Livermore National Laboratory students, 42; and nuclear weapons as deterrent, 91–92, 101; and red lines, 87, 96; and UN General Assembly, 30–31, 34–35. *See also* Atoms for Peace

el Qasim, Abdul Karim, and Baghdad Pact, 88

ElBaradei, Mohamed, on NPT, 80

Evaluation of the Effects of Atomic Bombing, 98–99

F Project, 27

F-4, 108

F3EAD cycle, 181

Faisal II, 88

Fat Man, 35; design test of, 27, 31; and Lawrence Livermore National Laboratory students, 43; and The Nth Country Experiment, 43; spread of information on, 30

federally administered tribal areas (FATAs), 135, 216

Federation of Atomic Scientists (Federation of American Scientists), 37

Fermi, Enrico, and first self-sustaining nuclear chain reaction, 26–27

Fernandes, George, 74

Financial Action Task Force, 151

Fissile Material Cutoff Treaty, 75

fissile material, 45–51

fission, definition of, 25

"flexible response," 94, 95, 108, 203, 231–34

Fordow Fuel Enrichment Plant (FFEP), 62

Foreign Assistance Act of 1961, 149

Foreign Policy and Nuclear Weapons (Kissinger), 5

Forrestal, James, 100

"fortress America," 90

France: and Dien Bien Phu, 31, 87; and irregular forces, 125; and nuclear option in Algiers, 112

Franck Report, 28

Franck Report, 28–29

Franck, James, 28

Franklin, Benjamin, 30

Frey, Karsten, *India's Nuclear Bomb and National Security*, 33

Friedman, Thomas, on "democratization of technology," 172

Frisch, Otto, and fission weapons study, 26

Frontier Corps, 126, 138

Frontier Crimes Regulations (FCR), 135, 138

Fuchs, Klaus, and nuclear information to Soviet Union, 30

Fuel Enrichment Plant (FEP), 62–63

Fulbrook, Mary, 167

Fulda Gap, 7

"Functioning Core," 144

G-8 Global Partnership against the Spread of Weapons and Materials of Mass Destruction, 12

Gaddis, John Lewis, 85

Gandhi, Indira, and Indian nuclear weapons, 33

Gareev, M. A., 164

Gates, Robert, 179, 204

Gendarmerie, 125

General Account of the Development of Methods of Using Atomic Energy for Military Purposes under the Auspices of the United States Government, 1940–1945 (Smyth Report), A, 37–41

General Treaty for Renunciation of War as an Instrument of National Policy, 188

Global Initiative to Combat Nuclear Terrorism (GICNT), 12, 191

Global Strike Command, 207

Goldberg, Jeffrey, 73, 76, 77

Gorbachev, Mikhail, 165

Government Communications Headquarters, 186

Great Wall of China, 122

Greenglass, David, 30

Gromyko, Andrei, 49

Groves, Leslie, 37; and Auer uranium processing plant, 46; and *Smyth Report,* 40

Gul, Hamid, 71

Gurkhas, 126

Hadrian's Wall, 123

Hahn, Otto, 25

Hall, Theodore, and nuclear information to Soviet Union, 30

Hamza, Khidhir, and *Smyth Report,* 40–41

Haqqani Network, 71

Harmon Committee, and *Evaluation of the Effects of Atomic Bombing,* 98–99

HatfXI/NASR missile system, 76

"Head of the District, The" (Kipling), 137

Hecker, Siegfried S., 58–59

Hezbollah, 9, 61, 112, 184

Hindustani Fanatics, 134

Hinton, Joan, and Chinese atomic bomb, 30

Hirbat Zachariah, 108

Hobbes, Thomas, on the individual and the state, 188

Hoover, Herbert, 90

Huntington, Samuel, 142, 158, 170

IAEA (International Atomic Energy Agency), 50, 51; and DPRK, 58; and HEU seizures, 67; and Iran, 16–17, 61–63; and nuclear forensics, 195; and nuclear material, protection of, 191, 192; on plutonium availability, 79; possible future roll of, 235

Il-sung, Kim, 85

Imperial University of Kyoto, 27

India's Nuclear Bomb and National Security (Frey), 33

Indian Mutiny of 1857, 134

"information revolution," 164, 165, 168, 170–71, 172

Institute for Science and International Security (ISIS), 59, 63

interdiction operations, 12, 13, 178–81, 232, 234

International Atomic Energy Agency. See IAEA

International Committee of the Red Cross, 214–15

International Convention on the Suppression of Acts of Nuclear Terrorism (ICSANT), 191, 192

international law, 120, 176–77, 179, 230, 235

International Military and Education Training program, 150

IR-1m, 62, 63

IR-2m, 62, 63
IR-4m, 63
IR-5m, 63
IR-6m, 63
IR-8m, 63
Iran (Islamic Republic of Iran): and 1979 Islamic Revolution, 61, 89; and Baghdad Pact, 88; and Khan, 69; and nuclear capability, 16–17, 60–66; and nuclear program, disruption of, 183; and Osama bin Laden, 139; and Quds Force, 184; and Saudi Aramco, 184, 186
Iraq: invasion of, and trustworthiness of US national security officials, 24: US-led invasion of, 12, 13
Islamic Republic of Iran. *See* Iran
isotopes, definition of, 25
Israel, 12, 13, 19; and 1973 Israel-Arab War, 108–10; and Atoms for Peace, 50; and Iranian capability, 63–64, 183; and nuclear option against Hezbollah, 112, 113; and nuclear program, 32; and South Africa, 34

"Jacksonian tradition," 214
Jamaica Constabulary Force, 126
Jeanloz, Raymond, 194
Jericho launcher, 108
jirgas, 136
Johnson, Lyndon, and nuclear option in Vietnam, 112
Joint Outline Emergency War Plan (Broiler), 99, 100
Joliot-Curie, Frederic, and chain reaction, 26
just war, and American tradition, 214–17

Kagan, Robert, and *Dangerous Nation*, 210
Kaiser Wilhelm Institute, 25
Kaplan, Robert, 171, 172
Kellogg-Briand Pact, 188
Kennedy, John F.: and Cuban Missile Crisis, 106–8, 178; and declaratory policy, 204; and "massive retaliation," 92–94; and scalable military capabilities, 93, 232
Kentucky rifle, 130
Khamenei, Ali Hosseini, 16
Khan Research Laboratories, 69, 76
Khan, Abduel Qadeer, 58–59, 68, 209. *See also* Khan Research Laboratories
Khan, Feroz, 15, 72, 73–74, 76, 77
Khan, Genghis, 128
Khariton, Yuly, 26–28
Khushab Plutonium Production Reactor, 69, 75
Khyber Rifles, 126
Kidwai, Khalid, 77
Kipling, Rudyard, and "The Head of the District," 137
Kissinger, Henry: and Duck Hook, 111–12; and *Foreign Policy and Nuclear Weapons*, 5–6; on international security model, 173; and *Nuclear Weapons and Foreign Policy*, 92
Korean War: and civilian casualties, 213; and Dulles, 89; and Truman rejection of MacArthur, 111; and US counterterrorism, 145; and US red lines, 84
Kristol, Irving, 156
Kurram Militia, 126

Lashkar-e-Jhangvi, 71
Lashkar-e-Taibai, 71; and attack on
    Indian Parliament, 74
Lawrence Livermore National
    Laboratory: and The Nth
    Country Experiment, 42; and
    nuclear forensics, 196; UCRL-
    4725, Weapons Development
    during June 1956, 44; *UCRL-
    5280, Weapons Development
    during June 1958*, 44
"left of boom," 17
LeMay, Curtis: and America's
    atomic program, 98–99;
    and Berlin Blockade, 104;
    and Cuban Missile Crisis,
    106
levée en masse, 159
Levey, Stuart, 150–51
Libya, and interdictions, 13; and
    Khan Research Laboratories,
    69; and UTN, 70
Life, and *Smyth Report*, 39
Lilienthal, David: and material pro-
    liferation, 47–48; and *Smyth
    Report*, 39
limited military options, 217–20
Lippmann, Walter, 188
Little Boy, 1; and South Africa,
    34
Lobban, Iain, 186
Los Alamos laboratory,
Los Alamos National Laboratory:
    and information to foreign
    governments, 30; and May-
    Johnson Bill, 36; national
    make up of, 27
Los Alamos Primer, The, 41
Lugar, Richard, and the Cooperative
    Threat Reduction program,
    12, 15, 67
Lusitania, 4

MacArthur, Douglas, and use of
    nuclear weapons during the
    Korean War, 111
Mackenzie, Ranald S., 133
MAD, 42, 94
Mahmood, Bashiruddin, 69; and
    Osama bin Laden, 70; *Dooms-
    day and Life After Death: the
    Ultimate Faith of the Universe
    as Seen by the Holy Quran*, 70
Majid, Chaudhry Abdul, 69; and
    Osama bin Laden, 70
Maliks, 135, 137
Manchester Guardian, 33
Manhattan Project: and Combined
    Development Trust, 45; and
    Franck Report, 28; and *Project
    Y: The Los Alamos Project*, 41;
    and *Smyth Report*, 37; and
    spread of information on
    fission, 30–32, 34, 36, 46
Mao Zedong, 31, 57, 85
Maréchaussée, 125
Mark 12, 101
Mark 3, 98
Marshall, George, 46
"martial races," 126
martial restraint, 217–20
Marx, Karl, 166
Massachusetts Institute of Technol-
    ogy, and *Progressive*, 44
"massive retaliation:" and John Fos-
    ter Dulles, 89–90; and John F.
    Kennedy, 92–93; legal standing
    for, 196; and terrorism, 113,
    163, 232
May-Johnson Bill, 36
May, Michael, 194
McChrystal, Stanley, 181
McMahon Act, 31
McNamara, Robert, and "flexible
    response," 93

McPhee, John: *The Curve of Binding Energy*, 24
Mead, Walter Russell, 167, 214
Mehsud, Baitullah, 147
Meir, Golda, 108–9
Meitner, Lise, 25
Military Application of Uranium Detonation committee, 26
Missile Defense, 10, 11
Mobruk, Saleh, 78
Monroe, James, 143
Morland, Howard, 43–44
Mowatt-Larssen, Rolf, 68
Mujahadee-e Khaq, 61
Musharraf, Pervez: and Abduel Qadeer Kahn, 69; and nuclear arsenal, dispersal of, 77; and Tenet, 201, 220
Muslim Brotherhood, 139
Mutual Defense Treaty, 89
"Mutually Assured Destruction" (MAD), 42, 94, 101, 198

N Project, 27
"nascent nukes," 14, 16, 56, 60–66, 223
Natanz plant, 62, 183
nation-state, 158–63
National Academy of Sciences, 194
National Defense Authorization Act (NDAA), 149
National Intelligence Council, 169
National Security Archive, 112
National Security Council report NSC-30, *United States Policy on Atomic Warfare*, 99
National Security Council report NSC-68 (1950), 143
NATO, 86, 94
Negev Desert nuclear reactor, 32
Nehru, Jawaharlal, and Indian nuclear program, 32

Netanyahu, Benjamin, 64
New Defense Technical Accord, 31
New Republic, 36
New York Times: and Siegfried S. Hecker, 59; and Stuxnet, 183
Newsweek: and Henry Kissinger, 173; and *Smyth Report*, 39
Nixon, Richard: and Israeli nuclear capability, 109; and nuclear option in Vietnam, 112; and Operation Nickel Grass, 110; and policy of deterrence, 95
No Fly List, 123, 138, 150, 152
"Non-Integrating Gap," 144
Non-Proliferation Treaty (NPT): and American "negative security assurance," 195, 236; and DPRK, 14, 58; and fissile material, control of, 51; and Iran, 60, 61; and nonmembers, 13; and World War II victors, 32
Nonproliferation, office of, 10
North Atlantic Treaty Organization (NATO), 86, 94
North Atlantic Treay, 86
North Carolina, and hydrogen bombs, 6
North Korea (Democratic People's Republic of Korea): and Graham Allison, 14; and cyberattacks, 186; and exportation of nuclear components, 80; and Robert Gates, 179, 204; and interdictions, 13; and Khan, 69; and nuclear weapons, 56–60; and Pakistan, 77; and Syrian reactor, 19, 179, 231; and US red lines, 85
NSC-30, *United States Policy on Atomic Warfare*, 99
NSC-68 (1950), 143
Nth Country Experiment, The, 42

nuclear forensics, 195–97
Nuclear Posture Review, 11, 204, 205
Nuclear Security Summits, 190
Nuclear Suppliers Group (NSG), 12
Nuclear Terrorism: The Ultimate Preventable Catastrophe (Allison), 14
Nuclear Weapons and Foreign Policy (Kissinger), 92
Nunn-Lugar Cooperative Threat Reduction (CTR), 12, 15, 67
Nye, Joseph S.: on centralization, 169; on global citizen, 170, 171; on soft power, 166

Oak Ridge National laboratory, and May-Johnson Bill, 36
Obama, Barack: and "global nuclear lockdown," 223; and Assad, 231; and coercive action, 185; and counterterrorism, 146–49; and critical threshold, 65; and IAEA on Iran, 62; and Levey, 151; and Mehsud, 147; and Middle Eastern politics, 149; on nuclear material, 190; and punitive expeditions, 127; on terrorists, and nuclear material, 78; on terrorists, and the state, 161; and unilateral military operations, 161
Ogarkov, Nikolai V., 165
Ogburn, William, 169
Operation Nickel Grass, 110
Operation Olympic Games program, 183, 184
OPLAN 312, 107
OPLAN 316, 107
Osirak nuclear reactor: Israeli raid on, 12

P-1 centrifuge, 69
P-2 centrifuge, 69
P-3 centrifuge, 76
P-3C Orion, 73
P-4 centrifuge, 76
P-5+1, 16, 63
Paine, Thomas, 142
Pakistan Atomic Energy Commission, 75
Pakistan Institute of Nuclear Science and Technology, 70, 75
Pakistan: and Frontier Corps, 126, 138; and India's acquisition of missile systems, 77; and National Defense Authorization Act, section 1206, 149; and nuclear capability, 68–78; and nuclear program, 15–16, 75; and plutonium, 75; and SEATO, 87, 88. *See also* federally administered tribal areas, Musharraf, and Pashtuns
Pashtuns, 71, 126, 133–38
Patriot PAC-3 system, 77
Peace of Westphalia, 9, 159, 175, 236
Peacemaker, The, 3
Peierls, Rudolf, 26
Pennsylvania Constabulary, 126
Pentagon's New Map, The (Barnett), 143
Petraeus, David, 150
Petras, Elizabeth McLean, 169
"Piffers." *See* Punjab Irregular Force
Pilot Fuel Enrichment Plant (PFEP), 61–62, 63
Plains Indians, 128–33
plutonium, 45, 67, 76, 79, 102
Progressive, and America's nuclear weapons program, 43–44

Project Y: The Los Alamos Project, 41
Proliferation Security Initiative (PSI), 12
proportionality in attack, 214
punitive expeditions, 127–28, 133
Punjab Irregular Force ("Piffers"), 137–38, 147
Putin, Vladimir, 191
Pye, Lucien, 159

Qom, 62, 63
Quds Force, 184

Reagan, Ronald, 95, 96, 165
red lines, 83–84, 230–31; and declaratory policy, 91, 203; and defense pacts, 86, 234; and Israeli policy toward Iran, 63–64; and nation-states, 187
Reidel, Bruce, 73
Report on the International Control of Atomic Energy, The. See Acheson-Lilienthal Report
Resolution 1540, 190
Resolution 1887, 190
Revere, Evans, 57
Rhee, Syngman, 85
Ridgway, Matthew, 146
Rio Treaty, 107
Roosevelt, Franklin Delano, 211, 226
Rosenberg, David, 100
Royal Canadian Mounted Police, 125–26
Royal Irish Constabulary, 125
Royal Newfoundland Constabulary, 125
Royal Ulster Constabulary, 125
Ryokichi, Sagane, 26

sabotage, and nuclear containment, 182–84

Sadat, Anwar, and 1973 Israel-Arab War, 110
Safeguards Agreement, 61
Salehi, Ali Akbar, 63
Sanger, David, and *Confront and Conceal*, 183
Sanqiang, Qian, 30
Sarkozy, Nicholas, 62
Saudi Aramco, 184, 186
Schelling, Thomas, 83
Scots, 126
Second Line of Defense program, 124
Selden, Bob, 43
Sepoy, 134
Shangri-Law Dialogue, 204
Sharp rifle, 132
Sherman, 213–14
Siemens systems, 183
SIGINT, 53
Sikhs, 126, 134, 135
Single Integrated Operational Plan, 100
Sino-American Mutual Defense Treaty, 89
Sino-Indian War, 33
"Smiling Buddah," 33
Smyth Report (A General Account of the Development of Methods of Using Atomic Energy for Military Purposes under the Auspices of the United States Government, 1940–1945), 37–41
Smyth, Henry De Wolf, 37, 75
South Waziristan Scouts, 126
Southeast Asia Treaty Organization (SEATO), 87–88
Soviet Union: and Berlin Blockade, 103–5; and cold war, diplomacy during, 91; and cold war, manpower during, 90; and

cold war, spending during, 165; and Cuban Missile Crisis, 106–8; and DPRK, 58; and Kissinger, 6; and Los Alamos affiliates, 30; and market economy, 166; and nuclear option in Afghanistan, 112; and nuclear proliferation, 49, 50, 51; and red lines, 230
Stalin, Joseph, 85, 104
Strategic Plans Division (Pakistan), 72, 77
"Strategy Hits a Dead End" (Brodie), 83
Stuxnet, 183, 184, 188
Suez Crisis, 31
"Suicide or Surrender; Humiliation or Holocaust," 93, 231
Sum of All Fears, The (Clancy), 3
"supercriticality," 26
surveillance, 51, 73, 147, 181
Symantec, 183
Syria, 13, 18, 108–10, 216, 227, 231
Szilárd, Leó: and Smyth Report, 39; and Franck Report, 29; and nuclear chain reaction, 26

Taliban, and Pakistan, 71. See also Pashtuns
Tatsusaburo, Suzuki, 26
Taylor, Maxwell, and The Uncertain Trumpet, 93
Taymiyya, Taqî ad-Dîn Amḥad ibn, 134, 140
Tehrik-e-Taliban, 147
Tel Nof, 108
Teller, Edward, 101
Tenet, George: and Majid and Mahmood meeting with Osama bin Laden, 70; and Mowatt-Larssen, 68; and

Musharraf, 201, 220; on al-Qaeda nuclear procurement, 79
Tennessee Valley Authority, 47
terrorism, definition of, 119–22
Terrorist Screening Center, 152
Texas Rangers, 131, 148
Third Temple, 108, 109
Thirty Years' War, 159
Thirty-Eighth Parallel, 85
thorium, 45, 46
"Three No's" doctrine, 13–15, 24, 56, 60, 67, 79
Thucydides, 31, 188
tier mondisme, 142
Tochi Scouts, 126
Tolman, Richard C., 37
Tonkawa, 131, 133
Transcontinental Railroad, 132
Treaty of Medicine Lodge, 132
Treaty of Mutual Cooperation and Security, 89
Trinity Event, the, 27, 28, 30
Trojan plan, 97
Truman, Harry S.: and Berlin Blockade, 104–5; on freedom, 143; and nuclear energy, control of, 235; and nuclear option, non use of, 111; on nuclear proliferation, 35, 39, 98; and proliferation, 46–47, 99; and red lines, 87; and Smyth Report, 39–40; and speech to Congress, 35; and the Atomic Development Authority, 189; and use of nuclear weapons during the Korean War, 85, 89, 111, 215

U-235, 27, 65
UCRL-4725, Weapons Development during June 1956, 44

UCRL-5280, Weapons Development during June 1958, 44

Umma Tameer-e-Nau (UTN; Reconstruction for the Islamic Community), 69, 70

UN Atomic Energy Commission (UNAEC), 47

UN Security Council Resolution 1267, 152

UN Security Council Resolution 1540, 12, 190

UN Security Council Resolution 1887, 190

UN Security Council Resolutions 1874, 12

Uncertain Trumpet, The (Taylor), 93

United Kingdom's Terrorism Act of 2000, 119

United States Code, 120, 175–77

University of Chicago, and May-Johnson Bill, 36

unmanned aerial vehicle (UAV), 146, 161

uranium-235, 25

uranium–233, 45

uranium, 45, 46, 48, 64

US Atomic Energy Commission, 61

US national security bureaucracy, 12

UTN, 69, 70

Vemork, 182

von Clausewitz, Carl, 6

Wahhabism, 134

Wallace, Henry, 39

Washington Post, 147

Washington Times, 151

Weber, Max, 167

West Bank barrier, 123

Wilson, William Julius, 169

Wohlstetter, Albert, 83, 94

Yamamoto, Isoroky, 5

Yongbyon plant, 14, 15, 58

Zel'dovich, Yakov, 26–27

Zhob Militia, 126

ABOUT THE AUTHOR

Benjamin E. Schwartz has served in a variety of national security offices within the US government, including positions in the Department of State, Department of Defense, and Department of Energy. In the Office of the Secretary of Defense, Mr. Schwartz served in the Special Operations and Combating Terrorism and Countering Weapons of Mass Destruction offices. Prior to his work in defense policy, Mr. Schwartz worked in the Department of Energy's Office of Intelligence and Counterintelligence. He is a graduate of the Johns Hopkins School of Advanced International Studies and Swarthmore College. His unclassified publications have appeared in *The American Interest*, *Orbis*, and various other news outlets.